AMERICA
WALKS INTO A BAR

Gentlemen you are welcome sit down at your eafe. Pay what you call for & drink what you pleafe

WIL^M. GORDON

CHRISTINE SISMONDO

AMERICA
WALKS INTO A BAR

A SPIRITED HISTORY OF

TAVERNS AND SALOONS,

SPEAKEASIES AND

GROG SHOPS

OXFORD
UNIVERSITY PRESS

OXFORD
UNIVERSITY PRESS

Oxford University Press is a department of the University of Oxford.
It furthers the University's objective of excellence in research, scholarship,
and education by publishing worldwide.

Oxford   New York
Auckland   Cape Town   Dar es Salaam   Hong Kong   Karachi
Kuala Lumpur   Madrid   Melbourne   Mexico City   Nairobi
New Delhi   Shanghai   Taipei   Toronto

With offices in
Argentina   Austria   Brazil   Chile   Czech Republic   France   Greece
Guatemala   Hungary   Italy   Japan   Poland   Portugal   Singapore
South Korea   Switzerland   Thailand   Turkey   Ukraine   Vietnam

Oxford is a registered trade mark of Oxford University Press in the UK and certain other countries.

First published in the United States of America by
Oxford University Press
198 Madison Avenue, New York, NY 10016

First published as an Oxford University Press paperback 2014

Library of Congress Cataloging-in-Publication Data
Sismondo, Christine.
America walks into a bar : a spirited history of taverns and saloons,
speakeasies, and grog shops / Christine Sismondo.
p.   cm.
Includes bibliographical references and index.
ISBN 978-0-19-973495-5 (hardcover : alk. paper); 978-0-19-932448-4 (paperback)
1. Bars (Drinking establishments)—United States—History.
2. Drinking customs—United States—History. I. Title.
GT3803.S57   2011
394.1'30973—dc22   2010040111

1 3 5 7 9 8 6 4 2

Printed in the United States of America
on acid-free paper

This book is for Kilgours'—
and all the lovely people
who have made it what it is.
You know who you are.

CONTENTS

ACKNOWLEDGMENTS

I'd like to thank the following barflies and scholars: first, Peggy Hageman, one of the most supportive and encouraging people I have ever had the privilege to call my friend. Peggy helped me sort out my thoughts and early versions and even introduced me to the next person on this list—Ethan Bassoff, superagent.

Ethan has been everything I hoped an agent would be and more. And, of course, he got me together with Timothy Bent, the editor whose insight and enthusiasm have been absolutely invaluable. I can't imagine this project without Tim or, for that matter, Mally Anderson, whom I also cannot thank enough for her time and energy.

Then there are the people who have listened to me drone on in bars and/or helped me with my research. James Waller and Jim O'Connor each lent a generous ear and helped me with research sources. Karen DeCrow took the time to help me with a first-hand account of her efforts in the battle to democratize the institution by raising rabble in bars. Jose Sarria spoke to me at length about San Francisco in the 1950s and 1960s and the incredible part he played in the history leading up to Stonewall. Brian Rea, who has done endless primary research on bars, cocktail lounges and other drinking establishments, has helped me to no end. Add to that the efforts of A.K. Sandoval-Strauss, who paved the way for American bar research with his ground-breaking work on the American hotel. Thomas Pegram was extremely generous with his time, as were Ann Tuennerman, Kevin Richards of the Sazerac Company, Jon S. Handlery of Handlery Hotels, Heather Leavell of the Peabody Historical Society, Katherine Molnar of the Historic Review Commission of Pittsburgh, John Potter of the Connecticut Historical Society, Ghyslaine Leroy of Corbis, Bernard Rosenthal, Ed Cray, and Peter Mancall.

There are many, many scholars who did the tough legwork before me and whose work I draw upon: Andrew Barr, David Conroy, Wayne Curtis, Tom Goyens, Ray Oldenburg, Madelon Powers, W.J. Rorabaugh, and Peter Thompson are just a few who have so brilliantly covered the tavern and saloon in the past.

Many professionals in the industry, such as Jim Meehan, Sasha Petraske, Katie Stipe, and Phil Ward, also inspired and helped me grasp the importance of the American bar, taking time out to speak with me about the current struggles facing the institution. A few of the most outstanding bartenders who have inspired and informed over the years are Nabil Scherief at Il Bistro, Murray Stenson at Zig Zag, Jeffrey Morgenthaler at Clyde Common, and Takaaki Hashimoto at B Flat. There are many others, of course, too many to mention. We can't even remember all the names. Closer to home, there's York University in Toronto, which helped through research grants, and I'd like to thank people there such as Steven Bailey, Lorraine Code, and Patrick Taylor for their continued support.

Last but hardly least are those who have politely listened to the thesis for this book and the minute details about its progress. Family first: parents Sergio and Liane Sismondo, brother Sergio Sismondo, and Khadija Coxon have gone above and beyond the call of duty. Same for Chandra Edwards. Helene and Paul Eberts and Amy Vigorita were extraordinary in helping me think through the project and, in particular, the value of association. Apologies for the rants and sincere thanks for all the encouragement and feedback are also due to Joe Alexandrovitch, Joan Allen, Suzanne Alyssa-Andrew, Paul Ayers, Sean Aylward, Simon Beggs, Ryan Bigge, Kevin Brauch, Sandy De Almeida, Lloyd Dilworth, Ann Fitzpatrick, Siobhan Flanagan, Paul Gallagher, Garvie, Adrian Griffin, Christine Hooper, Sue Ketcheson, Andrew Kilgour, Peter Kilgour, Andrea Ledwell, Hugh Leighton, John and Mary MacMillan, Sara Marino, Bill and Carol Martin, Janet Milligan, Scott Mochrie, Fred Newey, Sharon O'Rourke, Anne and Nick Pashley, Donna and Kennedy Pires, Jessica Polzer, Sherry Roher, Dana Rourke, Sanjay Talwar, Ron Thompson, and, of course, Uncle. And thank you to whomever else I have missed.

Finally, finally, there are those people I live with—the ones who find their lives both neglected and taken over whenever I have a new project (which is pretty much always). Myles, nearly a feral child now, has learned to fend for herself and rarely complains. Thank you, Myles.

And none of this could ever have happened without Al, whom I suckered into another journey with the promise that a book about bars would be practically recreational. Nothing I can say can possibly convey how important his help and support was in the creation of this book and, so, I won't even try. Except to say that it's not just the book that I couldn't have done without him. Thank you for everything—always.

PROLOGUE
A
LITTLE
KID
WALKS
INTO
A BAR

WHERE DREAMS COME TRUE

The Highland Room bar and lounge at San Francisco's Hotel Stewart
(now Handlery Union Square Hotel), 1961. Image courtesy of Jon S. Handlery.

It was the highlight of any family trip—better than cable in the room, the swimming pool, better even than being allowed to order pancakes for breakfast and Coke with dinner.

The hotel bar was magic. It was where adults seemed to wonderfully transform from tightly wound disciplinarian micro-managers into lively, indulgent, joyful humans. It was like the *Invasion of the Body Snatchers*— in reverse. In the bar, you could find smiles everywhere, strangers giving away loose change simply to bring a thrill to a child's face, doting waitresses and their endless provision of sodas and salty snacks. The couches were rich and velvety; the brightly colored menus were full of exotic fare.

To some, so early an early introduction to bars will fall somewhere between scandalous and tragic. In defense of my parents, though, they had little choice. They frequently traveled on business and, rather than leave me at home or alone in a hotel room, they brought me with them to the place where they met colleagues and clients to close deals and solidify relationships.

As soon as I could get into bars on my own, I made it my mission to get into as many as possible. I wanted what so many people wanted—a place where you could simply drop in and stand a decent chance of running into somebody you knew.

Before long, I found that place, a Toronto neighborhood bar called Kilgours'. I wound up working there and, almost indiscernibly, grew to be a part of a community. It spanned several bars—the dive two doors down with the little pool table and the big slushy margaritas; the faux-British pub on the next corner that catered more to the student crowd; the nineteenth-century hotel, a block the other way, which, on Saturday afternoons, gave over its large main room to a spirited jam session where locals rocked and little kids danced. When Claire was unable to pay for her cancer treatments, patrons and coworkers staged a benefit. When Joe lost his job, cooks would accidentally make steaks for fictional customers, then slide the mistakes his way. We all made sure to rotate buying drinks for those down on their luck so they could stay in the circle.

There are bars like this all over North America. They are the places that serve as the subject of fondly considered memoirs, such as J. R. Moehringer's *The Tender Bar*; the places romanticized by authors such as Pete Hamill and Jack London and Walt Whitman. They're the bars cherished by sociologist Ray Oldenburg, who has shown that the neighborhood tavern is an invaluable place where the community unwinds from the stresses of daily life and people bond with folks they would otherwise never meet.

When the Eastern seaboard went dark at 4:11 PM on August 14, 2003, Kilgours' was crammed by five. Many of us simply headed there as though on some homing device. Kilgours' had also been packed two years earlier, on 9/11. We filtered in and out, looking for answers about friends who worked in lower Manhattan. We speculated about our own safety, whether this was the beginning of something stronger and whether or not anything would ever be the same again. We were there to reach out to fellow humans.

There are countless other bars about which similar stories can be told—and they reach down into our shared history. Americans have always walked into a bar: It is where the freedom to associate has been traditionally exercised.

As I hope to show in this book, the bar has been one of the places in which America and Americans have struggled for self-definition, establishing the rights of its citizens to express themselves and effect change and to do so in groups. Freedom of association gave rise to the countless progressive movements that, over the years, have been implemented there—from the founding fathers and original revolutionary leaders to the Jeffersonian political reformers who battled to keep the new American democratic experiment honest after independence. From labor leaders and social reformers who denounced monopolies and the exploitation of a seemingly endless supply of immigrant labor throughout the nineteenth century, to the early organization of middle-class communities in disenfranchised populations, such as segregated black Americans living under Jim Crow laws. And, more recently, from those who rose up against the systemic discrimination against lesbian and gay communities to the feminists who struggled for social change and demanded to be let into the bar—which, at the time, was effectively the boardroom of American business. This is not to say that everything that began in bars has been rights-expanding and noble. The Nazi Party organized in beer halls and, here in America, corrupt machine politics were maintained through a system of saloons for nearly a century. Lincoln's assassination was planned in a tavern.

Bars are where people gather and talk. And drink. And alcohol leads to more talking, more drinking, and, under certain circumstances, a heightened level of outrage and commitment to action. Since its early beginnings as a humble one-room tavern with a simple wood bench for visitors, the bar served as an extension of the town hall—an American innovation and its earliest great contribution to democracy. At times, it *was* the town hall. Going at least as far back as the early eighteenth century, when some Boston rebels began agitating in smoke-filled taverns, groups denied access to legitimate and sanctioned forms of political representation have taken to the saloon.

In an age when everything from tapioca to quilting has been touted as an overlooked agent that has helped shape history, it's tempting to soft-sell the importance of the American bar. Like its close cousins, the coffee-houses of Paris and London, however, the bar was where the public proved itself—often with less sobriety—capable of economic and political self-determination.

It may be hard imagining bars as serving the same critical function in this age, when we frequent them to enjoy relatively bourgeois pursuits—sampling haute-cocktail creations at the spate of New York bars such as Milk and Honey, Angel's Share, PDT, and Death & Co. It's tasty and fun and can't help but seem a little frivolous compared with the Sons of Liberty meetings, Democratic-Republican insurrections, Anarchist bomb plots, labor movements, feminist sit-ins and the events leading up to Stonewall, the cornerstone for the gay pride revolution.

Yet America still struggles with the public space that is the bar. In 2006, for example, when the Hurricane Katrina Relief Bill was passed, a rider was originally attached that excluded bars from applying for aid or tax breaks on the grounds that they contributed nothing to the community. Nothing. Many in New Orleans will tell you the opposite was true, especially those who sought refuge in bars over the many weeks of chaos. In New York and other urban areas across the country, an aging and gentrifying population repeatedly clashes with bar clientele over a number of issues, including the noise, brawls, and bodily fluids that will sometimes spill from these fun houses. The struggle manifests itself in court-induced closures and polarizing neighborhood battles over issues such as babies in bars, sexual assaults, and proximity to places of worship.

No doubt that there are legitimate concerns over the competing needs of urban dwellers—between those who still feel bars poison those who can't help themselves and those who value them as spaces where grassroots programs are nourished. When I first stumbled on a few seemingly disparate events that spilled out of a bar, tavern, or saloon—the Revolution, Shay's Rebellion, labor movements, Anarchism—I decided to embark on a pub crawl through American history. Early research uncovered no end to these seemingly disconnected events becoming connected. It almost seemed as if everything that had ever happened in America had happened in a bar. These events no longer seemed disassociated. The inner logic of the tavern rabble-rousers was, in fact, what produced the early American public sphere. And, after the Revolution, America continued to redefine itself in that same space, be it the country's numerous taverns, saloons, juke joints, grog shops, blind pigs, speakeasies, night clubs, and, eventually, post-prohibition bars of all stripes.

America, as we know it, was born in a bar. And the struggle over the tavern has been more than just a struggle over where to drink and with whom. It has been the struggle over a nation's destiny.

AMERICA
WALKS INTO A BAR

A PILGRIM WALKS INTO A BAR

TABERNAE MERITORIA

The Romans were pioneers in developing the
"local." In this mural from Pompeii, patrons are
enjoying a game in the tavern.

Upon all the new settlements the Spaniards make, the first thing
they do is build a church, the first thing ye Dutch do upon a new
colony is to build them a fort, but the first thing ye English do, be it
in the most remote part of ye world, or amongst the most barbarous
Indians, is to set up a tavern or drinking house.[1]

So wrote Captain Thomas Walduck in 1708, in a letter to John Searle, a
nephew in London. We don't know a lot about Walduck—only that
he was well-traveled, well-read, and fairly frank about his disapproval
of his own country's colonial practice in Barbados and elsewhere. In
between letters to the Royal Society in London, in which he tried to further the cause of science with his own amateur naturalist observations,
he indicted the colonial slave planters, claiming that the island's "glory"
was "barbarity and ill gott wealth."

What Walduck could not know, however, was that the same Tavern-
First approach he ridiculed would turn out to be an integral aspect of
one of the most successful empire-building strategies ever.

At first glance, the Tavern-First Method may seem like a strange
way to run an empire—with everybody drinking in taverns instead of,
say, taming the land or subjugating the native inhabitants. But the
British, divided by bloody and seemingly irresolvable religious differences at home, were at least united by this strategy for settlement
abroad.

Truth be told, this wasn't entirely confined to the Brits. North American Moravian settlers adhered to a similar philosophy, a fact confirmed
by the retelling of a debate in the German Protestant settlement of Naza-
reth, Pennsylvania, in the 1740s. Townsfolk and church elders were arguing over which should come first, tavern or church. The townsfolk—and
the tavern—won out, their case eloquently stated with this evocative
summation: A town without a tavern is like *Hamlet* "without the ghost."[2]
Taverns were so closely tied to community identity that a settlement
could not be considered whole until it established its center.

These varied utopian Protestant colonists intent on creating a "city
upon a hill," could have built their new settlements any way they liked,
and the Puritan settlers may well have initially considered a tavern-free
society. Their later Quaker counterparts certainly did, but then changed
their minds. In his first draft of the Fundamental Constitution of Pennsylvania, for instance, William Penn, recognizing the subversive nature
of "Taverns" and "Playhouses," barred both. Somewhere between his

first and final drafts, however, Penn must have realized utopia could not be dry, that taverns were going to be crucial for the colony's development. And so, instead of barring them, he devised one of the first comprehensive sets of state-licensing guidelines. It was strict, stipulating the following: No profanity, no gambling, and no drinking "healths" (toasts to another's fortune and well-being). It also called for a fixed-price system for both quarts of beer and meals; last call at eight in the evening; and, in a remarkably clear and early recognition of how the tavern was a potentially dangerous public forum, a prohibition against defamation of character, the spreading of false news—and sedition.[3] This was Penn's attempt to control what he understood was going to be a necessary evil.

Taverns were absolutely critical for the new settlers' survival. Establishing the tavern was the first priority—not just the first choice—of every colony. For starters, they could temporarily substitute for absent infrastructure. The first dedicated official government building in New England wasn't erected until 1658, in Boston; until then, all legal and government proceedings took place in taverns and meeting-houses, like the one in Dorchester, Massachusetts, where the country's first town hall meeting was held in 1633. Nor was this unique to the Puritan and Quaker settlements. One of the more prominent examples of a licensed house of entertainment doubling as a more serious institution was the Stadts Herbergh Inn, or City Tavern, on the East River in New Amsterdam (today's lower Manhattan), which was, simultaneously, the central market for traders and merchants, a public auction house, the prime location for the posting of public notices, and, eventually, in 1653, the official city hall. The tavern was a de facto courtroom, the first colonial post office, a library, a news center, the town hall, community center, and, on days when the meeting-house was too cold, a church. In Medford, Massachusetts, there are numerous late-seventeenth-century town records that indicated a meeting was "moved to the house of Samuel Sadey, innkeeper, by reason of the cold." Also in Medford, it was decreed that "names posted on several tavern doors" was enough notice to summon jurors to a trial.[4] In most settlements, court itself met in the most convenient and respectable tavern; in Charlestown, Massachusetts, in 1700, there is a record of the Superior Court being held at "Sommer's great room below stairs."[5] The tavern was everything to everyone while they were waiting for the proper structures to be built.

At first, though, the most important function the tavern fulfilled was as the way-station. Although travel was limited in early colonial days—as a result of poor roads, danger, and expense—those who did travel needed rest stops. The tavern was the transportation hub for every town and travelers stopped there to refresh themselves and, if they had such luxuries, their horses. Sometimes it was for a mere pit stop, sometimes the stay was overnight, but the significance cannot be overstated. In fact, some of the earliest colonial legislation mandated that each town institute a tavern and even tavern-hater Penn had changed his tune by 1685. Rather than banning them, he now spoke with pride of Philadelphia's seven "ordinaries"—another term for a tavern, derived from the practice of selling a prix-fixe meal at the same time every day. They were not only the mark of a world-class colonial settlement but laid the groundwork for empire-building.

To give proper credit where due, erecting taverns in new settlements was not, strictly speaking, the original brainchild of the British colonists. During their empire's expansion, the Romans developed an institution called *tabernae deversoria*—a class of inns that catered more or less exclusively to travelers. These were set up roughly every fifteen miles along Roman roads as rest stops to accommodate military and commercial travel. Distance was literally measured in taverns. The tabernae were distinct from another worthy Roman institution, *tabernae meritoria*, which also maintained barrooms and entertainment, but served a local clientele who came out for diversion.[6] While the tabernae were a major factor in the empire's expansion, like many innovations, they also had a negative and unintended consequence. The wine served in these taverns was often adulterated with *sapa* (a syrup simmered in a lead pot), which, in time, led to the widespread lead-poisoning that some have argued contributed to Roman vulnerability when it came time for the Barbarians to invade.

Ultimately, the Roman empire faded away—but not the tabernae deversoria, an updated version of which proved an absolute necessity for travel in burgeoning pre-industrial Europe. Before the institution of this network of taverns, travelers were often forced to rely on the hospitality of monasteries. This probably sounds more austere and joyless than it was, especially for those with means. Regardless of Christian prohibitions on drunkenness, the brothers and padres were generally happy to indulge guests, especially the wealthier tier of travelers. When tenth-century Northumbrian King Eadred was invited to the Abingdon monastery, the Bishop of Winchester made certain the entire party was supplied with mead the entire day, from a vessel that miraculously never grew empty. The chronicler, Wulfstan of Winchester, also noted that the Northumbrians got drunk "as they tended to," attributing the intoxication to the Northumbrian character rather than the bountiful supply of monastic hospitality.[7]

This worked adequately throughout the early Middle Ages but, after the Black Plague had decimated the population and sparked economic growth and personal freedom for the survivors, a spate of privately run early public houses was established by entrepreneurs in the latter half of the fifteenth century. This coincided with a division between public and private, which was becoming more entrenched in Tudor England thanks to "enclosure"—the division of commonly used land into private plots and, increasingly, dedicated spaces that were developed to accommodate strangers. With this, the British alehouse was established—one of the very first semipublic places in the Western world and the earliest incarnation of the pub, short, of course, for publican. Historian Iain Gately argues that the pub was one of the first places where common people enjoyed freedom of speech and that it became the "nucleus of popular culture."[8]

If the tavern was of great social and political import in England, it was going to play an even bigger role in "New England," where, as we've seen, it had to stand in for every other missing institution. Taverns also just happened to be the most likely place in which a colonist could find a beer. And locating a steady source of beer was the first thing on every colonist's mind, since, for him, beer was a staple. In crowded pre-industrial England and throughout most of Europe, where safe drinking water was scarce, beer was—by far—the healthiest option.

Brewing was not only important to the Brits and the new Americans. Some historians argue that harnessing fermentation was a crucial technology dating back to the days of the Fertile Crescent and now rank it as one of homo sapiens' all-time important inventions. Without it, we might never have succeeded in the shift to our new non-nomadic lifestyles.[9] Agriculture and fermentation seem to have enjoyed a symbiotic relationship. According to historian Tom Standage, without brewing, excess grains in boon times would simply have rotted and gone to waste. Beer was a way to preserve crops and make a virtue of that fermenting grain. More important even than extending the life span of the grain was the role it played in extending the life span of those who tended to the grain. This prehistorical period was when people began drinking beer regularly, since it was the safest way to rehydrate. Clean water was hard to come by even before overpopulation became an issue in many regions, especially in warmer climates. Others have suggested that the desire to brew beer may even have been the motivating force behind the development of agriculture that marked the end of the nomadic lifestyle. Even if they didn't understand the specifics of water-borne bacteria—and wouldn't until Antonie van Leeuwenhoek's experiments with microscopes in 1674—people had learned that, once you turned water into beer, it was a lot less likely to lead to fatal illness and, so, the need to secure grains for fermentation.

Establishing taverns and micro-breweries, then, was a vital tradition by the time it reached the shores of New England in the early seventeenth century with the arrival of settlers in ships such as the *Mayflower*. The *Mayflower*'s crew, incidentally, was in a right panic over beer supplies even before it had sight of the coast. The ship's beer stores were low and everyone understood the gravity of the situation. Initially, Captain Christopher Jones dipped into his private stash to help slake his cargo of Pilgrims, but his generosity came to an end when he saw that giving more would leave his crew desperately short for the return voyage. This pending shortage may well have forced Jones to cut the trip shy of its original destination—the area at the mouth of the Hudson River where the Pilgrims had a Royal charter to settle. Jones called it quits at Plymouth Rock in what is now Massachusetts, over two hundred miles up the coast. Beer-wise, the good captain might've been better off sticking to the original plan. Had he been able to find his way to the Dutch settlement in nearby New Amsterdam, he should have been able to replenish his stores at the Block and Christiansen brewery, which had been established in 1612, eight years before the *Mayflower*. While the Dutch may have been the first to have a proper full-scale brewery, it was hardly the first North American beer, since the Roanoke Island settlers were making maize beer as early as 1585—after which they promptly lost themselves. Long before that, even the pulque-drinking Aztecs were hooked on a beer made from the maguey plant, from which mescal is now derived. Tesquina and chicha—both fermented corn drinks—were also brewed in pre-Columbian times.

Despite some concerns, water in the relatively sparsely populated New World was, in most cases, just fine, especially in New England, where cold weather limited pathogenic bacteria. One Puritan settler by the name of William Wood, in fact, notes that the water was not so "sharpe" as that back home, remarking on its mouth-feel and hues.

North American water, Wood writes, was "of a fatter substance, and of a more jetty color; it is thought there can be no better water in the world." Nonetheless, however delicious, water was never going to prompt the Pilgrims to abandon beer, as Wood indicates with his final disclaimer: "Yet I do not prefer it before a good Beere."[10] Ale remained a central feature of the settlers' culture and also an important source of nourishment, often standing in for or accompanying what we now call the most important meal of the day—breakfast. Similarly, what some now refer to as a "barley sandwich" made a good replacement for lunch, a mid-afternoon snack, even dinner. In his 1674 *New England's Rarities Discovered*, English traveler John Josselyn wrote that "we made our beer of Molosses, Water, Bran, chips of Sassafras Root, and a little Worm-wood, well-boiled," and a score of other ingredients including "Cat-mint, sow-thistle, Liquorice, Anny-seed and Fennel-seed." After some further adulteration, boiling and cooling, he advised that it be drunk "letting it run down your throat as leasorely as possibly you can; do thus in the morning, in the Afternoon, and at Night going to bed."[11]

As well, if a colonist happened to feel a little tender after a mid-day meal of beer, the prescribed remedy would have been . . . another beer. Beer was frequently taken to facilitate digestion and settle the stomach and the same medicine was prescribed for anxiety, weakness, and blood ailments. Beer was superfood, something taken as a preventative health measure for its perceived nutritional effects and panacea combined, and daily consumption was as important a part of a healthy regimen as exercise and leafy vegetables are today. In fact, when American insurance agencies were first established, drinkers paid a lower rate—as much as 10 percent lower—than nondrinking clients.[12]

As alcohol historian Andrew Barr points out, the moment the colonists secured a reliable source of beer, they wasted little time minimizing their water intake. On top of all of water's previous image problems (brackish *and* a potential killer), it became associated with deprivation. In fact, learning that there were early beer shortages while the first breweries were being established, was all some would-be Pilgrims needed to hear before banishing any further thoughts of migration.[13] Indentured servant Richard Frethorne wrote to his parents from Jamestown that "as strong beer in England doth fatten and strengthen them, so water here doth wash and weaken these here [and] only keeps [their] life and soul together."[14] Many of the first breweries were small and are lost to history, but there were several in Massachusetts Bay and Virginia, including one run by a Robert Sedgewick of Charles-Towne.[15] As soon as these breweries were up and running by the 1630s, colonists had their consumption back up to an estimated six gallons of absolute alcohol per year. The average American drinks about half that now.[16]

The variety of drinks made from that six gallons was pretty impressive, too, and a testament to the creativity of the settlers. Beer itself was made out of birch bark, sassafras, spruce, and even twigs, which were boiled and added to malt, roots, pumpkin, or apple, and fermented. According to a ballad that dates roughly to 1630, known simply as "Our Forefather's Song," colonists complained about "New England's annoyances" but consoled themselves with this: "We can make liquor to sweeten our lips; of pumpkins, parsnips, of walnut-tree chips."[17] In some places, *metheglin*—a Welsh name derived from the words "healing" and "liquor"—was very popular. Essentially, this was mead enhanced with spices like lavender, cloves, chamomile, and nutmeg.

While the cocktail as we know it (with ice, liquor, and an alteration in flavor produced by bitters and sugar) wasn't invented until the early nineteenth century, there were a number of mixed beverages in colonial times—with names such as the Calibogus, Bombo, Whistlebelly and Cherry Bounce—that might be described as proto-cocktails. Being both powerful—by percentage alcohol—and served warm, these concoctions would probably not suit contemporary tastes, but their names make them ripe for rediscovery. Topping the list, surely, would be the Rattle-Skull, another colonial favorite, made from brandy, wine, port, nutmeg, and lime.[18]

Modern molecular mixology is foreshadowed by the libation known as the "Bellowstop." One Canton, Massachusetts, tavern-owner seems to have been the author of this particular version of "flip"—a colonial favorite, typically made with strong beer, dried pumpkin, molasses, and rum. His version involved four "huge spoonfuls" of a rich mixture of cream, eggs, and sugar added to a nearly full quart of bitter beer and rum. He then "thrust the iron poker into it," and whisked up another freshly beaten egg in order to "get the froth to gush over the top of the mug."[19] The December issue of the 1704 *New England Almanac* suggests its popularity:

The Days are short, the weather's cold,
By tavern fires tales are told,
Some ask for dram when first come in,
Others with flip and bounce begin.

"Dram" is easy enough, deriving from a Scottish measure for a little over an ounce of whiskey, or whisky, as it was spelled there. For its part, "bounce" was made by infusing fresh cherries in rum for a full year until they were completely dissolved. In addition to flip and bounce, colonists might have enjoyed a Meridian (brandy and tea), Sangaree (Madeira, sugar, and nutmeg), or the slightly vile-sounding Sitchell, which combined whiskey, water, molasses, and vinegar.

Cider (originally spelled *cyder* or *syder*) was a common drink in the mid- to late 1600s and, before long, people had worked out how to make the stronger applejack and cider brandy by distilling the fermentation. The earliest incarnation of this was known as hard cider or, occasionally, "winter wine," which was concocted by freezing cider and removing the top layer of nonalcoholic ice, revealing a pool of potent applejack liquid. Before that innovation, colonists might have enjoyed a "Stonewall," or a "Stone-Fence," which was cider fortified with rum and thought to have been named for its kick, as in how drinking one might have the same effect as running headlong into a wall. By contrast, Samuel Sewall (1652–1730), notable traveling justice, Salem Witch trial participant, and diarist who was so kind as to supply social historians with minute details of his day-to-day life, went the other way with his cider. Rather than trying to make it stronger, he mellowed it out with sugar, nutmeg, and cream, transforming it into "sillabub" or syllabub, a traditional English dessert dating back to the late fifteenth century, originally made with wine or ale and raw milk freshly squeezed from the cow's udder into an ale pot. In that Sewall was noted for his somewhat anomalous sobriety, this was likely less popular.

The improvisational creativity of their keepers meant that taverns began to assume the same role originally filled by the Roman *tabernae*. In addition to accommodating travelers, they were also helping sate locals' desire for diversion with a night of flip and bounce. Without taverns, the colonies' trade routes and government regulation would simply have shut down, or never taken root in the first place. And, as in Roman times, distance was again measured in taverns and routes determined accordingly.

Yet for all the functions the tavern provided, it also produced one inevitable and undesirable problem, namely drunkenness. Although this would seem a predictable result for a population that per capita annually consumed an average of six gallons of alcohol, drunkenness was not generally considered an acceptable outcome. Or, as sober and thoughtful

Puritan minister and politician, Increase Mather, once said: "Drink is, in itself, a good creature of God, and to be received with thankfulness, but the abuse of drink is from Satan; the wine is from God, but the drunkard is from the Devil."

This is not a uniquely Puritan take on the paradox of drinking. There has been a prohibition on extreme drunkenness since the Bible, starting with Noah—not merely the savior of humanity and all those pairs of animals but also the inventor of wine. Pleased with his innovation, as the story goes, Noah proceeded to get a little tight one night, then passed out cold—and naked. When his son, Ham, found Noah in this undignified state, he and his brothers helped cover him up. Japeth and Shem were careful not to look but Ham, it seems, sneaked a peek. For this, Noah doled out a curse on Ham's son, Canaan, that he (and all Canaanites thereafter) should live a life of servitude.[20]

This is not the only biblical caution against drunkenness. There are passages warning that drink will lead to sloth, poverty, and violent behavior. "Wine is a mocker, strong drink is raging: and whosoever is deceived thereby is not wise," says Proverbs 20:1. And Leviticus 10:9 warns that drinking in the "tabernacle of the congregation" might even result in death. Puritan settlers, trying to be faithful to the word of King James, faced the tough task of maintaining the indispensable institution of the tavern while simultaneously limiting the devil's influence. They tried to walk this fine line with legislation regarding taverns that fell into two main divisions—laws designed to encourage the institution of taverns and the laws designed to control them.

In 1637, the General Court of Massachusetts, the highest authority next to the governor, decreed that each town was to choose a responsible community member to sell "wine and strong water lest the public suffer from lack of public accommodations." Connecticut followed with a 1644 decree that ordered one "sufficient inhabitant" per town to set up an ordinary, since "strangers were straitened" when they wanted to get a little less straight. One Dutch visitor to Hartford in 1639, noting this "straitening," remarked that the difference between his culture and that of the English was that the latter were very sober, "drinking but three times at a meal." It's hard to know if this was said tongue-in-cheek or not, since this same visitor also said of the punishment: "When a man drinks to drunkenness, they tie him to a post and whip him as they do thieves in Holland."[21] It's likely no sarcasm was intended. Dutch settlers in New Amsterdam didn't seem to need laws to encourage the institution of taverns, since one of every four buildings was already devoted to the sale of liquor or tobacco.

Back in Massachusetts, the county courts decided in 1656 that they could not only legislate the *necessity* of a tavern but fine the residents of offending tavern-free towns.[22] This was no idle threat, either. Concord was hit with a fine in 1660 and Newbury was twice docked before a valiant local by the name of Hugh March before it finally opened a public house.

Often a condition was attached to a license, regulating, for instance, where a tavern was to be located or what secondary purpose it should serve. In 1651 Boston, a John Vyall was granted a license, "provided he keep it neare the new meeting house," from where, none other than Increase Mather preached.[23] In 1636, in Cambridge, Deacon Thomas Chisholm opened his own tavern next door to his parish. Taverns were almost certainly used for the occasional religious service, especially on those winter days when the frigid meeting-house failed to warm up, even with members carrying foot-stoves with live coals. Taverns, always warm with the body heat of its inhabitants, definitely accommodated chilled worshippers in the noon break between morning and afternoon services. It was also typically used for "seating the meeting"—when it was decided in which row each member would sit, according to social rank. It was not considered blasphemous or indecorous for important church business to take place in a tavern, since antipapal religious reformers rejected any suggestion that some houses were more legitimate than others. God was present in all of them.

When the tavern wasn't being used as a de facto meeting-house, it often doubled as a courthouse. And even when a dedicated courthouse already existed, many towns granted licenses for tavern-keepers to open up next door so that trials could be held there on cold days and small disputes settled "out of court."

Tavern court chambers were small rooms that held roughly twenty people. The fanciest ones, mainly in well-populated urban areas, often had elevated judges' benches. In Boston, there were two major courts— John Turner's Tavern and George Monck's Blue Anchor. And while both of these provided respectable and well-run chambers, there were numerous examples of miscarriages of justice arising from the informality of the general set up. On occasion, there'd be a clear conflict of interest. One such case involved a Virginia hostler (another word for tavernkeeper) named Charles Hill, who allowed patrons to run up huge bills on credit. When patrons failed to pay, Hill, who also happened to be the county jailer, would arrest and lock them up in the tavern, now doubling as a jail. From there, patrons would frequently "escape," prompting Hill to turn to the county court for reimbursement for his unpaid tabs. Naturally, his argument would be that it was the *county jailer's* fault the debtors had escaped.[24]

It wasn't at all uncommon for people to hold multiple offices as Hill did. A colonial tavernkeeper might also be the deacon, the constable, the surveyor, a selectman or tithing man. The latter made for a curious double role, since it was the tithing man's job to root out unlicensed drinking houses and fine tavernkeepers for serving drunken patrons. David Conroy, another tavern historian, has unearthed tales of justices who held both offices in colonial Massachusetts, where there were no laws barring the practice. In Watertown, one individual who was both a selectman and tavernkeeper for twenty-seven years was found to display a very "tolerant attitude toward drinking," since he dismissed almost all of his cases of public drunkenness.[25] While simultaneously selling alcohol and enforcing public drinking laws would seem an obvious conflict of interest, few jurisdictions attempted to legislate against the practice, despite the occasional critique like this one: "Drunkenness is decried from almost every pulpit, but what justice punishes drunkenness?"[26]

Although little effort was put into fixing this problem, a good bit of legislation aimed at improving the quality of accommodation was enacted, so that circuit-riding judges weren't subject to the colonial equivalent of the flea-bag motel. Complaints about some taverns ranged from raucousness, to having to sleep on the floor, to being nearly "eat up alive with buggs." One step up from sleeping on the floor was shared accommodation, when taverns with more lodgers than beds simply assigned two or three strangers to a single bed. Traveling memoirist Francois Jean de Beauvoir, the Marquis de Chastellux, summed it up thusly: "After you have been some time in a bed, a stranger of any condition (for there is little distinction), comes in to the room, pulls off his clothes, and places himself, without ceremony, between your sheets."[27]

Then there was the food. Sarah Kemble Knight, an early diarist, wrote of the many and varied taverns at which she stayed, often complaining of atrocious meals. Once, she reported she was served a "twisted thing like a cable, but something whiter." Whatever it was, the serving woman laid "it on the bord, tugg'd for life to bring it into a capacity to spread. The result was "served in a dish of Pork and Cabage."[28]

Having been regularly exposed to similar conditions in the line of duty, traveling magistrates were instrumental in standardizing tavern beds and fare, requiring, for example, that Maryland tavernkeepers have at least four "good feather beds" and "in any place where the county Crt is kept, eight ffeather or fflock beds at the least . . . and that they shall suffer noe drinking or gaming upon the Sabbath Day."[29]

Then, of course, there was the concern over the amount of alcohol consumed before, during, and after judicial proceedings and whether it might mar judgment. In some places, where the bottle was passed around freely and tankards of cider were readily refilled, there were those who were distressed that a justice might become "mellow in his cups," since, as alcohol historian W. J. Rorabaugh explains, drunken juries led to a greater rate of acquittals.[30] If John Turner's in Boston was any indication, though, few paid much attention to quantity control. There, witnesses and justices were served wine in quarts, despite a law prohibiting wine served in any quantity more than half a pint at a time.[31]

The fact that so much important civic and divine business was held in taverns meant that legislation typically specified that a respectable member of the community be there to run it. And, in order to keep things operating on the up and up, incentives were used in many regions. In Virginia in 1677, it was decreed there could only be two taverns per county—thereby guaranteeing lucrative monopolies. In Maryland, land grants, tax exemptions, and monopolies were given to upstanding community members who ran the ordinaries that had been deemed so severely lacking in 1662. In all states, tavern legislation was involved and constantly changing. In Virginia after 1638, there was more law on the books regarding the licensing of taverns than there was on "roads, land titles, care of the poor and general law and order."[32]

Many laws were less favorable to the tavernkeeper, such as those meant to keep order and discourage drunkenness. As early as 1633 in the Massachusetts Bay colony, before taverns were declared vital, fines and other punishments were imposed upon publicans "in whose howse any were found or suffered to drinke drunck," just as it still is illegal to serve people to the point of intoxication. (Early settlements in New England look positively quaint in comparison to Virginia, where ministers were singled out and forbidden from giving themselves to "excesse in drinkinge or riot.") In addition, they were warned against "spendinge their tyme idllye by day or night,"[33] indicating another aspect of concern over the emerging Puritan drinking problem—that there was almost as much cultural anxiety regarding what wasn't being done (namely, work) as there was over the drunken "rioting" that taverns occasionally produced. Later, toward the close of the seventeenth century, Nathaniel Saltonstall of Haverhill would complain that those who cried "povertie" spent much time and "their entire estate at such blind holes," and, further, that taverns were plagued with "pernicious loitering" and the foolish "firing and shooting off of guns."[34] In a preamble to a 1637 law regulating taverns, Puritan leaders expressed worry over the "waste of good creatures of God" and the "mispense of time."

Even before legislation, there were recorded incidents of tavern loafers and drunkards being punished, generally by shaming. Early tavern historian Alice Morse Earle tells of a James Woodward of New-Towne (now Cambridge, Massachusetts) who, in 1632, after having been caught "drunke," was "sett in the bilbowes," a handcuff device similar to "stocks," allegedly conceived in design capital Bilbao, Spain. When attached to both feet and hands, bilbowes managed to cause both humiliation and pain.[35] For the following year, there's record of a Robert Coles being fined ten shillings (roughly a hundred dollars today) and forced to stand with a sheet of paper on his back with the word "Drunkard," written large, for the crime of "abusing himself shamefully with drink."[36] The 1633 "drinke drunck" legislation, therefore, had seemed a necessary response to Massachusetts Bay colonists such as Woodward and Coles, who had been "distempering themselves" with drink, selling to servants, and even selling to people who were already distempered, "thereby causing much disorder, drunkenness and misdemeanor."[37] Not that the legislation had much effect on behavior. In 1638, the courts fined one William Reynolds for having got so drunk that he "lay under the table" and vomited "in a beastly manner" at his host's home.[38]

Some of the anxiety about it all had to do with concerns over sex outside of the confines of marriage, which was, then as now, a lot more likely to happen with alcohol. Punishments here were often harsh. In 1639 in Ipswich, Massachusetts, a man was whipped for copping a feel under a "girles coat." In another instance, also in Ipswich, Margery Rugs was lashed for having convinced George Palmer to "commit folly." It's interesting to note that Palmer wasn't punished. Perhaps pleading a case of the "drinke drunck," he maintained that he'd been unable to resist Margery's allurements.[39]

We can imagine the many debates surrounding what constituted the state of "drinke drunck." Drunkenness, after all, remains contentious even though we've achieved an understanding about blood-alcohol content. Maryland, apparently undaunted by ambiguities, forged ahead and defined the actual state. In 1638, its legislators agreed that drunkenness was characterized by a "noticeable perturbation of any organ of sense or motion." In Massachusetts, an attempt at a more refined definition was made in 1646: "And by Drunkenness is understood a person that either lisps or faulters in his speech by reason of overmuch drink, or that staggers in his going, or that vomits by reason of excessive drinking, or cannot follow his calling."[40]

To prevent any of this from happening, patrons' attempts at getting "glaiz'd" were thwarted (or, at least made more of a challenge) by some of the country's very first drinking laws. In 1646 in Plymouth, Massachusetts, the maximum amount of wine that could be served at any one time was a half-pint. By today's standards, that seems fairly generous—roughly a third of a contemporary wine bottle—another indication of the volume consumed in the colonial era. Closing time was also set at nine in the evening, except for people who were visiting from somewhere else. Out-of-towners were free to imbibe for as long as they wished; locals were banned from drinking for more than an hour at a time.[41] (Talk about your happy hour.) Then again, they probably considered themselves lucky since they'd previously been allotted only thirty minutes. (Talk about your happy half-hour.)

At one point in Boston, residents were fined if they were found drinking in local taverns at all, part of an attempt to reduce the number of houses of entertainment from twenty-six to ten. The same rationale had led the Romans to divide the *deversoria* from the *meritoria* and was clearly an attempt to ensure taverns were used primarily for business, not pleasure. It was also surely the birth of the road trip.

Keeping track of who was from abroad and who was local and, among the latter, whose time was up, was the tavernkeeper's job. Neglecting to do so, or allowing patrons to get inebriated on premises, would result in a fine assessed per drunken patron or, in the worst cases, a revoked license. One tapster in Dorchester, Massachusetts, was caught serving patrons to the point of inebriation and as punishment ordered to surrender two gallons of his "stronge water" for the "benefit of the poor."[42] On top of that, starting in 1670, lists of problem drunkards were in circulation and tavernkeepers were required to refuse service to those "habitual tipplers," even if their tippling had occurred elsewhere.

One group automatically granted honorary membership on this list were Indians. Later the list would gradually be extended to include other racial groups, as well as indentured servants, sailors, and, eventually, women. The laws that would bar most of these from taverns were justified by the generally accepted view that these groups were unusually prone to becoming drunk.

This is not to say that the upstanding were always sober and the downtrodden always drunk. Far from it. Along with the many individual accounts of people vomiting under the table, set in bilboes, or forced to wear the scarlet letter "D," the extensive legislation governing drunkenness suggests that it occurred across the board. Increasingly though, there developed a fictional divide between those who had mastered the art of drinking well and drunkenness, which happened mainly to Indians, sailors, and other marginalized groups, but never to white men of high social standing. (We realize the use of the term "Indian" is problematic. However, since the legislation of the time refers to Indians, it seems confusing to switch back and forth to Natives or First Nations' Peoples. In addition, in a later section, there is an antidrink movement begun by a political group that called itself Natives or Nativists, referring to second- or third-generation British settlers. To avoid further confusion, therefore, we will employ the term used most frequently in the contemporary records.)

Indians, in particular, were nearly always portrayed as drinking to drunkenness and, once drunk, behaving raucously. In 1636 Plymouth, it was made illegal to sell alcohol to Indians unless as medicine and, by the end of the 1660s, many communities had similar laws on the books. Punishments for noncompliance ranged from the confiscation of spirits (since any alcohol an Indian possessed was, by definition, contraband) to the jailing, and sometimes whipping, of the offender. In some cases, the rationale was clearly spelled out in the legislation—that it "caused disorder and offended colonists." In Maryland, a limit on sales to Indians was put in place on the grounds that it made them "drunk and mad" and that the result would be a war between Indians and settlers.[43] The most commonly expressed fear over excessive drinking among Indians was that it led to "rioting." Over time, this term has come to refer to angry crowds causing damage; during the colonial period, it had a broader usage that included "generally unrestrained." And restraint was a key aspect of the Protestant model for success and domination. As identified by future governor of Connecticut Gurdon Saltonstall in the 1690s,

immodest or garish clothing, dancing, drinking, singing, personal ambition, and family discipline were all tightly regulated so as to "give
check to those wretched Principles, of Pride and Contradiction, Disorder and Confusion."[44]

Initially, it was Indian rowdiness and rioting that was most feared
and, therefore, most heavily pathologized. Always aware that violent
conflict was a threat as they continued to encroach on Indian land, settlers were petrified of the natives—and with fair reason. In 1675–1676,
the bloody conflict between colonists and natives known as King Philip's
War helped cement the settlers' fears. More than half of New England's
settlements were attacked and almost eight hundred colonists lost their
lives in the Indians' response to settlers moving into their lands, particularly in western Massachusetts and Rhode Island. In Brookfield, Massachusetts, the entire town of eighty-two had to take refuge in Ayers'
Tavern, which Indians, acting like "wild bulls," attempted to burn to the
ground—twice. Between rain and efforts by firefighters, the tavern was
saved (during the siege, two sets of twins were born in the tavern,
bringing the Brookfield population up to eight-six).[45] The use of taverns
as garrisons—as with the Ayers' in Brookfield and Major Thomas
Fenner's in Providence—was a useful strategy for colonists against the
Indians, who lost some three thousand during the hostilities.

To what degree this stereotype of drunken Indians (more specifically,
drunken *violent* Indians) was based on truth is still a matter of intense
debate in scholarly circles, although a few misconceptions have been
put to rest. For instance, the popular notion that Indians are less able to
metabolize alcohol than Europeans has been rendered false. Attempts
to prove this have failed, as has the quest to identify a genetic basis for
alcoholism. Among other problems with the theory, it makes the all-too-
common mistake of identifying all the populations who lived on both
American continents before Europeans as a monolithic "race." Other
theories have been advanced to account for the widespread reports of
Indian drunkenness. Historian Andrew Barr contends that the "firewa-
ter myth" could well be a result of different cultural mores. Indians consumed large quantities of drugs such as tobacco and other inhalants in
spiritual ceremonies to find enlightenment by "devouring" the spirit
contained. A bottle of liquor, then, would have been seen as something
to be consumed in its entirety in order to achieve an altered state—not
something to drink semimoderately throughout the day (the acceptable
"dram" drinking of colonial America) and somewhat less moderately at

social occasions. Less acceptable, of course, was binge drinking, which, nevertheless, was becoming more popular all the time, judging from the many New England laws lamenting the rampant drunkenness "fallen out at the inns and common victualing-houses."

There's some anecdotal evidence to support Barr's theory. As early as 1630, Indian alcohol consumption was something French settler Paul Le Jeune of the St. Lawrence Valley thought worth noting. "The Savages have always been gluttons," he writes, "but since the coming of the Europeans they have become such drunkards . . . Give two Savages two or three bottles of brandy, they will sit down and, without eating, will drink, one after the other, until they have emptied them."[46] Forty years later, in describing colonial New York, Daniel Denton writes that Indians "do not care for drinking, unless they have enough to make themselves drunk." European settlers might have simply failed to realize that alcohol was used, as historian Peter Mancall writes, in "spiritual and psychological quests . . . to achieve a greater sense of personal power."[47]

In addition to the cultural differences, there was the aggravating factor that some tribes might have had limited experience with fermented beverages (some, but not many, would have consumed fermented corn and spruce beers) and were not prepared for the introduction of distilled spirits, obviously a much more intense version of alcohol. Aftershocks from the introduction of spirits were not unique to North America, either. The Brits took at least thirty years to adjust to *genever* (Dutch gin), easily traceable from the five Gin Acts aimed at controlling vice and debauchery passed between the years 1729 and 1751. After that time (and considerable moral panic over fifteen thousand gin palaces—about one for every forty-five residents), however, gin-soaked Londoners learned to drink it for what it was—namely, *not* beer.

Still others have speculated that Indians learned to drink from the "wrong" types of colonists—sailors and fur traders.[48] This theory, though, reinforces the precise prejudice against marginal groups and their alcohol established during early colonial days. The notion that Indians would have picked up civilized habits had they learned to drink from respectable town elders and not *couriers de bois*, perpetuates the idea that there were two types of drinkers: degenerate drunks and those who had mastered "the art of drinking well."

While it's quite possible that the intense fear colonists felt toward the Indians was a factor in an overreporting of drunkenness, as were cultural factors and inexperience with alcohol, raucous behavior did occur regularly in some Indian tribes. Lurking beneath the surface in all this, however, is the problem that, at least in the early days, the alcohol being abused came directly *from* the Europeans, who needed to trade it for Indian goods. In fact, there's even evidence that alcohol was used by British settlers to gain an upper hand in negotiations for land. Chief Miantonomah of the Narragansett tribe was said to have been plied with liquor in order to secure his loyalty to the British colonists at Samuel Cole's tavern in Boston—the town's first tavern of any note, established in 1634, directly across the street from Governor Winthrop's residence.

There were those who simply ignored and defied the laws prohibiting the sale of alcohol to Indians or took advantage of lax regulations. One generous colony was Maryland, which limited the sale of alcohol to Indians to a gallon of wine or five gallons of cider per day. In Massachusetts, residents provided a bushel of corn and three quarts of wine to any Indian who delivered a dead wolf. There were also laws that exempted some traders from prohibitions on exchanging alcohol with Indians.

That there was a "wrong" type of drinking also implied there was a "right" type of drinking—one that town elders and the colonial society elites clearly had mastered. Almost certainly there's a grain of truth to the idea that, given a tight-knit colonial community and its harsh punishments for straying outside of established rules for behavior, there may have been a greater sense of decorum. But it's impossible to accept the oft-advanced argument that almost all early English settlers were temperate social drinkers, and for two main reasons: the sheer volume of alcohol consumed and the extensive and elaborate tavern-licensing laws.

As we've seen, the settlers drank sizeable quantities of alcohol throughout the day and to mark nearly every occasion—weddings, funerals, harvests, births, ordinations, the openings of new buildings, and, most especially, training days. These latter centered around afternoon military drills meant to maintain the colonists' defenses against Indians. As these afternoons progressed, however, the volunteer soldiers tended to fight one another after getting "drunk as David's sow," an early American expression meaning beastly drunk. Cotton Mather (son of the aforementioned Increase) complained that these had degenerated into "little more than drinking days." Like most everything else, training days were centered on taverns, especially since the captain of the local militia was often a "tapper of strong waters," too. By evening, so many strong waters had been tapped, men were indiscriminately firing into the air.

So, regardless of how close-knit and family-oriented the community, there was plenty of drunkenness, confirmed by the many reports, both official and unofficial, of people abusing themselves with drink and the assorted punishments meted out and, as mentioned earlier, the amount of legislation designed to control and prevent public drinking and drunkenness. Forty pieces of legislation were introduced in Massachusetts alone over the course of a hundred years.

In fact, one of the very first edicts to an American colony was a demand sent to Governor Francis Wyatt from the London Company in 1622 for a "speedie redress" of the shameful amount of drinking taking place on Virginia plantations, where an estimated half of the colonists' income was being spent on alcohol.[49] Nonetheless, it was the Indians and indentured servants who were singled out as the primary groups that couldn't handle their alcohol. As a result, antitavern and strict licensing legislation (with a view to limiting that drinking) was introduced swiftly in all colonies. In Virginia two early laws were explicitly aimed at controlling the indentured servant population—one limiting the number of taverns per county, the other the amount of credit that could be extended to anyone other than the aristocracy. Such measures were also meant to reduce escape attempts by indentured servants working out commuted sentences on plantations, where conditions were generally inhumane. Fleeing truants would often use ordinaries, on credit, to try to wait out their period of indenture.

In the late 1660s, Virginia began enacting stricter tavern legislation to discourage the use of ordinaries as an escape route for indentured servants by limiting the credit for patrons who were "neglecting their callings" and, having "contracted debts beyond their abilities of payment," sought to abscond "out of the country to the detriment of the publique." Nathaniel Bacon Jr., one of the country's first reformers, attempted to outlaw all ordinaries, except those in Jamestown and near the York River ferry. In 1691, further measures were required, apparently, since it became illegal for tavernkeepers to give credit for more than three hundred pounds of tobacco (enough to buy about ten gallons of wine), except to those who were masters of at least two servants. And in 1710, having cleared the official ordinaries of all but the gentry, Virginia lawmakers went after illegal "disorderlies" and unlicensed tippling houses where "not only the looser sort of people resort, get drunk, and commit many irregularities, but servants and negroes are entertained and encouraged to purloin their masters' goods for supporting their extravagance."[50]

Despite supposedly mastering the "art of drinking well," many of the colonial Virginia gentry got drunk enough to alarm authorities. However, they apparently weren't committing "irregularities" and therefore weren't as severely punished, thanks to a 1699 revision to Virginia law that reduced the monetary fine for drunkenness from ten shillings to five. For those who couldn't afford to pay the fine, by contrast, the punishment was made *more* severe. Where drunkenness was once punished by a three-hour visit to the stocks, now it would merit ten lashes "laid upon his or her beare back." The law specifies that the lashes should be "well laid on."[51]

Maryland made nearly identical revisions to its laws at around the same time. In addition, though, if tavernkeepers there made it their "practice to draw in and entertain the seamen" and give more than five shillings credit to their sailor patrons, they would lose the amount they were owed. That's what you got for encouraging sailors to "ruin" themselves with drink (and in the process, their wives and children, as it was suggested in a 1712 Virginia Act).[52] This two-tiered judgment of problem-drinkers brings to mind Dylan Thomas's definition of an alcoholic as "somebody you don't like who drinks as much as you do."

Landlords of the taverns were supposed to monitor, curtail, and, in some cases, prohibit the accompanying rituals that were seen to encourage raucous drinking. In Massachusetts in the mid-seventeenth century, there was much controversy surrounding "drinking healths"—the practice of toasting to your drinking companion's health, the queen's health, or anyone else's health. Although this practice seems pretty innocent at first glance, one round necessitated a reciprocal round (so as not to seem to be welching), and each toast inevitably led to the next, more ambitious one, especially in cases in which barroom orators were trying to outdo one another with clever verses and songs. Toasting brought out both the group's camaraderie and competitiveness. (We imagine the last toast of the night being particularly eloquent.) Drinking healths transformed the tavern from a place where a colonist could come in for a refreshing pint (the ideal) into a place where he could get caught up in the colonial version of a drinking game. Increase Mather claimed that "healthing" obliged men to drink a large quantity of liquor "as an Indication of their Praying for the Prosperity of such a Person."

This, Mather argued, was a heathen activity and merely the flip-side of wishing someone ill with an evil potion. It also smacked of the same idolatry that dissenters accused Roman Catholics of in their worship. The seemingly extreme reactions to healthing suggested the suspicion that it was akin to transubstantiation—a severe charge in New England.[53] Finally, it also led to heated conversations among merry-makers— possibly dangerous and potentially seditious.

Governor John Winthrop, better known for his "city upon a hill" sermon, in which he articulated the ideals of the Puritan settlers and laid the groundwork for "American exceptionalism" (the contentious notion that the country is unique for its egalitarian ideals), was actually one of the first Americans to wage a "war" on drinking healths, a practice he felt was tearing his community apart. In 1630, Winthrop began his war on toasts with a plan to lead by example, disallowing them in his own home. In declaring his intention to give up healths, he pointed out that they were out of fashion anyway, having grown "little and little to disuse." As historian Ernest H. Baldwin points out, this observation was probably more fantasy than reality since, nine years later, perhaps dismayed that his house was one of the few places where health-drinking was actually in disuse, Winthrop had to abolish "that abominable practice of drinking healths" over the rest of the region. Those who persisted paid a fine for stubbornly engaging in an activity that led to "drunkenness, quarrelling, bloodshed, uncleanness, misspense of precious time."[54]

In 1645, the law against toasting was taken off the books as Winthrop's idealized image of the new community ultimately lost out to the reality that tavern rituals and the camaraderie and community-bonding that resulted—drunken or not—were far too important to colonial life to simply give up. But neither would it be the end of America's first moral crusade. In 1663, the law was back in Massachusetts, this time, "for the special benefit of shipmasters who, while their ships rode at anchors in colonial harbors, were wont to punctuate their toasts with cannon shots."[55] Pamphlets against healths were circulated in 1682, detailing 120 separate incidents in which toasting had led to immediate divine punishment, including one story of a woman who was hoisted into the air by the devil after drinking a health.[56]

Winthrop and other moral arbiters were also concerned about the songs that tended to accompany the celebrations. While most of the surviving colonial songs are clean enough for a schoolhouse (mostly variations on existing English songs such as "Greensleeves" or "The Girl I Left Behind Me"), there were plenty of vulgar ditties making the rounds at the time. One such bawdy example is the early-eighteenth-century "My Husband's a Mason":

My husband's a mason, a mason, a mason.
A very fine mason is he.
All day long he lays bricks, lays bricks, lays bricks.
At night he comes home and lays me.
Tra la la.
At night he comes home and lays me.
My husband's a butcher, a butcher, a butcher. A very fine butcher is he.
All day long he stuffs sausage, stuffs sausage, stuffs sausage.
At night he comes home and stuffs me.
Tra la la
At night he comes home and stuffs me.[57]

Surprising as this song might seem to those who might have assumed Puritan entertainment mainly took the form of quilting, it's actually relatively tame. Compare it with "The Sea Crab" (this version circa 1620–1650), which tells of a fisherman who stored his day's catch in the chamber pot—but neglected to warn his wife.

The good wiffe, she went to doe as shee was wont;
Up start the Crabfish, & catcht her by the C—.

When the fisherman tries to intervene, the crab pinches his nose with its other claw. The fisherman then yells for his kids to get the doctor to pry "your father's nose and your mother's cunt apart." There are several other verses in which the predicament is described in equally colorful ways.

Increase Mather had his concerns about the bawdy songs and recitations, although both he and son Cotton clearly worried about the big picture, too—that drunken sociability and easy discourse at the tavern could undermine the social order.[58] The Mathers were, of course, correct in their suspicions. Drinking and discussing politics *were* disruptive to the social order—and made even more dangerous by groups trying to impress one another with both oratory and drinking prowess. The war on toasts and efforts to keep bawdy drinking songs out of taverns was part of an attempt to redefine drinking into two categories—healthful drinking and drunken fits. But it was also an early recognition of the radical potential of toasting, which was destined to become a major part of the rebellions of the next hundred years and, ultimately, the revolution that was to reshape not only the nation but also political philosophy in the Western world.

Increasingly antidemocratic legislation limiting toasting and freedom of association endorsed by Winthrop, Mather, and others was a result of the paradox the tavern embodied in colonial society, namely, that the same institution that was absolutely necessary for the smooth running of the colony was rapidly becoming a place for dangerous political debate. With the eyes of the world upon it, the "city upon a hill" had a clear mission and little room for dissenting views on how the vision should be realized. Attempts at repression, however, both by Puritan and British colonial leaders in other settlements, would ultimately backfire and lead to the fight for independence, self-determination, and the freedom to associate—in bars.

2

A DISSENTER WALKS INTO A BAR

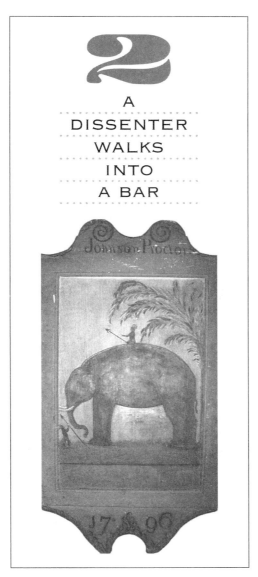

JOHNSON PROCTOR TAVERN SIGN

*Johnson Proctor was a descendant of John Proctor, the tavern-owner
from Salem who was hanged during the witchcraft delusion. The tavern and farm
remained in the Proctor Family until 1851. This sign is circa 1800 and was inspired
by a wealthy Salem merchant's purchase of a two-year-old Indian elephant that
toured America. Image courtesy of the Peabody Historical Society.*

Despite considerable antitavern and antidrink legislation introduced year after year throughout seventeenth and early eighteenth century New England, taverns and drinking were unquestionably on the rise. When attempts were made to limit them, taverns behaved, instead, like a hydra and multiplied. Despite Boston's effort to halve the number of taverns, the number nearly doubled between 1675 and 1681.

Worse was a near epidemic disregard for laws designed to reduce drinking. One visitor to Boston in 1682 remarked that the laws looked like "Scarecrows, compared to their habits," and that the "worst drunkards" could easily find company, "for all their pretences to Sobriety." As we've seen, of the many antidrink taboos being ignored, healthing was right up there with the best of them. When Increase Mather had attacked the practice some years earlier, a major component of his qualms stemmed from what he called the "witchiness" of toasting healths. What real difference was there, he argued, between wishing friends well with a pint and wishing enemies harm with a voodoo doll?

One of the better-known accused witches—and she just happened to also be widely known as a tavern-owner, too—was one Mrs. Bishop (we'll get to her first name later), who kept a tavern of the same name, Bishop's, located near Salem Town. Some nights, to the horror of the neighbors, Bishop's degenerated into a place of "great prophainness" and "iniquity" and it was rumored that patrons frequented Bishop's to play shovel-board and drink fermented apple juice into all hours of the night. In those days, this meant after 9 PM—"last call" in 1690s Massachusetts.

Bishop's may well have been doing worse than simply serving after hours. While licensed only to sell cider to out-of-towners, some locals persisted in hanging around with Bishop and her guests in defiance of the law and "remained up late at night, playing checkers and drinking and being merry."[1] Checkers and shovel-board, like all "Sports of the Innyard," including "dicing, tally, bowls, billiards, slidegroat, shuffle-board, quoits, loggets [and] ninepins,"[2] were all strictly prohibited in licensed establishments. Apparently the slidegroat playoffs would get particularly rowdy.

A couple of clarifications might be in order here: first, the distinction between "Salem Town" and "Salem Village," the latter being a more rural community to the northwest. The Village's attempts at gaining autonomy would actually cause much of the tension that resulted in the looming trials. We should also explain the apparent prominence of women tavern-owners. One might expect women to have been pro-hibited from running taverns in Puritan New England, but, in many ways, the era was actually less restrictive than the Victorian era when it came to gender roles. Obviously, women did run taverns, and, even though there was often a condition attached that a male overseer or guarantor be involved, women were granted tavern licenses in most of the original colonies, especially if they were widowed and might, oth-erwise, have become a burden on the community.

Another clarification or two will certainly be in order as we get back to Bishop's tavern, where all the partying was about to come to an end. Accusations of witchcraft will do that. According to one familiar version of the story, a tavern-owning woman named Bishop was hanged on Gal-lows Hill, June 10, 1692, making a tapster the first victim of the Salem witch hysteria. But it has taken many historians many years and much research to sort this out—a confusion rooted in a mix-up involving two women named Bishop, Sarah and Bridget—and a third named Sarah Osborne. The two Sarahs owned taverns—Bishop's obviously, but also the Ship tavern that Osborne ran in Salem Town.

Bridget Bishop did not own a tavern but was well known for having a tight "red paragon bodice." It's often, but mistakenly, thought that this bodice had been used in examinations as evidence of her wanton char-acter, but was really being examined to see if it was a garment for a voo-doo doll. In any case, Bridget was the one executed that June 10. She was not the first to die as a result of these chaotic times, however. That would have been Sarah Osborne who was one of the first three of some twenty citizens eventually fingered for witchcraft. She would die in prison on May 10, a month before things hit a fevered pitch. The tavern owning, shovel-boarding Sarah Bishop was similarly arrested, exam-ined and jailed but, with husband Edward, broke out of prison that August and escaped town.

Sarah Osborne had married a man named Robert Prince, who him-self had inherited the tavern. Upon his death, Sarah was left to run the Ship, considered the best tavern in town. There was just one problem with her newfound fortune, namely, that Prince's sister Rebecca, now a member of the prominent Putnam family since her marriage to John Putnam Jr., argued, with the support of her in-laws, that she should have some share of the Ship's profits. The amount of money at stake was probably fairly substantial since Salem Town was a prosperous center, and the Ship was where all notable Salem visitors stayed, making it the most powerful business center in the region. Almost all Salem Town trade would have been conducted on its premises and the proprietor would have had a significant amount of power and knowledge over the town's affairs—an important public office. For instance, some ten years before the witchcraft trials began, meetings regarding the specifics of the construction of the Salem town hall had taken place at the Ship, where, in fact, all town meetings would be held until the hall was finished. Even with the hall completed, the Ship still would have been the forum for many business and political matters—sometimes because it would have represented a less formal arena for discussion; other times, simply because it was warm.

While some were staying warm in the Ship over the long, cold winter of 1691–1692, a group of girls, including twelve-year-old Ann Putnam Jr. (Rebecca's niece), Abigail Williams and Elizabeth Parris were keeping themselves entertained by practicing magic at the Parris homestead under the tutelage of their domestic slave, Tituba. Before long, the girls' "spectral sightings"—along with their seizures and contortions—would provide the basis for the trials to come.

Tituba was new to the community, imported by Samuel Parris, the new minister hired by Salem Villagers so that they would no longer be dependent on Salem Town for all their godly needs. Parris, leaving failed business ventures in Barbados, brought with him not only his family, slave and some stern religious convictions, but also a modest library containing Cotton Mather's 1689 publication *Memorable Providences, Relating to Witchcrafts and Possessions*, an extraordinary early true-crime account of the case of Goody Glover, a Boston Irish washerwoman who was tried and executed for witchcraft.[3]

Many historians have argued that the names of the accused had been suggested to Ann Putnam (and by extension, the other girls) by her family. Sarah Osborne, Sarah Good and Tituba had been the first, rounded up on the first day of March 1692, for examination at Nathaniel Ingersoll's ordinary. At least that was the plan until it became apparent that not all the curious gawkers would be able to cram themselves into Ingersoll's tap room. The very first hearing of the trials was moved to the town hall, although later inquests into "witchiness" were held in taverns—the Globe Tavern on Essex Street in Salem Town, for instance. And while Ingersoll's lost out on the dubious distinction of being first, the tavern remained the unofficial host for the proceedings. Guards and out-of-town justices stayed there and, over cakes and cider, visitors and locals congregated to rehash the day's events. The tavern buzzed with speculation throughout the entire affair.

By June, Osborne was no longer one of the main subjects of conversation, however. She had died in prison on May 10, 1692, a month before the slew of accusations against so many others, most of whom, as it turned out, were feuding with the Putnams. The feud was rooted, in part, over what may well have been colonial America's worst commute. By the middle of the seventeenth century, greater Salem sprawled over a fairly large area, but the only meeting-house serving the public's religious needs remained in Salem Town. For those on the furthest outskirts of Salem Village, that meant a three-hour walk—each way—one made even more miserable during the unforgiving Massachusetts winters. Members of the church were expected to make the trek twice a week and the full implication of this will be obvious to any contemporary commuter: it wasn't simply the walk that was a burden, it was the opportunity cost. Travel time took its toll on the productivity of the farmers, who not only had to give up a day's work twice a week, but also had to choose between leaving their farms unprotected on those days or spending money on some heathen of a guard who wasn't concerned about his soul's final destination. Salem Village was very much a western frontier. Indian attacks were still a serious threat and the memory of King Philip's War remained vivid.

Salem Village farmers, therefore, had been campaigning for their own church for some time and, led by the Putnams, managed to pull it off in 1689 with the hiring of Samuel Parris. Religious self-determination, however, is relatively easy compared with the attendant problem of how to finance it. The failed merchant-turned-preacher had to be promised a salary and abode in order to be lured to the frontier. The hiring committee which decided on his generous incentive package was headed up by Nathaniel and John Putnam, two other close relatives, and Deacon Lieutenant Nathaniel Ingersoll. On top of promises of firewood and other supplies, the Putnam-led group offered Parris ownership of the town parsonage, the adjoining barn, and two acres of land—despite a prior village resolution that the parsonage would always remain communal property. Outraged that the community's public space had been turned private, some villagers complained that not only was the offer essentially illegal but, further, had been made in secrecy. Nobody other than the Putnams and Ingersoll was privy to the decision until after it was too late to rescind.

The donation of the parsonage might have been the most grievous offence, but the kindling that stoked the fire was, literally, kindling. When Parris demanded that the residents of Salem Village bring him firewood, he was simply ignored. This act of noncompliance was, in essence, America's first tax revolt. Just who was behind this early "rebellion" remains unclear. However, we can find ample anti-Parris activity going on at Bishop's tavern, owned by Sarah and Edward Bishop, in addition to the merry-making and shovel-boarding. This popular house of entertainment was rather conveniently located on Ipswich Road, smack-dab in the middle of that arduous commute between the rural farming area of Salem Village and the meeting-house in Salem Town. The Bishops weren't the only entrepreneurs to figure out that Ipswich Road was prime real estate. There were several taverns on this major thoroughfare, from the very north end of the road, where the Bishops, Joshua Rea, and Walter Phillips had hung out shingles, all the way to the southern tip and hostler John Proctor. All were Putnam enemies, all had signed a petition opposing the installation of Samuel Parris, most were opposed to the witch trials, and many were later accused.[4]

Proctor, the model for the character of the same name in Arthur Miller's play *The Crucible*, had a tavern license to sell beer, cider, and liquor that his father had applied for in 1666 on the grounds that his house was "in the common roadway." Presumably, John Proctor Sr. was already letting people rest and refresh en route to Salem Town and, seeing as he had a built-in clientele, decided it would make sense to offer public accommodation and make a little money off the deal. Like the Bishops, he was granted a license to sell—but, again, exclusively to travelers, not to locals who might be tempted to engage in tavern-loafing when their time would be better spent working to build a model society.

How closely Proctor's son, John Jr., stuck to this particular rule is anyone's guess. But, since he would later get into trouble for drinking "'til piffled," fighting with his wife, selling alcohol to Indians, and accepting property in exchange for drink (another illegal activity), it's easy to imagine him serving a few ciders to locals. Proctor not only raked it in at the till but, with multiple properties and business interests, was one of Salem's rising merchant class—a group that felt a little less constrained by the restrictive social order than the farmers who resided further afield. With tradesmen, craftsmen and even the occasional farmer, all using the tavern as a rest stop, the Ipswich Road merchants were worldly in comparison. Proctor and allies would have felt more closely aligned with Salem Town, and almost certainly less than inclined to provide for Samuel Parris and his family.

At the root of the Salem hysteria and tragedy, then, was a long-standing dispute between urban merchants and rural farmers. This entailed debates over the tax structure and the redistribution of income and, finally, political and religious self-determination, all of which polarized residents of the geographically distinct Salem Town and its rural "suburb." In other words, the Salem Witch Trials were a preview of many of the same battles that would define American politics throughout history and continue to do so—rural versus urban, reactionaries versus progressives. It was a micro-version of the Red and the Blue. And the taverns in which they drank.

Regardless of whether or not the tax revolt was specifically organized in the Ipswich Road taverns, they were certainly progressive and anti-Putnam centers of resistance. Three of the tavern-owners were among those eventually accused and several others proved to be very vocal dissenters during the trials. Proctor, along with his wife, Elizabeth, and a stunning eleven other members of his family, were all arrested on suspicion of witchcraft—a particularly rigorous persecution of his family that suggests he was a very special target for the Putnam/Parris clan.

Perhaps Proctor invited such singling out because he was particularly vocal. Early on, he offered the moderate suggestion that all of the *accusers* should be hanged. He then threatened to beat his servant Mary Warren—like the preteen girls, she had begun to have spectral sightings of her own—if she continued to testify and produce fits at the trials (evidence of demon possession). After Proctor's own arrest, he would continue to display a disobedient streak, writing to Increase Mather and four other Boston ministers, pleading for intervention. Although Increase had apparently moderated his views about heathen activities and was against the use of spectral evidence (the hearsay reporting of ghosts' accusations was used to convict many of the accused), he did not respond to Proctor's plea. Mather's son, Cotton, however, had no qualms about including spectral evidence and chronicled the trials in his new incendiary true crime book, *Wonders of the Invisible World*. His sensationalist journalism helped keep the horror and hysteria alive in places like Ingersoll's tavern, where ever-percolating public opinion helped guide the outcome.

While Cotton Mather's writing is often credited with strengthening support for witch-hunting, Proctor's writing campaign and his protestations of innocence did not effect any change and he was hanged on August 19, 1692. His pregnant wife, Elizabeth, fared better, even though one of the young girls had testified that the ghosts of two dead men had appeared, alleging her guilt. One had apparently said that Elizabeth had bewitched him as revenge for a difference they had over the price of cider; the other ghost claimed he had incurred her wrath over an unpaid bar tab. She was convicted and sentenced to death but her planned execution was postponed until after she delivered her baby. The delay saved her life and she was freed in May of the following year. Having been convicted as a witch, though, her rights as a person had been revoked. As such, she had no claim to her dead husband's estate and lived in poverty for many years. While the historical record will not permit certainty as to any specific conspiracy against Parris taking place in Proctor's or Bishop's taprooms, it is clear these were prime centers of anti-Putnam activity. The fact that the Ipswich tavernkeepers were so disproportionately targeted makes them some of the first victims of an authoritarian backlash against the political power the tavern was beginning to exert.

Salem, however, was not the first place where taverns and their owners began to flex their political influence. In Philadelphia in 1684, legislators bandied about a local excise tax on liquor (an excise refers to a tax on a specific product, usually local, and a levy that the producer is expected to pay, then pass on to the consumer). A group of merchants, half of it publicans, immediately petitioned the council and won. Two decades later in Philadelphia, Samuel Carpenter, owner of the Globe Tavern and brother Joshua, a brewer and owner of the pre-eminent Tun Tavern, led another early tax revolt, simply refusing to pay William Penn what he said they owed the state.[5]

In an attempt to control taverns and the radical political ideals that were beginning to ferment inside them, legislation was ramped up to ensure that the most disenfranchised members of society weren't allowed to congregate and organize in taverns. Of particular concern were slaves and, accordingly, there were severe restrictions on serving "black or Indian" slaves, as well as indentured servants, throughout the colonies. In seventeenth-century Manhattan, however, slaves were subject to slightly less deplorable conditions than elsewhere and, in fact, frequented taverns quite regularly. This state of affairs was the fleeting legacy of Dutch colonization and slave exploitation that allowed slaves some limited rights and freedoms, including the right to work for wages, accumulate property and, on occasion, petition for full or partial freedom.

Just before the end of Dutch rule in 1664, some 75 petitions for full emancipation were granted to those who already had partial freedom, increasing the population of freedmen in the city who mingled with slaves who "enjoyed" relatively humane living conditions.[6]

Things began to change after the New York Slave Revolt of 1712, in which some two dozen black slaves, after a reported tavern rendezvous, wound up killing nine whites, five of them slave-owners. The violent outburst was blamed, in part, simply on the amount of freedom other black slaves seemed to enjoy in mixing with freedmen. Hysteria over the possibility of another occurrence prompted an almost immediate introduction of that year's "Black Code," which reduced conditions for slaves in New York to a par with those on Southern plantations. The code explicitly prohibited relationships or transactions between slaves and freed blacks, and outlawed the assembly of more than two slaves at a time. The code was amended again in 1730 to specifically target the persistent problem of slaves still managing to gain access to public spaces, mainly taverns. It dictated that no person should sell "rum or other strong Liquor to any Negro Indian or Mulato Slaves or Slaves."

But just as many had defied laws prohibiting healthing, so did New Yorkers ignore laws aimed at curtailing black patronage in taverns. There were at least ten New York drinking establishments regularly serving slaves in the early eighteenth century, two of which—John Romme's Tavern near the Battery, and Oswego, a tavern on the Hudson River near Trinity Church and owned by tapster John Hughson—became infamous. Hughson was indicted and convicted, not long after Oswego's grand opening, of serving a multi-racial patronage, in the winter of 1740–1741. On top of that, Hughson had also become known as one of the city's most notorious fences, ever-eager to help move stolen goods (his tavern's name was derived from an upstate Indian trading post near Lake Ontario). Nonetheless, his greatest offense remained his stubborn insistence on serving black patrons, many of whom were slaves and therefore, by definition, forbidden to congregate in a tavern. Hughson's brazen disregard for the laws continued even after his conviction (for which he was let off as a first-time offender) and Oswego went on to become a huge hit among slaves for its Sunday after-church "great feasts," consisting of mutton, goose, rum, cider, and punch. The place was lively throughout the week, slaves popping in en route to and/or from household errands, and known for dancing, live music, cockfights, and frank discussions about the harsh conditions under which they lived.[7]

There were other taverns that served slaves, but Hughson's was one of the most notorious "disorderly" houses of the day, thanks to its also being a brothel, one in which Margaret Sorubiero—also known as Salinburgh, also known as Kerry, also known as the "Newfoundland Beauty"—worked. Everyone knew her as "Peggy." Sorubiero accepted both black and white clients and would become scandalous for having a child with a black slave named Caesar. In 1741, Peggy's paramour was involved in a robbery and stashed the stolen goods at Oswego. When the authorities came to the tavern looking for the conspirators, they happened upon Mary Burton, a sixteen-year-old indentured servant who worked for the Hughsons, who was more than happy to give up the name of everybody involved in the robbery, the fencing, and, it would turn out, just about anyone whose name she'd ever even heard.

This event, unfortunately, coincided with several others that already had tensions running high in New York. First, it was the tail-end of the harshest winter in anybody's memory. Second, there was the matter of the five captive "Spanish Negroes," who, despite their vigorous claims of being freedmen, had been shackled upon arrival and sold as slaves. Their vows of vengeance over the injustice were still ringing in New Yorkers' ears when people began to grow alarmed over a series of fires— some small, some large, some perhaps set accidentally, others probably set to create a distraction for thieves. New Yorkers feared, however, that these were a coordinated attack of some sort, possibly signaling a second slave conspiracy.

The first fire hit the governor's house at Fort George on March 18, 1741. Four more fires, in relatively prominent peoples' homes or businesses, struck in less than three weeks. When four more fires broke out on April 6, one at a property owned by wealthy businessman Adolph Philipse, where a black man was seen running away, all it took was for one witness to cry out, "A negro, a negro!" for a full-fledged racial panic to overtake the city.

Mary Burton had been quite happy to finger the people she felt were involved in this apparent slave conspiracy, too. The teenager claimed to have once overheard Hughson plotting something with slaves and saying that when it was done, he'd be "king," while Caesar would be "governor" and Cuffee (Adolph Philipse's slave) would have untold riches. Cuffee would also be identified as the man seen running from the fire at Philipse's. According to Burton, Cuffee had also bragged that "in a short time" the wealthy Philipse would have "less" and he would have "more." Apparently,

Burton had also overheard slaves talking in the tavern when, in the midst of a heated discussion about whether or not to kill all the slave-owners, one had said, "God damn all the white people." Only one slave objected to this, on the grounds that his particular master was "too good" to kill. Even Hughson had been heard to say (although not necessarily on that particular occasion) that the country was not good and that there were "too many gentlemen here, and they made negroes work hard."[8]

Some historians contend that, rather than being a politically motivated slave revolt, the conspiracy Burton overheard and testified to may well have been a Hughson attempt to organize an early crime syndicate. Apparently, he'd been working to unite the city's two main gangs, the Fly Boys, whose main headquarters was at Romme's, and the Long Bridge Boys, led by Prince, a slave who worked out of Oswego. If Hughson could have arranged for some cooperation between the two, he might have been able to divide up the territory and become the central commander ("king") of the syndicate. His second-rank "governors" would include Caesar, Prince, and Cuffee—a triumvirate, incidentally, sometimes known as the "Geneva Club" for having once been caught stealing Dutch gin. That was not, however, how it was perceived by Daniel Horsmanden, Frederick Philipse (father of Adolph), and Chief Justice James DeLancey, three of the principal players in the criminal proceedings for what came to be known as the Slave Conspiracy of 1741. After Burton turned in Caesar and the Hughsons, she was quick to implicate Romme, Prince, Cuffee, and an ally of Cuffee's named Quack. Romme, perhaps thanks to his familial relationship with a prominent politician, was allowed to leave New York for the South. The rest were not so lucky. Caesar and Prince were hanged first, while Cuffee and Quack were burned at the stake by a crowd of angry New Yorkers, despite the fact they had been offered reprieve on the condition they confess in full—which they had.

Hughson, along with his wife, Sarah, and Peggy, the Newfoundland beauty, were all hanged next. Hughson's body was left to next to Caesar's for New Yorkers to view and, in one of the more bizarre twists in an already bizarre tale, witnesses swore that Hughson's body turned black and Caesar's white. In the end, as Burton kept naming names, 152 people were arrested. The five vengeful Spanish negroes were of course hanged, as was a Roman Catholic priest by the name of John Ury.

This mass delusion is a clear indication of the level of hysteria over race and safety in eighteenth-century New York. The tragedy grew from the anxiety over taverns that defied the law and allowed slaves a place to assemble, drink, and air grievances. Throughout the conspiracy trials, it became clear that Hughson's ambitions to become boss of the city's first crime syndicate were of minimal concern when compared against his tavern practices. For illustration, in Hughson's court proceedings, Justice Philipse, took issue with the idea that it could ever be "lawful to sell a penny dram or a penny worth of rum to a slave, without the consent or direction of his master." He pointed out that this was "directly contrary to an act of assembly now in force, for the better regulating of slaves," a reference to the 1712 Black Code.[9] But it was Justice DeLancey who most neatly summed up New Yorkers' anxieties when he attacked Hughson at his sentencing for running a tavern that was "guilty of not only making negroes their equals but even their superiors by waiting upon, keeping with, and entertaining them."[10] Hughson was literally demonized throughout the trial and was called the "devil incarnate" and an "arch rebel against God."[11] Little wonder, perhaps, New Yorkers had visions of his body turning black after death.

Some say the conspiracy was criminal, others that it was political. In reality, the truth might be somewhere in between. The Geneva Club's plans were the result of racial and class inequality, widespread food shortages, a severely depressed economy, and another cold, harsh winter. In addition, it seems clear that the airing of grievances in Hughson's tavern and his choice to supply the venue was political in its own right and an act that slave-owners *should* have feared.

The swift and brutal reaction was overtly political as well. Public hangings and burnings were warnings to both white tavernkeepers who might subvert the "natural order" and make "negroes their equals or even their superiors." The laws that this "devil incarnate" had broken were not simply there to prevent criminal conspiracy but also to keep blacks out of taverns, which, increasingly, were becoming the colonies' radical political centers.

Of course, the radical politics spilling out of taverns was, often as not, shrouded in an alcoholic haze. One such example of violent agitation was the Philadelphia Election Riots of 1742, in which Anglicans reacted aggressively to allegations that the city's Quakers were planning to rig an election by "bussing in" German immigrants—not legally eligible to vote—from surrounding rural regions to support Quaker candidates. Opposing the Quakers was the Proprietary Party, supported by many of Philadelphia's Anglicans.

Aggravating the situation were many of the same problems that plagued New Yorkers before the slave conspiracy a year earlier—a shortage of bread, general price increases, an unusually cold winter and Britain's ongoing war with Spain. What made matters worse in Philly, however, was the fact that the Quakers, as pacifists, had refused to support the war effort, which didn't win them any friends among the city's sailors. In the early morning hours of Election Day, sailors were already hanging out at Peter and Jonathan Robinson's Indian King, once one of Philadelphia's most respectable taverns. A rumor spread that, there, sailors were rallying support for a plan to "knock down the Broad brims" outside the polls.[12] We might think of Philadelphia as relatively quiet compared to tavern-infested New York, but it, too, had its edgy side. A few years before, at the Red Lion Tavern in Elbow Lane, one patron put down a wager that he could down a gallon and a half of Cyder Royall in ninety minutes. He did, then died on the spot.[13] Quakers were thought to be an entirely sober group, but were, in fact, not. One of the more popular drinks at the time was named a "Stewed Quaker."

Two Quakers, Thomas Lloyd and Israel Pemberton Jr., by all accounts entirely sober, went to the Indian King to try to calm things down. There, Lloyd and Pemberton found a Captain Mitchell buying rounds and shouting "every man his dram; and then march." His fears confirmed, Lloyd asked Mitchell to stop agitating his fellow sailors but the captain refused. Lloyd then appealed to tavernkeeper Robinson to cut off any sailors who "appeared too warm." Robinson responded in the tradition of America's best defiant keepers, swearing he would "serve who he pleased," then proceeded to pour a "large glass of rum" for Captain Mitchell.[14] (It could have been worse; it could have been a "Stewed Quaker.")

At ten in the morning somewhere between fifty and seventy sailors, post-dram, marched to the courthouse and started swinging. Quaker and German voters took shelter inside. The riot ultimately backfired as the public, horrified at the violence from the anti-Quakers, sided with the pacifists, who won the election handily.

As the Salem Witch Trials, the Slave Conspiracy in New York, and the Philadelphia Election Riots demonstrate, the role of the tavern was central but unfocused. And, just as authorities were coming to understand that role and beginning to look frantically for ways to control it, a group of radicals in Boston saw an opportunity to harness its power and bring it in line.

A REBEL WALKS
INTO THE BACK
ROOM OF A BAR

PINE TREE TAVERN SIGN

The owner of the Pine Tree Tavern was making his political allegiances clear to all potential patrons when he painted a liberty tree on the sign, indicating that he was sympathetic to the Sons of Liberty—if not one himself. Image courtesy of the Connecticut Historical Society.

Its reproduction now located on Boston's Union Street, the Green Dragon came to be known as the "headquarters of the American Revolution." Yet, as important as it was, the Dragon was but one of many taverns—and hardly the first—in which revolution was conceived, discussed, plotted and orchestrated.

As should by now be clear, politics and taverns have always shared a bed. The tavern was a social space where the public gathered to discuss the news, legal cases, religious and local political issues. Political action grew naturally from this set of circumstances and the events of the previous chapter—John Proctor's persecution, Philadelphia's early tax revolts and election riot, and the Slave Conspiracy in New York—were but the first of many political struggles that would define America's larger quest for self-determination.

Much of the tavern-related activity was sketchy and chaotic—but not all of it. In fact, there was a strain of political action in colonial taverns that was out and out respectable and reasoned. Some of this rationality may have stemmed from the tavern's more auspicious early usages—not only as a watering hole but also as a classroom and lecture hall. At Philadelphia's Indian King Tavern in 1749, for example, a Swedish pastor preached sermons on the second and third Sunday of every month. That same tavern would host lectures given by travelers just returning from Europe. Another lecture titled "The Divinity of Jesus Christ"—this time at Aaron Aorson's Nassau Street tavern in New York—was given by a man "more than 30 years an Atheist."[1]

As revolutionary and progressive as this might sound, it was nothing compared with the fiery potential of the live performances that were occasionally presented in taverns. Most settlements had prohibitions on theater from the outset, since theater was objectionable both on religious grounds (it was from the "Devil-Gods," according to Increase Mather) and on political grounds (because, as William Penn had explained, it was an art form aligned with revolutionary political thought and sedition). These prohibitions went unenforced rather quickly, however, and failed to be reinstated when many other repressive tavern licensing restrictions were dropped in the early eighteenth century. Before long, taverns even doubled as theaters. Aside from Punch and Judy shows, performances of *Richard III* and *The Beggar's Opera*—a satire aimed explicitly at British politicians—were mounted in taverns. Many plays became politically charged in the actors' interpretations and led to near-seditious discussions afterward.

Not all of the entertainments were so highfalutin', of course. About ten years before the pastor from Sweden turned up at the Indian King, the same venue boasted a cat with "one head, eight legs and two tails; and from the navel downwards it has two bodies of the female kind." Its preserved corpse may have crossed paths with an African leopard, which was on tour in Boston and Philadelphia taverns in 1743 and 1744. Other times, other taverns, patrons would be treated to the spectacle of the "white negro," a girl with grey eyes and white woolly hair. Or maybe orangutans, a "Large Sea Dog," baboons and crocodiles, not to mention the "Learned Pig," who could not only read and spell but also add, subtract, multiply and divide. For those of even less discerning tastes, there'd be entertainments like musical clocks, camera obscuras, cockfights and, perhaps the best of all, The Female Sampson, who lay "with her body extended between two chairs, bearing an Anvil of 300lb on her Breast" while two men pounded the anvil with sledge hammers.[2]

But when the entertainments weren't leaning toward the freakish, the lectures, sermons and theater performances helped spark discussion and spawned a new colonial phenomenon—clubs and associations. One such club was the Junto, (named after a mistaken interpretation of the Spanish word "junta," which was thought to simply mean "join" but actually can mean "assembly") established by Benjamin Franklin in 1727. The Junto's meetings were held in the Indian King, the very same space that would become home to conjoined cats, Swedish pastors, and stewed sailors getting pumped for their Election Day rumble against the Quakers. When Franklin frequented the Indian King, however, it was run by a respectable hostler by the name of John Biddle and its taproom was the very picture of civilization, a place where elevated discourse could thrive. Franklin devised the Junto as a society for the study of "useful" arts and decreed that, at the monthly meetings, "every member, in his turn, should produce one or more queries on any point of Morals, Politics, or Natural Philosophy (physics), to be discuss'd by the company." In addition, every member had to write an essay on a topic of his own choosing four times a year. Although the Junto met in a tavern and we know that Franklin had a taste for good beer, he apparently saw it as distinct from the rampant tavern-haunting that he critiqued as a waste of time. Franklin promoted his tavern club (and similar organizations), as well as the establishment of libraries, as healthy alternatives to the tavern. Apparently, he was a man who enjoyed contradictions. The Junto, incidentally, would eventually grow into the American Philosophical Society, it, too, born in a tavern.

Similar clubs sprouted up throughout the eighteenth century. Later, French writer and traveler Alexis de Tocqueville, commenting on the many associations and clubs, noted that "Americans of all ages, all conditions, and all dispositions constantly form associations."[3] Many of the clubs were instituted to facilitate communal education, which, since there were so few formal institutions for higher learning, was practically the only real option early Americans had. Philadelphia, for example, had no college until 1740. Franklin's meetings therefore represented the height of the city's intellectual life. In rural areas, the colonial tavern often doubled as a mini agricultural college, a place where farmers met to exchange tips. In urban areas, patrons were more likely to discuss high-minded affairs—philosophy and the arts—though few stuck so closely to the agenda of productive, sober debate and essay-writing as the Junto members did.

Dr. Alexander Hamilton, a traveling physician from Maryland who conveniently kept a diary recording his experiences, used tavern clubs as a way to introduce himself to like-minded society in foreign parts. In Boston, he was delighted with the "abundance of men of learning" he met at the Sun Tavern's Physical Club, where he and the members "drank punch, smoked tobacoo" and engaged in "agreeable conversation." In New York, though, Hamilton's hopes of meeting with people who could hold him in polite and enlightening conversation were often dashed. He was surprised, for instance, to discover that, at the Philosophical Club, "no matters of philosophy were brought upon the carpet." At Robert Todd's tavern, in which meetings of the Hungarian Club were held, he noted that some of the "toapers" seemed to think that "a man could not have a more sociable quality or enduement than to be able to pour down seas of liquor and remain unconquered while others sunk under the table." Throughout New York, instead of finding enlightenment, Hamilton was bombarded by young "whoreing rakes" who kept drinking healths to themselves and talking "smutt." He did qualify the smutt, however, as "polite." A few days later at a tavern called Waghorn's, Hamilton wrote that he met up with a "drunken doctor so intoxicated with liquor that he could scarce speak one connected sentence."[4]

By 1753, a young Whig, (Tories and Whigs were the American extension of the British two-party system, the Tories being the less liberal of the two) named William Livingston, later to be governor of New Jersey, began tackling what had become a problematic (but standard) aspect of politicking—the practice of buying drinks for voters at the polls. This widespread ritual was known as "treating" or, as Livingston called it, "Election-jobbing." He argued that it was one of the many rituals which, though "it may claim the Authority of Custom," was threatening one of New York's "constitutional privileges," and that it made people "venal, vicious, insensible of private Virtue, and of public Glory or Disgrace." Livingston was careful not to accuse anyone of outright bribery, since he didn't want to offend anybody in office who likely got there with a little election-jobbing of his own, but was clear that the practice would lead to nothing less than the downfall of society.[5]

"Swilling the planters with bumbo" (a contemporary drink made with rum, water, sugar and nutmeg, made popular in the Royal Navy), as the practice was sometimes called, was not simply a part of the New York political landscape but common across the colonies, accepted by most, and well on its way to becoming a long-standing American tradition. Even the Puritans celebrated Election Day with alcohol—nothing less than a full holiday on which it was customary to discuss events over drinks. While Puritan election days probably started out fairly civilized, it didn't take long for them to become fortified. Despite the violence and the concerns that many tavernkeepers were dispensing both alcohol and political influence, there were few laws that prohibited the mixing of the two. A couple of notable early exceptions: In 1705, a Virginia law outright prohibited alcohol at the polls and a 1678 Maryland law decreed that tavernkeepers couldn't also hold political office.[6]

More commonly, though, elections were pretty wet. It was standard for politicians to buy votes by spreading the "bumbo," not to mention Scotchem, Whistle-Belly Vengeance and Rum Switchel. And Fish House Punch if they were in Philadelphia. George Washington's liquor bill for his 1758 campaign is frequently cited as evidence of the regularity of this practice. Despite the fact that Virginia (where he was running to represent his people in the House of Burgesses) was one of the few colonies that had explicitly banned alcohol at the polls, Washington's good cheer amounted to the spreading around of forty-seven gallons of beer, thirty-four gallons of wine, two gallons of cider and three and a half pints of brandy. No election would have been complete without rum punch, of course, and, in this case, seventy gallons of it. That's a pretty hefty bar tab—especially as there were only 310 registered voters in the district.

John Adams complained about the practice: "An Artful Man, who has neither sense nor sentiment may by gaining a little sway among the Rabble of a Town, Multiply the Taverns and Dram shops and thereby secure the Votes of Taverner and Retailer of all, and the Multiplication of Taverns will make many who may be induced by Phlip and Rum to Vote for any Man whatever."[7] Of course, Adams had an axe to grind regarding alcohol and elections. While he won his 1766 bid for office in Braintree, Massachusetts, his colleague and political ally Cornet Bass did not share in the triumph. Bass won on his first ballot and might well have won the second if not for his supporters who, "after putting in their Votes the first Time, withdrew for Refreshment" at opponent Eben Thayer's tavern. Once properly refreshed, it seems they forgot to vote in round two. Adams' motivation aside, he certainly would have joined forces with Livingston, who was organizing his resistance to election-jobbing in that most obvious of settings—the tavern. It was Livingston's hope that the barroom might be reformed and reclaimed as a space for civilized discourse and, to that end, he instituted clubs like the Society for the Promotion of Useful Knowledge and the Society for Promoting Arts.

Some of this was an attempt to mimic the coffee-house and salon culture that was thriving in Paris and London at the time. In those caffeinated spaces, men of high social standing met, read and exchanged news, and engaged in the debate that would fuel coming political and philosophical changes in Europe and England. Some credit coffee-houses as creating an actual, self-defined "public." Through the individual discussions in clubs, coffee-houses, and salons, and the exchange of contentious viewpoints in newspapers (which were often read aloud and debated in these forums), private citizens came together to form a "public sphere," gathering a significant segment of that population that no longer would complacently and unquestioningly accept the authority of the state. This critical public sphere would ultimately challenge and then alter the prevailing orthodoxy of both the aristocracy and the church.[8]

In the colonies, the coffee-house wasn't nearly as powerful a force. Though there were actually plenty of them—Boston opened its first in 1670—many were serving as much alcohol as coffee. Not that French and English coffee-houses were entirely dry, either, but in the colonies, if a proprietor designated his establishment a "coffee-house," it was usually evidence of his hopes to serve a better class of people—not actual coffee.

The task of creating a public sphere in the colonies would therefore have to be left to the tavern and, as you might expect, the public sphere birthed in rum presented some significant differences from the one that grew out of the coffee-house. For starters, tavern patronage was, by eighteenth-century standards, pretty diverse. The coffee-house clientele, by contrast, was bourgeois and delineated by profession. In London, financiers frequented Lloyd's coffee-house; political radicals hung out at Will's coffee-house. Colonial taverns were also sometimes divided by profession: Taverns near docks catered to sailors; those adjoining courthouses, to lawyers. However, laws that fixed the price tavernkeepers could charge for a drink (instituted in most regions) made it nearly impossible for bar-owners to cater to upper-classes or certain professions. In Philadelphia, for example, where William Penn had instituted a fixed-price system as a tavern control, records indicate that early tax rebel Joshua Carpenter, who had become the second-richest man in town through opening the Tun Tavern as well as the first brewery, drank right alongside the shipyard workers at the Pennypot.[9]

Tavern historian Peter Thompson has shown that Philadelphia's taverns were especially democratic and egalitarian, largely as a result of Penn's licensing system. Dr. Alexander Hamilton dined in the City of Brotherly Love with "mixed company," including "Scots, English, Dutch, Germans, and Irish; there were Roman Catholicks, Church men, Presbyterians, Quakers, Newlightmen [Evangelicals], Methodists, Seventh day men, Moravians, Anabaptists and one Jew."[10] They all sat together at one long table, talking about the price of flour and the prospect of another war with France, all the while swatting away what was considered an unusual number of flies.

Philadelphia may have been exceptionally nonsegregated, but its type of tavern licensing system was far from unique. Massachusetts also had an early fixed-price system, regulating a ceiling of a penny per quart of ale, which led to a comparably democratic system. Similarly, starting in 1640, Virginia legislated the maximum price for a meal or beer, although that amount was measured in tobacco, not shillings.

Aside from featuring a relatively diverse clientele and egalitarian environment, the tavern also would have been radically different from the coffee-house in that its main commodity was liquor. Drunkenness was bound to lead to a different form of politics than coffee-drinking, since alcohol had a fundamentally different effect on the psyche. As philosopher and psychologist William James put it, the "sway of alcohol over mankind is unquestionably due to its power to stimulate the mystical faculties of human nature, usually crushed to earth by the cold facts and dry criticisms of the sober hour." Sobriety, James continues, "says no; drunkenness expands, unites, and says yes."[11]

Between the democratic and varied nature of the patronage and the elevated spirits, there was something distinctly populist about the tavern and the vein of the political discussion generated on its premises. This characteristic was noted (and critiqued) by John Hector St Jean de Crèvecoeur, a French-American writer and farmer who chronicled American society, when he wrote in the 1780s that men at a tavern "neither know nor foresee of what Eminent service" a potential political candidate might be. He complained that the populace only knew what was said of the candidate at the tavern, and that, even though it had no grasp of the political implications, the barroom debate elevated a man above his station and gave him a "high opinion of himself."[12]

While Crèvecoeur clearly did not see this as a virtue of American society, the fact that ordinary tavern patrons began to see themselves as part of an informed public, just as capable of making political decisions as those officially in charge, is key to the unique political will that was building throughout America at the time. And this was not an exclusively bourgeois public sphere wherein the rights of man were being debated. Rather, this was the domain of the common man, who felt almost as secure in his abilities as those who might have held debate in more genteel settings. The tavern man was ready for action, as we saw in Philadelphia in 1742. And the person who was beginning to understand the full promise of the rabble roused in the taverns and the tight relationship between politicking and alcohol was not a reformer like Livingston. Instead, he was a frustrated rebel in Boston, who saw the political deck stacked against him and his fellow colonists but also an opportunity to level the playing field in the tavern. That man was Elisha Cooke Jr.

Before Hancock, before Washington, before Revere, there was Cooke. Before Cooke Jr., there was an Elisha Cooke Sr., a Boston physician and politician, who worked to fight for colonists' rights and, as a result, was denied the political office of councilor that he won by popular election in 1693. His son would follow very closely in his footsteps—to the extent that he, too, had an election victory (1718) invalidated by the Governor—and soon began looking for other ways to gain power in what, to him, increasingly seemed a game rigged against the colonists.

Elisha Cooke Jr. had three major things going for him—his determined and passionate character; a fair bit of cash inherited after his father's death in 1715; and the fact that he knew his way around a tavern. Taverns were already shaping up to be a fairly major force in Boston politics. Francis Holmes' Bunch of Grapes Tavern on Boston's King Street (later State Street), for instance, had been a Whig stronghold since 1712, a place where like-minded citizens rallied against the monarch's absolute rule. Tories weren't welcome but this was fine with them, since they had their own taverns. Cooke, however, was the first to understand that the future didn't rest in either Tory or Whig taverns but, instead, in those frequented by the general population in the North End and around Boston's Long Wharf, the massive pier that accommodated the city's considerable sea trade. Cooke, therefore, set up his own bar on King Street and immediately began using it to win friends and influence people.

Cooke's was the meeting place for what became known as the Boston Caucus, a shadowy cabal that agitated for reform and came quite close, in fact, to open rebellion. The Caucus consisted of Cooke and his allies Oliver Noyes, John Clark, William Clark, and Thomas "Death's Head" Cushing (so named by political opponent Governor Belcher, for having very pale skin). At some point, perhaps as early as 1724, Samuel Adams Sr., also became mixed up with the group. The Caucus set the agenda of the Boston Town Meeting which, ironically perhaps, was New England's famed innovation and major contribution to democracy in America. Nevertheless, the Caucus also seems to have controlled the entire Boston electoral process by creating a voting bloc among the artisans, shopkeepers, and tavernkeepers that would consistently support their anticourt candidates. The Caucus selected candidates for what was informally known as the "popular party," putting up its own allies as candidates for selectmen and tax assessors, then working to mobilize its voter base. According to revolutionary correspondent Reverend William Gordon, each member would "furnish themselves with ballots, including the names of the parties fixed upon, which they distributed on the days of election." He continues: "By acting in concert, together with a careful and extensive distribution of ballots, they generally carried their elections to their own mind."[13]

The Caucus, however, also employed (and some say innovated) more nefarious methods for voter mobilization, namely, pamphleteering and, best of all, buying votes with liquor. Cooke would be accused of spending thousands of British pounds to secure votes throughout the 1720s. Staunch Tory Peter Oliver accused the Caucus of having picked up its popular support by spending some nine thousand pounds on liquor. Where he got this figure is unknown and, given that it translates into over a million pounds today, may well have been an exaggeration. Still, there *is* evidence of Cooke's land company one year spending a staggering half of its annual budget in taverns.[14] Although Oliver accused Cooke and cronies of securing votes through bribery, the whole scheme probably sounds far worse to modern readers than it would have to Oliver's contemporaries. The Boston Caucus wasn't a pioneer in this bribery technique, though it may have been the first to transform it from a haphazard process into a systematic method of power consolidation.

The Caucus became irretrievably associated with alcohol and was dubbed the "corkass" or "corkus" in contemporary accounts. Indeed, its very name is thought to have derived from either a bastardization of Cooke's House (referring to his tavern) or the Greek word "kaukos," which means "wine bowl." Aside from owning a tavern, Cooke was also known for his carousing and drinking to excess, falling over furniture and flying into violent rages. Although he was described as "genial" and "generous to needy people of all classes," he was most famous for being a "drinking man without equal."[15]

As the Caucus began taking over the reins of power in Boston, tavern licenses increased substantially, not surprising at all since they were being approved by the Caucus' own men. Prior to Cooke's rise to power over the years 1719–1722, fewer than a third of hopeful licensees were approved. After Cooke, over three-quarters of new applications were granted and, over the four years, the number of licensed taverns increased by eighty percent. This just happened to coincide with a new laxity in liquor laws, both on the local and regional level. Presumably this had nothing whatsoever to do with Cooke and his Caucus, since it happened everywhere in Massachusetts. Around that period, though, all of the regulations prohibiting dancing, singing, drinking healths, and nine o'clock closings failed to be reinstated. With Cooke's new network of tavernkeepers, indebted to him for their livelihood and no longer having to fear nosy selectmen or their undercover spies, the tavern, at least in Massachusetts, was poised to become more powerful than ever. Through this network, the Caucus grew ever more influential and, before long, even owned the House of Representatives.

The "popular party's" opponents fought back with pamphleteering of their own, hiring moralists like Cotton Mather (he and father Increase were long-standing political enemies of the Cookes) to write tracts against Cooke and allies. Rather than appeal to the constituency of their opponents, however, many of the pamphlets written by the governor's supporters must have accomplished the opposite, for they were actually insulting to Boston's working class. Mather, for instance, essentially asked that people resign themselves to their lot in life. Another pamphlet rebuked the "ordinary people" for their "foolish fondness of Forreign Commodities & fashions, excessive tippling in the taverns, laziness, sottishness, and a hunger for things above their station in life."[16] Cooke's party, with its excessive tippling in taverns, was looking better and better all the time.

It helped, too, that most of the tax assessors (Deacon Samuel Adams Sr., was one in 1724) selected by the Caucus and elected by the general public were pretty dismal at their jobs. Their inability to collect taxes efficiently, though, only served to make them *more* popular with those they were supposed to be collecting from. Between "treating" at the polls and misfiring with their tax collections, now *there* was a winning formula.

The tavern-based, rum-soaked Boston Caucus represents a major development for two reasons. The first is obvious—it was the precursor to the Sons of Liberty. Where Deacon Samuel Adams left off, his son, Sam the Publican, would pick up and the Sons of Liberty would fight the same tyranny the Caucus opposed—and by using many of the same techniques. The Caucus' second legacy perhaps provides a little less reason to celebrate: it was the first modern political machine. And this model of machine politics—which, typically, selected its own candidates, then ensured their election by corralling the support of poor urban voters through tavern and, later, saloon favors—would dominate American politics for almost three hundred years.

It didn't hurt the newly cemented relationship between radical politics and taverns that the main commodity in which taverns dealt—rum—was a major sticking point in the perpetual negotiations between colonists and their royal administrators. Alcohol would become one of the prime catalysts in the rebellion and eventual war for American colonial independence. Many of the Sons of Liberty were directly involved in importing alcohol (or raw ingredients like molasses), distilling it, or selling it in stores or, more frequently, in taverns.

To reduce it to a matter of rum makes the Revolution seem trivial—a war waged purely on behalf of the narrow interests of alcohol importers, makers, and retailers. It's important, however, to remember that rum was no ordinary commodity but, rather, one that practically drove the economy. Taxes that affected distillers, importers, and retailers affected the entire population. In fact, the 1733 Molasses Act (which imposed a six-pence-per-gallon levy on foreign molasses) brought the Boston shipbuilding trade to a complete halt. The effects rippled through all trades, too, to the point that many abandoned the depressed port for greener pastures. In the late 1730s and early 1740s, its economy decimated, Boston's population actually shrank.

This became a major factor in the politicization of taverns. Even though the entire economy was hurt, those who were hit hardest by a direct tax on the raw ingredients used to make cheap rum were obviously the most active in fighting the tariffs and militating for political and economic self-determination. Many of these actions were initiated by the Boston Caucus or its allies in taverns, whose keepers were taking increasingly active roles and prominent political positions. One of the more polarizing events was the Land Bank Crisis of 1741, an attempt by Samuel Adams Sr., and distiller John Colman to kick-start the economy by allowing people to borrow against the value of their property and circulate some much-needed currency. Adams and Colman printed their own money and issued it to nearly four hundred members from the Exchange Tavern. While the bank broke no laws, Governor Jonathan Belcher saw it as an affront to his administration and, concerned about a new currency with an uncertain value floating around town, declared it valueless and made all Land Bank directors personally responsible for any of the currency merchants had already accepted.

Adams, whose malting business was unable to come close to paying off his liabilities, was dragged through the courts until his death in 1748. John Adams, the Deacon's sober nephew, would much later note that the Land Bank fiasco had "raised a greater ferment in this province than the Stamp Act" (of 1765). And while the Land Bank Crisis certainly goes down as one of the Boston Caucus' failures, the rebels gained support in leaps and bounds, in part, because many saw the royal quashing as yet another instance of unjust interference.

By the late 1730s, Cooke's network of taverns covered not only Boston but extended well into the countryside. When tensions over the Land Bank were at their greatest in 1741, there were rumors that tavernkeepers across Massachusetts were organizing mobs and planning a march into Boston. While this never happened, the network of keepers and patrons, allied with Boston rebels and disgusted with the crown's seemingly arbitrary exercise of power, was in place and still active twenty-five to thirty years later, when revolutionary fervor came to a boil.

The politics being discussed in the taverns was increasingly anticourt, a result of the democratic and egalitarian nature of the social space, the depressed economy, and the fact that tavernkeepers had a natural interest in evading any new taxes that adversely affected the distilling industry. Accordingly, many tavernkeepers, registering their dissatisfaction with the crown, became heavily involved in smuggling; some taverns actually served as centers for smuggling networks. The Man Full of Trouble Tavern in Philadelphia had an underground tunnel running from the basement kitchen to Dock Creek for this purpose.

Other schemes may have been less concrete but were no less a problem for colonial administrators trying to staunch the flow of illegal molasses and other products making their way into America. In part, they relied on informants such as one George Spencer in New York, who ratted out fellow citizens in 1759. In retaliation, a rebel creditor had him arrested for outstanding debts. In escorting Spencer to debtor's prison, the deputy sheriff took the scenic route, stopping off at a tavern and ordering drinks. A mob promptly grabbed Spencer, tossed him into a cart and paraded the traitor, pelted with mud, through the streets of Manhattan.[17]

Even though New York was a loyalist stronghold, mobs were common and the political sentiment pouring out of taverns often turned violent. Manhattan had been a pretty rough town, known for its inebriated citizens long before Dr. Alexander Hamilton visited and noted how wet it was. It was, in fact, since the early days of Wouter Van Twiller's administration as Director-General of New Netherland in the 1630s, known as the "place where we all got drunk." (This, by the way, is exactly what the Lenape Indian word *Manahachtanienk* means and, while fun, is a false etymology for the name Manhattan.) Some attempts at regulating taverns had been made over the years, but the lack of arrests and punishments for public drunkenness, rather than suggesting a diminished number of drunks roaming the streets, is generally taken to mean local authorities had given up trying to enforce laws. On a slightly more conspiratorial level, some explain the lack of enforcement by pointing to the vast income taken in via taxation on the extraordinarily lucrative New York bar business.

In any case, when large groups of merchants began meeting at the Province Arms Tavern in the 1760s to discuss the sad state of the economy and form a Committee for Petitioning the Assembly and Parliament, while still others were meeting at the Queen's Head owned by Samuel Fraunces, the ingredients were in place for potentially violent action. Again, exacerbating the situation for tavernkeepers in particular was the decline in soldiers availing themselves of the amenities in major ports like Boston and New York after the end of the Seven Years' War. The colonial economy was in rough shape and heading inland was no longer an option, since King George III's Royal Proclamation of 1763—a gesture at establishing a lasting peace with the French—prohibited settlement west of the Appalachians. The colonists had no choice but to stay put and endure the depressed economy.

Then there were the war debts. England didn't really expect the colonists to contribute toward paying them off but rather, to defray the costs of the peace-keeping army that was to remain in North America, ensuring the safety of the colonists and British interests. To this end, Parliament instituted the Sugar Act (part of the American Revenue Act of 1764), devised to raise enough revenue to cover half the cost of the troops left behind.

At first glance, the Sugar Act seemed a piece of good luck for the colonists, since it reduced the tariff on molasses by half. However, in the thirty years since the passage of the dreadfully unpopular Molasses Act, nearly everyone had devised a way to avoid paying any taxes whatsoever. Some had developed elaborate smuggling tunnels, such as the one at the Man Full of Trouble Tavern, while others took to unloading ships in clandestine locations at very odd hours. Still others simply bribed the proper authorities. The 1764 legislation was meant to put an end to all that, giving customs agents greater powers and establishing a Customs Court for offenders. The message was clear: Rampant smuggling was not to be tolerated any longer.

In addition to the New York meetings, there were myriad gatherings beginning to take place in Boston, which, at the time, was nearly as soused and twice as agitated as New York patriots thanks to its wealth of taverns. Massachusetts Governor Thomas Pownhall, for example, had complained in the 1750s that every other house in Boston was a tavern. Even young patriots like John Adams concurred. Writing of his student days in Boston, Adams said, "Playing cards, drinking punch and wine, smoking tobacco and swearing. . . . I know not how any young fellow can study in this town."

The most prominent Boston meetings were taking place at the Green Dragon, the would-be headquarters of the American Revolution. The Caucus had moved to this Union Street tavern around 1764 and it was there that Samuel Adams Jr., (cousin to John Adams) gave long, rousing speeches on British tyranny for the benefit of both the Caucus and an increasing number of impoverished shipyard workers from the nearby docks, where employment was no longer as profitable as it had been during the war.[18] Sam "the Publican" Adams knew how to work a tavern. In fact, perhaps nobody understood the relationship between politics and the tavern better than he, having grown up privy to the back-room politics of the Boston Caucus. Adams had been quick to get into politics after graduating from Harvard but, after an auspicious start as a tax assessor in 1747, his career languished. He was more interested in strolling about town, dropping into taverns to talk local politics with keepers and patrons than in collecting taxes, working in his father's malt business, or building a solid political career. Ironically, professional inattention would serve him incredibly well during the Revolution, since the taverns gave him far more powerful allies than he might have gained through any other venture, however successful. While he still frequented the Bunch of Grapes, where Boston's more polite Whigs were urging moderate action through legal channels such as petitioning the Governor for legislative change, Adams also became a constant presence in taverns with a less sophisticated clientele and where more radical politics were discussed. And the most dramatic events of the coming fifteen years were going to come from the antics of those who drank healths, got drunk, and considered immoderate action.

Through his tavern politicking, Adams took his father's place in the Caucus as a leader whose stock only rose with his unwillingness to properly assess and collect taxes. (He wasn't the only one reticent about collections—another being John Ruddock, a shipyard owner and one-time leader of the Caucus, who was also notoriously dismal at this.) By 1760, the secret society was becoming a poorly kept secret. Caucus members were becoming more blatant with their activities, and the court party was rebuking the Caucus on record, calling it the "Junto" and charging it with operating merely out of self-interest.[19]

John Adams learned of the Caucus' existence in February 1763, and would go on to describe his uncle William Fairfield and cousin Samuel Adams, as well as Thomas Dawes, William Story, John Ruddock, and William Cooper as being engaged in smoking "tobacco till you cannot see," drinking flip and selecting "Assessors, Collectors, Wardens, Fire Wards, and Representatives" who were "Regularly chosen before they are chosen in the Town." There were others present that day but John Adams dismissed the rest as a "rude" and "undigestible" mass. Once the men were chosen, committees were sent to take the choices to the Merchant's Club, which would then be solicited for support. On this particular occasion, the Caucus met at Thomas Dawes's house but, other times, it met in taverns, often at the Salutation Tavern, which was becoming a political "it" spot.

With the passage of the Sugar Act in 1764, Sam Adams and the rest of the Caucus began to take more direct measures. Adams saw the institution of the new taxes as a threat to the future of colonists' rights and immediately wrote tracts against it that were published in sympathetic Boston newspapers. His calls to action and dramatic appeals to the people of Boston were then read aloud in the barroom of every like-minded tavernkeeper. Following that, the Boston Caucus wrote a demand for the repeal of the Sugar Act, citing it as being "Taxes laid upon us . . . without our having a legal Representation where they are laid." The patriots complained that the American colonists were no longer treated as free subjects but, instead, subject to the "miserable State of tributary Slaves."

Adams was not the only one holding forth in Boston's taverns. In the early days of agitation, James Otis Jr. was also emerging as a likely leader of the rebels. The bad blood between the crown and the Otis family had begun in 1760, when James Otis Sr. was passed over for the post of Chief Justice of Massachusetts by Governor Francis Bernard. Political principles notwithstanding, Otis Jr. was further motivated by the family feud to oppose the Sugar Act and, indeed, any measures imposed by the crown that he perceived as violating colonists' rights. For a few years, Otis rivaled Sam Adams for leadership and it was only Otis's increasingly erratic behavior that, over time, gave Adams the edge. Otis was often seen drunk in public and, one fateful evening in a tavern on King Street, he picked a fight with John Robinson, a customs officer Otis had only recently lambasted in an editorial in the *Boston Gazette*. He asked Robinson to step outside, but the latter refused and tweaked Otis's nose instead. This led to a tavern brawl in which Otis was clocked on the head. Whether or not he sustained permanent injuries to his faculties can never be known, but this marked the beginning of Otis's downfall as a Revolutionary leader. His behavior grew increasingly erratic and he was caught, the following year, vandalizing the Town House in a "mad freak."

The early center of political agitation against the Sugar Act was clearly Boston, since that was the port with the most extensive trade with the West Indies. The 1765 Stamp Act, which threatened to take taxation to a new level, spread the discontent throughout the colonies. It required that every legal transaction be subject to a tax, paid for by a stamp issued by the British government. This included tavern licenses, which would have cost twenty shillings—a little over a hundred dollars by today's standards. Playing cards or dice within the tavern would also become more costly—a new set of cards being taxed at a shilling; dice, ten times that. Reading, the other major tavern entertainment, was also to be taxed. Taxes on pamphlets and newspapers were relatively moderate but advertising space in a gazette was pricey—two shillings (ten dollars today) per ad. The costs associated with the new taxes were not nearly as inflammatory as the form of its delivery. The Stamp Act was the first tax levied directly against the colonies and would have been extraordinarily effective since it would have been nearly impossible to evade, as any document without the stamp would be considered null and void under British law.

Now the crowd turned ugly—first in Boston, then everywhere. In Boston, a group known as "the Loyal Nine" (almost all members of the most recent version of the Caucus) emerged and orchestrated much of the early political action. Thomas Chase, a distiller, was one of the members and the counting room of his distillery was used for the group's covert meetings. The key to the Loyal Nine's success was in its strategic and meticulous organization and ability to mobilize the tradesmen and artisans across Boston, accomplished by rallying tavern patrons. Likely working with Samuel Adams, who is often thought of as the "Loyal Tenth," the Nine managed to unite the rival North End Mob, led by Henry Swift, and the South End Mob, led by Ebenezer Mackintosh— long-standing rivals who even had an annual gang war. On August 14, 1765, however, Swift and Mackintosh would put aside their differences and, united under the leadership of the Caucus and the Nine, would mount the most shocking and effective protest against the British government to date.

Two thousand men took to the streets that day to protest the Stamp Act—impressive in that Boston's total population at the time was only fifteen thousand. The Loyal Nine orchestrated the event, providing the mob with effigies of Andrew Oliver, the local stamp distributor, and his brother Peter Oliver, a long-standing enemy of the Boston Caucus. A boot with a devil emerging from it represented Prime Minister John Stuart (the Earl of Bute) and, along with many other effigies, was hung on a tree near Boston Common, which came to be known as the Liberty

Tree. Over the next few years, many more would be planted all across the colonies. Swift and his North End Mob guarded the tree to make sure the symbols of dissent weren't removed, while Mackintosh led the Southies through the streets with yet more effigies of the stamp distributor. When they got to one of Oliver's buildings on the wharf—the one rumored to be the future site of the stamp-distribution office—the mob ripped it apart, then proceeded to Fort Hill, where more effigies of Oliver were burned and beheaded.[20] Smaller riots and disturbances ensued in the following days, including one in which Mackintosh led his roughs to the home of Lieutenant Governor Hutchinson, where they ransacked his book collection, destroyed furniture, and drank up his entire (and sizeable) wine cellar.

News of the riots spread quickly and sparked numerous town meetings across the colonies, most of which were held in taverns, such as David Reynold's in Bethlehem, New Jersey, and MacHenry's in Savannah, Georgia. In Portsmouth, New Hampshire, citizens burned effigies of the appointed stamp tax collector George Meserve until he agreed to resign, after which he was promptly cheered and carried off to a tavern to celebrate.

Presumably for the sake of posterity, tavernkeeper William Davenport kept the bill from September 25, 1765, the evening on which much of the town of Newburyport, Massachusetts, assembled at his Wolfe's Head Tavern to ease the "Greate Uneasyness and Tumult on Occasion of the Stamp Act." There are a few hot suppers on the bill but also an astonishing amount of punch and toddy. A *Harper's* magazine editor a century later, during a centennial celebration of the Revolution, commented that they had to "keep their spirits up by pouring spirits down," then estimated the quantities consumed that eve at about a gallon of punch per person. More than 85 percent of the bill was put on credit, including the breakfast and coffee for those who stayed through the morning.

The Frenchtown Tavern was the locus of resistance in Cecil County, Maryland. In Norwich, Connecticut, mobs threatened stamp distributor Jared Ingersoll in Captain John Durkee's tavern until he resigned. In Williamsburg, Virginia, Governor Francis Fauquier and aides actually fought with townspeople at Christiana Campbell's tavern. That's just naming a few.

The rowdiest taverns, by far, were still in New York—hardly surprising, given New York's reputation as a drink-soaked town. There, in September 1765, an angry crowd threatened to kill Maryland stamp officer Zacharias Hood at his temporary residence, the King's Arms Tavern. Cadwallader

Colden, governor of New York, had to offer Hood a bed in his house, saying he was "extreamly sorry for the occasion" which obliged him to "apply . . . for a Lodging." And would-be New York stamp distributor James McEvers preemptively resigned his post after hearing of the ruckus in Boston. Aware that New Yorkers were likely to react just as violently, he quit to avoid his house being "Pillag'd" and his "Person Abused."

Of course there were many attempts to guide the anger generated by the Stamp Act into traditional political channels. Most of these still took place in taverns but many were headed up by the more sober minds, mostly Whig supporters, who attended the clubs and societies dedicated to self-improvement and promotion of the arts and education.

The Stamp Act Congress took place in New York on October 7, 1765, and, while the nine delegates from the colonies officially met at City Hall, unofficial meetings were taking place at Burns's City Arms Tavern at Broad and Stone. Attempts to stage a peaceful protest would be centered at the City Arms, where James DeLancey organized a town meeting on October 31, attended by two hundred of New York's most prominent merchants. The businessmen swiftly agreed to a boycott of all British goods until the Stamp Act was repealed. This was known initially as the Non-Importation Agreement—the first boycott of the American Revolution. Later, after rioting became the norm, William Livingston joined DeLancey at the meetings and urged moderation, though the two were political adversaries. DeLancey had been one of the worst offenders in the election-jobbing practice that Livingston had so passionately opposed. DeLancey didn't just work hard in taverns, he played hard in them, too. Whigs even accused him of being addicted to keeping "low company," when he and aristocratic Tory pals such as Frederick Philipse went slumming. They were well known as violent, drunken rakes.

Livingston was losing the battle on tavern reform and civil obedience. Thoughtful, civilized debate, which would have been approved of by men such as Samuel Sewall, Benjamin Franklin, Dr. Alexander Hamilton, and friends, were on the wane in the ramp-up to the American Revolution. In New York, rioting began the moment the stamps arrived in the harbor. On the evening of the signing of the Non-Importation Agreement, a crowd assembled outside of Burns's Tavern and took to the streets with a raucous "funeral for liberty," to counter complaints that the boycott wasn't nearly radical enough. Worse rioting began the very next day—the official inauguration of the Stamp Act. Here, too, were the boots and devils and effigies of Governor Colden. Rioters seized Colden's private coach and raided the home of the British army's would-be enforcer Major Thomas James, who had threatened to "cram the Stamps down their Throats with the End of (his) Sword."[21]

Somewhere in the midst of all this, the New York chapter of the Sons of Liberty was born. Its public meetings were held at William Howard's tavern in "The Fields," (where City Hall is now) and its leaders clearly established—Isaac Sears, Alexander McDougall, Hugh Hughes, John Lamb, and Marinus Willett. Three of the founding five had connections to popular taverns in Manhattan. Like Sam Adams, these were men who were extraordinarily comfortable in a taproom. New York Sons of Liberty meetings were often chaotic, to say the least, and would frequently break up on account of drunken disagreement. Historian Benjamin Carp notes that the Sons of Liberty "accepted a certain level of disorder as a way of doing business—or politics—in taverns."[22]

Some order did arise from the chaos. Sons of Liberty chapters formed in taverns all across the colonies and a committee of correspondence was set up to standardize communication and other basic principles of organization. At least sixty-five riots ensued in over twenty-five different locales until the Act was finally repealed by King George III on March 18, 1766.

News of the repeal didn't hit the taverns of America until late May, but when it did, it created pandemonium. A completely disorderly celebration was had at William Howard's New York tavern, where twenty-eight separate toasts were drunk throughout the night. Other taverns across the city were jammed with liberty toasters, too. But victory had mellowed people's tempers and the mobs that poured out of New York's Fraunces' Queen's Head and Shepheard's Tavern, the Salutation in Boston and similar patriot taverns country-wide were relatively well behaved, despite their inebriation.

As we all know, however, revolutionary fervor did not die down simply because of this one concession. Although the Sons of Liberty resisted the urge to form a permanent political club and vowed, instead, only to reassemble should the liberty of the colonists be threatened again, it had become a political organization with tremendous popular appeal and influence. Nor would its members forget the methods by which they had so effectively resisted the Stamp Act: organization of a select few in taverns, followed by communication over a network of tavernkeepers and, finally, mobilization of the masses—again through taverns. These very same tactics would win them the Revolution.

A
REVOLUTIONARY
WALKS
INTO A BAR

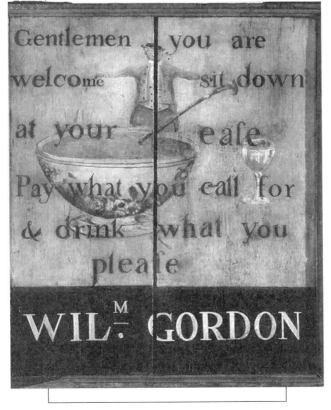

On the first anniversary of the Stamp Act's repeal—March 18, 1767—the colonists celebrated some more, although, this time, the national hangover was worsened by news that the Liberty Pole outside New York's King's Arms Tavern had been hacked down by a clutch of drunken British soldiers. Just as it sounds, this was a wooden pole garnished with a liberty cap or flag and used to signify Revolutionary spirit, just as the Liberty Trees were. The pole was reerected, this time its base fortified with iron. The soldiers' response to the new pole was to fire their muskets directly into Edward Bardin's tavern, another well-known rebel hangout. No patrons were hurt, but the incident marked the beginning of something that was going to become more common—small skirmishes between Redcoats and budding revolutionaries. These incidents became especially common when one or both sides were "limber."

In Boston, matters heated up considerably with the passing of the Townshend Acts, the brainstorm of "Champagne Charley" Townshend, a British politician renowned for eloquent oratory, both in parliament and coffee-houses, regardless of how many healths he had drunk. Several different acts, beginning in 1767, fell under the Townshend umbrella, but the most despised were the new duties on British paper, paint, glass, and tea. Sam Adams Jr. urged a general boycott but, while this garnered plenty of lip-service, many secretly continued to bag their tea from the East India Company. Others found smuggled alternatives, since there was no shortage of rebels devoted to bringing in as much of every coveted staple as possible—duty-free. One such tax-evading patriot was John Hancock, a wealthy Boston merchant and Adams's protégé, who had been won over to the movement during the days of the Stamp Act. It would be Hancock's tax troubles that ignited protest against the Townshend Acts.

In the summer of 1768, Hancock paid the customs agent for importing twenty-five pipes of wine (a "pipe" being a large cask that could hold nearly a thousand gallons) that had just arrived at Boston Harbor on his ship, the *Liberty*. Since a ship of its size was capable of carrying four times that amount, customs agents believed Hancock had managed to unload most of the wine before they'd arrived. When authorities seized the ship on suspicion of tax evasion on June 10, 1768, Boston rioting began anew. It continued in little disorganized bursts all summer but truly came into focus on August 14, the third anniversary of the day the Loyal Nine had led the first major Stamp Act protests. The major players celebrated at the Greyhound Tavern in Roxbury, Massachusetts, where

Adams and company hoisted a record-setting forty-five toasts, every one of which would have been considered treasonable by colonial authorities. Even the number of toasts was a tip of the hat to sedition, since it was a reference to issue number "45" of the *North Briton*, a publication in which British revolutionary politician John Wilkes critiqued George III for the Paris Peace Treaty that curtailed further western settlement in the Americas. Wilkes's screed earned him both seditious libel charges and the undying devotion of the colonists, particularly the Boston Sons of Liberty.

Hancock's tax troubles made news elsewhere, too, with many colonists feeling the customs agents had acted with too heavy a hand. Philadelphians jumped on the nonimportation bandwagon in March 1769; Virginians, that June. Initially, the debate and attempts to organize in Virginia had followed proper legal channels and members of the House of Burgesses (the lower house) were considering a nonimportation agreement. This all came to an end, however, when British governor to Virginia, Norborne Berkeley, simply shut down the House of Burgesses— and, with it, legitimate political debate. However, just as Elisha Cooke and his Boston Caucus pals had resorted to extra-legal tactics when their legitimate attempts at reform from within were shut down, so did Virginia protestors, among them George Washington, Thomas Jefferson and Patrick ("Give me liberty, or give me death") Henry. They reassembled with others at the Apollo Room of the Raleigh Tavern in Williamsburg, Virginia—a locale in which Henry was doubtless comfortable in that he'd been a barkeeper, as had his father. It was there that they soon voted to join the other colonies in nonimportation.

New Yorkers, meanwhile, were doing their level best to make sure the boycott was being respected. At Bolton's and Sigel's taverns, Isaac Sears organized an assembly of merchants to elect a team of inspectors responsible for patrolling the wharf. The strategy of employing physical intimidation proved extraordinarily effective in persuading people to give up their foreign luxuries and imports dropped to about a quarter of what they had been.

When Adams and company assembled at Lemuel Robinson's tavern in Dorchester, Massachusetts, in August 1769, they were well aware of the groundswell of support throughout the rest of the colonies. To celebrate the difference a year had brought to the political landscape, they enjoyed three barbecued pigs and another forty-five toasts, many of these with John Hancock's wine. Nobody asked Hancock if he'd remembered to pay the duty. Also on hand were Paul Revere, Dr. Joseph Warren, James Otis, John Gill, and Benjamin Edes, and, while the occasion was no doubt lively, John Adams wrote in his diary that, despite forty-five toasts at Robinson's: "To the honor of the Sons, I did not see one person intoxicated or near it." "In the Sudds" or not, the last of the forty-five toasts (or fifty-nine, if you consider the party had actually begun with fourteen by the Liberty Tree in Boston), promised "strong halters, firm blocks, and sharp axes to such as deserve either."

By 1770, New York's Bardin's Tavern—the one Redcoats fired into a few years earlier—had changed its name to the Montayne. The more things changed, though, the more the politics remained the same. The Montayne was still headquarters for New York's Sons of Liberty and the contentious Liberty pole that Sears, Lamb and McDougall had erected in a nearby field was still standing. And the Redcoats still wanted it down. When gunpowder initially failed to do the job, the flummoxed "Moon Ey'd" soldiers smashed the windows of the Montayne, trashed the interior, and assaulted an employee. Spirits buoyed, the soldiers eventually managed to blow up the pole, then piled its remnants at the bar's steps. A few days later, Sears roused a mob—including many angry sailors—from a number of other taverns and led it to Golden Hill (currently around John and Gold Streets) and another clash with the Redcoats. Sailors were particularly prone to revolutionary fervor, since they were experiencing a double-dip recession: business at the docks was slow and, worse, many British soldiers were moonlighting, picking up odd jobs at sea. At the Battle of Golden Hill on January 19, 1770, one sailor was killed and several on both sides severely wounded.

On January 30, the Liberty boys put up yet another pole, this time outside Vandenbergh's tavern near the East River. (The Sons of Liberty had to give the Montayne a reprieve from revolutionary activities, since its owner was tired of having his tavern raided and had declined the honor of hosting the Sons' annual Stamp Act repeal party.) The new, improved pole was considered practically indestructible, given that it was sunk twelve feet into the ground and housed within an iron cage. The pole's residence at the Vandenbergh, though, would be short-lived, since the Sons of Liberty soon felt it necessary to establish their own headquarters/tavern to stop endangering the lives and properties of others. Accordingly, they bought a place they named Hampden Hall (after English Civil War hero John Hampden) and installed Colonel Henry Bicker as tavernkeeper—a clear beginning of the institutionalization of the New York Sons of Liberty.

Generally, the Sons of Liberty were extraordinarily successful in controlling their followers by mobilizing them in taverns. There were times, though, when the crowd turned into a mob under nobody's control. One such mob resulted in the Boston Massacre, which occurred on March 5, only a couple of months after the Battle of Golden Hill. It began with alarm bells that indicated a British sentry—a Private White—was under attack. Scores of people spilled out of nearby taverns to discover the altercation was between the Redcoat and a boy, a wig-maker's apprentice who had followed the soldier outside his shop to continue a dispute over the bill, only to get rapped with the butt of White's musket. While reinforcements arrived for White, the crowd grew in size and emotional outrage—a "motley rabble" that John Adams described as "saucy boys, negros and molattoes, Irish teagues and outlandish jack tarrs." They began pelting the soldiers with snowballs.

What happened next is not entirely clear, but it's said that a sailor named Crispus Attucks upped the ante by throwing a stick that hit a private named Hugh Montgomery, who responded by firing his musket into the crowd, prompting other soldiers to do likewise. Attucks was among three who were shot and immediately killed, while two others were fatally wounded and died shortly after.

The event was obviously fueled by the tensions of the previous weeks, months and years, including, in all likelihood, an article published in the *Boston Gazette* that very day that questioned the legitimacy of the seizing of Hancock's *Liberty* (although the event was almost two years old, it was still a hot topic). Attucks is believed to have been in one of those taverns where the *Gazette* might well have been read and discussed.

While the Massacre could hardly have been planned by the Sons of Liberty, the rebels lost no time in using it to underscore how a callous British administration had set up conditions whereby such tragedies were possible, even likely. News of the subsequent trials and extremely lenient sentencing of the soldiers (many were acquitted) spread via newspaper and word of mouth to taverns full of sympathetic patrons, including the Four Alls tavern in Philadelphia, the Raleigh in Williamsburg, the Queen's Head in New York, and the Sabin Tavern in Providence, Rhode Island, a "house of boarding and entertainment for gentlemen" run by John Sabin and the soon-to-be setting for another major radical, proto-revolutionary event.

Patrons at Sabin's had been talking for months about the HMS *Gaspée*, a customs ship that had been patroling Narragansett Bay on the orders of

King George III. The *Gaspée* was commanded by Lieutenant William Duddingston of the Royal Navy. Duddingston had a reputation for "petty tyranny," and was known to search every single vessel and hold it for inspection, even when clearly full of fresh fish. On June 9, 1772, Captain Benjamin Lindsey, at the helm of the *Hannah*, refused to pull his ship over for inspection and instead hightailed off. The *Gaspée* followed and, lured into shallow waters, was grounded and forced to await the next high tide.

Lindsey wasted no time heading to Sabin's to inform patrons that included John Brown and Abraham Whipple, prominent Providence merchants and traders. They and twelve others rowed out to the *Gaspée* with a view to ensuring that it never made if off the banks. While Sabin stayed back to tend bar, fellow tavernkeeper Joseph Bucklin went with the rebels and, reportedly, shot Duddingston, as others boarded the *Gaspée* and set it afire. Duddingston pulled through but his ship did not. Other than rioting, this marked the first major "direct action" orchestrated by patriot rebels.

The second was hatched in the Green Dragon, America's best-known revolutionary tavern, a large two-story brick building near the intersection of Union and Hanover. Originally called St. Andrew's Lodge, the Green Dragon's name derived from a patinéed copper dragon that, along with a Masonic compass and square, adorned the entrance. Its main floor rooms were used primarily for political and educational clubs, like those regularly attended by Dr. Alexander Hamilton, William Livingston, and Benjamin Franklin. The basement, though, was home to the Boston Sons of Liberty, the secret society that, as we've seen, had grown out of the Loyal Nine, which in turn had descended from the Boston Caucus. It was there that Edward Proctor, Paul Revere, Joseph Warren, and others hatched the Boston Tea Party. As the song goes:

Rally, Mohawks!-bring out your axes!
And tell King George we'll pay no taxes
On his Foreign tea!
Then rally boys, and hasten on
To meet our Chiefs at the Green Dragon.
Our Warren's there, and bold Revere,
With hands to do and words to cheer
For Liberty and Laws!

Sam Adams, always careful to play a behind-the-scenes role, did not get mentioned in this ditty, although he was almost certainly instrumental in the plotting of the Tea Party. There are few records to prove this since most conspirators tend not to take careful notes.

That said, we have some evidence that suggests that the Green Dragon was indeed the "cradle" of the revolution. There exists a sketch of the tavern by an anonymous artist with a caption that reads: "Where we met to Plan the Consignment of a few Shiploads of Tea, December 16, 1773." There's also an entry in the Green Dragon's books that indicate the tavern was closed on both November 30 and December 16 of that year. The first date is the day after the first general town meeting regarding the tea; the second, the very day of the Party itself. There's also this explanation: "(N.B. Consignees of Tea took up the Brethren's time)." This is all further substantiated by testimony from Paul Revere himself, who wrote that, in the fall of 1774 and winter of 1775, he and upward of thirty men, "formed ourselves into a committee for the purpose of watching the movements of the British soldiers and gaining every intelligence of the movements of the Tories. We held our meetings at the Green Dragon Tavern."

Revere's "spy patrol" was less about intelligence and more about intimidation as his gang of thugs blocked the unloading of the tea. Since British law demanded that all goods not unloaded and cleared by customs within twenty days had to be returned to England, the original strategy was simply to force the tea to take this round trip. Similar protests in Philadelphia and Charleston had managed to get tea turned back through the intimidation of the tea consignees, who had been given a monopoly on its eventual distribution. In New York, the local crew of teamsters who blocked the tea's disembarkation had been organized at Samuel Fraunces's Queen's Head Tavern, where the Committee of Vigilance and the Sons of Liberty first plotted, then marched to the harbor to block the unloading of the ship *London*. The captain of the *London* would later wind up at the Queen's Head, where he was forced to make a public apology for trying to deliver such an unpatriotic cargo. Undoubtedly, a few toasts would have been required as well.

Back in Boston, however, intimidation was not working quite so well. Governor Thomas Hutchinson, once part of the effort to crush those involved in the Land Bank and the man who had his wine cellar emptied by mobs during the Stamp Act riots, stubbornly insisted the tea be unloaded. While tea consignees in other ports had been easily intimidated into resignation, here they were largely from Hutchinson's family (sons and others related through marriage) and subject to considerable pressure from him to stand firm.

We all know how this story turned out. The Boston Tea Party has long eclipsed the *Gaspée* affair as the defining moment of revolutionary action against British tyranny. The standoff in Boston eventually led to the dumping of the tea—a direct action if ever there was one—and, compared to a ship's return trip to England, one that represented a far worse loss to the crown and the East India Company.

There has always been some difference of opinion as to whether or not the Tea Party was entirely conceived in—and executed out of—the Green Dragon. Some submit that the plan was hatched in Boston's Salutation, located at the corner of Hanover and, logically enough, Salutation. Also known as the "Two Palaveres" (for a sign depicting two colonists meeting), the Salutation had been bought by rebel William Campbell in 1773, and many soon considered it to be the new home of the Boston Caucus. The truth may be forever smudged. Whether or not all aspects of the Tea Party protest were literally plotted in the basement of the Green Dragon, as oral and anecdotal evidence suggests, or spread across a handful of rebel havens, it's absolutely certain that almost every protest, alliance, and direct action was planned in barrooms across the colonies. Public opinion was orchestrated, tracts were written, and decisions made in the back rooms. In the front rooms, crowds of merchants, mechanics (meaning skilled workers), and artisans got to read and hear these arguments and debate their merits.

There were loyalist taverns, too, although many of these changed allegiances as evidence of British injustice mounted. The shift was on when signs reading "King's Arms" or "Crown Tavern" were replaced with ones that said "Congress" or "Liberty Tree." John Adams was one of the first to write about the power of taverns and to document how the general debate was playing out in the rebels' favor. In his diary, for example, he recounts spying on a meeting in Shrewsbury, Massachusetts:

> I sat in total silence to hear them. One said "The people of Boston are distracted." Another answered, "No wonder the people of Boston are distracted. Oppression will make wise men mad." A third said "What would you say if a fellow should come to your house and tell you he was come to take a list of your cattle, that parliament might tax you for them at so much a head? And how should you feel if he was to go and break open your barn, to take down your oxen, cows, horses and sheep?" "What should I say?" replied the first; "I would knock him in the head." "Well," said a fourth, "if Parliament can take away Mr. Hancock's wharf and Mr. Rowe's wharf, they can take away your barn and my house."

Adams's observations could hardly have been unique; similar conversations were taking place in countless taprooms across the colonies. And it was largely through word of mouth—guys talking in a bar—that news of the Boston conflicts spread. British colonial authorities knew taverns were being used as both communications channels and as recruitment centers, but there was little that could be done at this late stage. In the *New-York Journal*, an editor wrote for the need to suppress "tippling houses," which "subsist only by furnishing the Means of Drunkenness to Servants and mean disorderly People." He advocated limiting the number of licenses to two hundred. Similar measures were debated for the suppression of these "hot-beds of sedition" but, clearly, the barn door had been left open for too long.[1]

Next came the so-called Intolerable Acts, passed in 1774 and obviously not known by that name in British Parliament. Officially, they were comprised of four separate laws: the Boston Port Act, the Quartering Act, the Administration of Justice Act, and the Massachusetts Government Act, each of which accomplished something the colonists found . . . well, intolerable. For one thing, the port of Boston was to be closed until the East India Company was reimbursed for spilt tea. Second, tavernkeepers were forced to accommodate any homeless British soldiers and then seek reimbursement from local government. Third, soldiers or administrators accused of harassing colonists were to be tried in England instead of where the crime took place. And, finally, there'd be severe limitations placed on the power of local government—namely, the much-cherished Town Meeting, which had been firmly in the pocket of the rebel caucuses for many years. The Massachusetts Government Act held that such meetings could only be run once a year and that, even then, only local politics could be discussed.

News of the passage of the Intolerable Acts took weeks to arrive but, when it did, reaction was swift. Boston, as usual, was first off the mark, its leaders agreeing upon an immediate boycott of all British goods, not simply tea, paint, paper, and glass. Even though the Acts were aimed squarely at the rebels, the punitive measures were offensive to all colonists. Paul Revere barreled off on one of his early rides to inform New York of Boston's resolve, which prompted James DeLancey and his faction to consider a total nonimportation plan, and sent the more radical Sons of Liberty, led by Isaac Sears and Alexander McDougall, off to the Queen's Head for strategy discussions. Revere's ride also helped Sears realize the importance of intercolonial communication. He spent an entire evening with William Goddard at Drake's Tavern, devising plans for an established route of transmission between rebel taverns. Dabney Carr established a Committee of Correspondence from the Raleigh Tavern in Williamsburg, which also happened to be where a proposal for a Continental Congress was put together (again, after a session in the House of Burgesses was dissolved when it began bordering on the radical).

That first Continental Congress was eventually scheduled for the City of Brotherly Love, which had changed dramatically since the days when William Penn touted the "seven ordinaries for the entertainment of strangers." To many, though, the tavern scene in Philadelphia had gone too far. Benjamin Franklin estimated there to be about one hundred licensed establishments, meaning that, given all the unlicensed locales, places in which to drink probably made up a tenth of the city—a tavern for every twenty-five men. Everyone's gravest concern was for Helltown, one of America's first clearly defined "red-light" districts, which stretched between Race and Arch Streets, and from 3rd Street to Penn's Landing on the Delaware River. Race Street, incidentally, had come by its name honestly: it was essentially a mini-track along which tavern patrons—after getting down their bets—would race their horses.[2]

Bad as the drinking and gambling were in the Quaker City, the most severe moral panic was fostered by indentured servants, slaves (both escaped and still captive), the poor, the apprentices, and the prostitutes who assembled in Helltown to play dice, watch cockfights, and consume opium. Franklin referred to the dangers embodied in Helltown's "Nurseries of Vice and Debauchery" and warned they were growing in number. Obviously, there were a few "civilized" taverns about but, between Helltown and a raucous port area where very thirsty sailors hung out at places such as the Indian Queen, there were grumblings from the elite for a civilized tavern in which discussion of politics didn't always degenerate into bar brawls. In 1772, then, Philadelphia residents Captain Erkuries Beatty and Samuel Powell convinced fifty-two friends and allies to stake twenty-five dollars apiece toward construction of a tavern for the better members of local society. The institution of the nation's first private drinking club marked the beginning of the end for the democratic and egalitarian landscape for public houses in Philadelphia.

This presupposes that bar brawls only happened in taverns that catered to the poor and working classes, never among the elite. James Otis's confrontation with that customs officer in a Boston tavern speaks to the fallacy of the assumption. So, too, do countless other incidents, including a noteworthy duel in Charleston, South Carolina, that involved Dr. John Haley and Peter DeLancey—a member of that same DeLancey family that became a New York political dynasty. It seems there'd been a "Quarrel of several Years Standing between them, which always broke out afresh upon them being heated with Liquor."[3] Mostly, this stemmed from the fact that Haley was a Whig; DeLancey, a firm Tory. On August 15, 1771, they'd have their last argument. After drinking together much of the day, both went home to get their guns, met again at a small room at John Gordon's tavern, called for a bottle of wine, and shut the door. "Immediately afterwards, two Pistols were heard." DeLancey died, but not before twice missing, and while Haley was eventually exonerated in court, the verdict divided Charleston and was hotly discussed across the colonies.

Philadelphia's new private club was christened the "City Tavern" and was remarkable for its elegance, impressing visitors with a barroom, coffee room, two kitchens, spacious accommodations for strangers, and large club rooms. The public areas were well stocked, not just with so-phisticated libations such as Madeira wine, slings, toddies, and flips but also with newspapers and pamphlets for the edification of its members. It was as close to the Platonic ideal of what a tavern should be, both to moderate Whigs such as William Livingston and elites such as Dr. Alexander Hamilton. The City Tavern represented a haven for those hoping to distinguish their manner of drinking and talking politics from that of the lower classes at rowdy taverns, whereas, in all truth, their behavior was nearly identical, even if the elites believed that they had mastered the "art of drinking well."

In September 1774, the City Tavern was thus the obvious choice for the unofficial location of the Continental Congress. George Washington made the City his first stop upon arrival in Philadelphia, having heard so much about it, while John Adams, who might not have been so inclined, himself, was "whisked off" to the tavern in the early going. It was there that Washington and Adams met for the first time.

The official Congress, attended by delegates from twelve of the thir-teen colonies (Georgia was absent), took place in Carpenter's Hall— itself a compromise from the Pennsylvania State House offered by conservatives, who still hoped to see reconciliation—but much of the business involving Sam Adams, Patrick Henry, Benjamin Franklin, Thomas Cushing Jr., and even William Livingston, was conducted in the bar and club rooms of the City. There, representatives of the colonies cemented a meaningful bond that allowed them to agree upon a firm and total boycott of British goods, a demand for the repeal of the Intolerable Acts and, perhaps most important, the resolve to create militias in each colony—war preparations, in other words.

The British were quick to catch the drift of things and, in short order, began plotting their own preemptive measures to thwart the militias and seize their arms. Two of the first raids were planned in Massachusetts—Concord and Lexington—where the British hoped not only to break up local squadrons but also to capture Sam Adams and John Hancock, who were hiding in Lexington. In Concord, Wright's Tavern was destined to continue to play a major role in the fight for American independence. Already, Wright's had distinguished itself as the meeting place for the Provincial Congress, from which delegates were sent to Philadelphia, and at which resolutions were passed to defy British authority. On April 18, 1775, it was used by the "minutemen" for the organization of Concord's local militia, which, thanks to Paul Revere, was well aware the British were coming. (Historians point out that Revere may have stopped in Medford for a quick drink of rum en route— "Revere's midnight tipple," they call it.) When the British arrived, their first order of business was to occupy Wright's, and there, a Commander John Pitcairn stepped to the bar and ordered himself a brandy. He also pricked a finger, dripped some blood into his drink and offered a toast that rebel blood would be shed that day. Pitcairn, incidentally, would die not two months later at the Battle of Bunker Hill.

The day before, in Lexington, rebels were gathering at the Munroe Tavern, operated by William Munroe, Captain John Parker's orderly sergeant. There, patriots were tipped off by one Solomon Brown, who spotted soldiers and immediately hightailed it to the bar with the news. Fearing for the safety of Adams and Hancock, who were in hiding in a nearby parsonage, the patrons mobilized to protect the heroes. Patriot John Parker then rounded up the rest of his minutemen and sent them to the Buckman Tavern, run by John Buckman, a member of the Lexington Training Band. They sat out the night awaiting instructions to meet the British army on Lexington Green. In the early morning of the 19th, the British were surprised to find the rebels ready for battle. While only eight men died at Lexington, over 150 died on the first day of fighting. And some of the blood, indeed, was rebel.

Militias were readying themselves across the colonies. In the territorially disputed area between New Hampshire and New York that would later become Vermont, the Green Mountain Boys had armed themselves and gathered at the Catamount Tavern in Old Bennington. The Boys had a long head start on animosity and rebelliousness, since they had been resisting New York's attempts to control a section of land known as the New Hampshire Grants for over a decade. The Catamount was so named for its outside décor—a twenty-foot pole on which was mounted the skin of a mountain lion, bared teeth menacing and facing toward New York. Shifting their attentions from New York to the British, brothers Ethan and Ira Allen managed to lead over a hundred of their Green Mountain friends to Fort Ticonderoga, which they captured on May 10. The victory was doubly significant in that it not only netted large quantities of British munitions but also interrupted an important link in the British army's chain of communications.

Less than a month later, in New York, Marinus Willett, a man who had been involved in the original defense of Fort Ticonderoga (*for* the English and against the French during the Seven Years' War), could be found celebrating the fort's capture. Doubtless this would have been at Drake's Tavern, where there were daily rebel meetings, including one that hatched a plan to intercept troops transporting arms to Boston. Following that plan's success, Willett and compatriots hid the munitions in yet another tavern, this one owned by one Abraham Van Dyck.

By 1775, Drake's had become the new hangout for the New York Sons of Liberty, whose members were growing frustrated that support for revolutionary activities they kept hearing about in Boston, Philadelphia, and even in the South wasn't shaping up as quickly in New York. There were many rebels in the city, yes, but there were also a huge number of Loyalists living there, including one John Case. Frequented by sailors in addition to patriots, Drake's was well known for heated antiroyalist discourse—but apparently not by Case, who wandered in one night. Sears and McDougall immediately began attempts at getting the Loyalist to recant, but he refused and, in fact, grew more cantankerous about his loyalty. A visitor noted that, had Case expressed such sentiments in Connecticut, he'd have been put to death.

The Drake's patrons weren't quite so violent but did confine Case to a chair in a corner, defusing the potentially volatile situation by turning it into a drinking game. Anyone who got sucked into a conversation with Case had to buy the room a bowl of toddy. When later complaining about his evening's abuse, Case said that he'd been threatened with a branding from a hot iron and insisted that the Sons of Liberty were simply violent thugs, not freedom-fighters as they claimed. Sears partially confirmed Case's story when he said that it was only the would-be victim's age that had saved him from a red-hot gridiron.[4]

In March 1776, the Drake's patrons were again roused to action when it was discovered that the printer Samuel Loudon was about to release a pamphlet that attacked Thomas Paine's *Common Sense*, a runaway best-seller since its publication that January and the most rousing and important piece of pro-American and anti-British propaganda at hand. Those who couldn't afford their own copy could count on bumping into it in a tavern, where it was read aloud repeatedly. Historian Gordon S. Wood called it the "most incendiary" piece of propaganda ever written. Free of high-brow references and Latinate terminology and written in plain English, Paine's *Common Sense* (written with a little help from the revolutionary doctor Benjamin Rush) seems to foreshadow George Orwell's ideas about politics and the English language long before Orwell was alive to put them into print.

Paine's masterstroke involved a tale about a tavernkeeper in Amboy, New York, who failed in his duties, both to his child and to the Revolution, by wishing that the inevitable conflict with England be postponed until after his death. Paine makes clear that the correct moral choice would have been to rush to battle, so that there could be peace in the son's lifetime, if not necessarily the father's. Back at the Drake, then, after many rounds of "rumbo" (slang for rum) a "fuddled" mob poured into the streets and made its way to the printer Loudon's, where the rebuttal was rooted out and destroyed, pamphlets burned and printer smashed.

Drake's was used as a recruitment center, as were hundreds of other taverns over the next two years—most following the blueprint set up many years before by the Boston Sons of Liberty. Recruitment began with the tavernkeepers, who tended to be pro-independence as a result of the many taxes they'd been subject to over the years. Along with rebel leaders, they would rouse their patrons, who were likely further convinced by an inspiring reading of Paine's *Common Sense* and other tracts.

But a brief glance at the records reveals that taverns served many diverse functions—both officially and unofficially. Some suggest that Thomas Jefferson rehearsed the *Declaration of Independence* in mid-May 1776, with colleagues at the Raleigh Tavern in Williamsburg. He may have written a more final version at the Indian Queen in Philadelphia— a glass of Madeira at his side. The *Declaration* was circulated quickly and widely through the traditional channels—the network of taverns that formed the telegraph line of the era. In New York, recitations of Jefferson's tract led to riots; elsewhere, such as at the Bunch of Grapes in Boston, it was merely cause for serious celebration.

Philadelphia's Tun Tavern was used to recruit the marine forces for the Revolutionary War, which would eventually evolve into the United States Marine Corps. At the Catamount, the Green Mountain Boys turned the bar into a military tribunal and, after convicting a Loyalist of being on the wrong side, hanged him in an adjacent field—presumably in sight of the mountain cat skin.

On some brighter notes, at the King's Arms (promptly renamed the Eagle Tavern) in Williamsburg, proprietor Jane Vobe showed her support for the cause by giving free food and drink to Continental soldiers throughout the entire war. Soldiers were frequently welcomed into taverns and fed as generously as possible. Other taverns continued to act as organizing centers for less violent action. Tondee's tavern in Savannah, Georgia, for example, was the site of the election of delegates to the Second Continental Congress. Boston patriots, en route to that same Congress, enjoyed a welcome reception—and innumerable toasts—at every tavern they stopped. And at the Indian King Tavern in Haddonfield, New Jersey, the General Assembly ratified the Declaration of Independence in 1776.

As yet another indicator of the tavern's importance, a number of battles were named for them: The Battle of Spencer's Tavern in Virginia; the Battle of Torrence's Tavern in North Carolina; the Battle of Paoli Tavern near Philadelphia; and the Battle of Vanbibber's Tavern in Beaufort, South Carolina. The revolutionary forces initially mobilized to fight the British actually fought them in or near the very same taverns in which they'd been politicized and recruited. So vital a part of the Revolution, taverns, the original centers of dissent, also served as recruitment centers, hiding places, communications hubs, supply dumps, and safe havens. Taverns had earned a place of honor in colonial culture: They were also now revolutionary heroes. It was only fitting, therefore, that the majority of celebrations over the eventual patriot victory would take place in taverns, too. These began in October 1781, in places such as Mann's tavern in Annapolis, Maryland; the Globe in Portsmouth, New Hampshire; and, of course, Philadelphia's City Tavern, where there was an "elegant banquet" and numerous toasts once it became clear the British were giving up. The celebrations didn't end until 1783, when the last British soldiers left New York.

November 25 of that year became known as "Evacuation Day" and, as the last Redcoats departed, George Washington's troops marched into New York. The local Sons of Liberty waited at the Bull's Head Tavern to welcome him as he came through Harlem. Further south, Washington's company was met with a formal welcome at Cape's Tavern on Broadway. After that, it made its way down to "Black Sam's" Queen's Head—a natural spot for a victory celebration, given Samuel Fraunces's multiple contributions to the war effort. The Queen's Head had actually been a war casualty, taking a cannonball through the roof in 1775, but repaired by the end of the war. The evening's celebrations included thirteen toasts—one for each of the colonies, and another on which the wish was for a "close Union of the States" to "guard the Temple they have erected to Liberty."

Washington liked Fraunces's so much (housed in a former DeLancey residence, it was one of the most elegant taverns in New York) that he returned there in December to give his farewell address to his troops and, again, to celebrate his inauguration in 1789 as the first president of the Union. At the inaugural ball, they drank Barbados rum—known to be the best rum of the day and probably the reason one of the era's most popular expressions to describe an intoxicated friend was, "He's been at Barbadoes."

The Queen's Head would continue to thrive, although we imagine it wasn't quite the same without "Black Sam" (as Fraunces was known because of his mixed West Indian ancestry). He sold his tavern in 1785 after Washington hired him to become the first Executive Steward to the President, a position he took very seriously. "[H]e may kill me if he will," he is quoted as saying about Washington, "but while he is the President of the United States, and I have the honor to be a Steward, his establishment shall be supplied with the very best of everything that the whole country can afford."

For this brief period of mirth and revelry, the tavern was an uncontroversial and uncomplicated institution. Notable among the many veterans who returned home and hung out tavern shingles of their own was Davy Crockett's father, John Crockett—one of many patriots who continued the proud tradition of maintaining the democratic community centers of the nation. Tavernkeepers such as Black Sam were rewarded for the roles they had played during the war and, while he may have been the only one invited into the president's office, many others who had helped win independence in smaller ways held the respect of their communities and were recognized as heroes in their own right.

5

A FEDERALIST WALKS INTO A BAR

The victory celebrations were short-lived, however, and the very same things that made taverns so valuable to the revolutionaries—gathering places for the exchange of news and the discussion of grievances and handy centers for political mobilization—would now make them dangerous to the leaders of the new country.

Even before the last bowl of punch was drained on Evacuation Day, the thirteen colonies and their various political factions had started to observe the profound political differences they shared. And, just as the political ideas that shaped the American Revolution were hashed out and refined in a bar, so, too, would be the new problems facing the infant nation.

The dominant subject in the debate about American self-determination involved federalism versus states' rights—then, as now. An integral aspect of the issue was the recurring clashes between an increasingly powerful urban merchant class and traditional agrarian values. Add to this the usual catalyst for political and social upheaval—economic hard times. By the mid-1780s, much of America was in a depression, thanks, in part, to a well-intentioned sanction on goods shipped by British vessels, a proto-isolationist policy aimed at encouraging domestic growth.

In western Massachusetts, this depression was in full force by the summer of 1786. Many veterans had returned home to their farms and— if they were lucky enough—to a meager pay for their service in defeating the British. Payment was made in Continental paper notes, which were quickly devalued to about 10 percent of face worth—an early example of hyperinflation. Desperate veterans sold these notes to speculators, who bought them when they were nearly worthless, then managed to convince federal regulators to legislate that the notes be honored at full value, thereby making their money back ten times over. It was America's first major financial sector bailout.

There was still, however, the matter of how to pay for the redemption of the paper notes and that problem was solved by raising taxes—in this case, land taxes, which hit rural farmers disproportionately. Cheated out of their military pay once, many veterans were now being asked to pay higher taxes to subsidize the very speculators who had profited off their misfortune. Add to this the generally dismal economy and many honored heroes—men who had fought at Concord, Lexington, and Bunker Hill—were now finding themselves in debtors' prison. The details of the machinations weren't lost on the victims of this scheme, either. This was an extraordinarily informed and vocal public, thanks to thirty thousand copies of newspapers printed weekly in New England and the network of taverns in which they were read.[1]

So committees were formed and petitions circulated, looking for tax relief in these areas but, when no compensation was forthcoming through standard legal channels, some took to extralegal action. They did so, once again, in the local taverns of the area—many of which, as mentioned, were now run by veterans themselves. The taverns filled the same role they had during the Revolution, except that, after the war, the speed with which they evolved from communications centers into vortexes of dissent and recruitment and then finally into drill halls, was lightning fast. And tavern patrons were quick to act when they discovered the injustices heaped upon local farmers.

Those who rose to resist this systemic discrimination became known as the Massachusetts Regulators. They met at Clark's Tavern in Hubbardston and Merrick's Inn in Princeton, where they initially planned not to overthrow the system but, rather—and hence their name—to reregulate it so that inequities in the tax structure wouldn't unfairly punish farmers. At these taverns (as well as at least a half-dozen others), new militias were recruited and, once specific court dates were known, plans set for direct action, the majority of which was peaceful and orderly. This was the beginning of "the Regulation," in which activists, en masse, would shut down the courthouses on the dates of local debtors' trials. On August 29, 1786, fifteen hundred Regulators managed to close the Court of Common Pleas in Northampton. About two weeks later, the protest was even more impressive. Through a network of taverns, Regulators managed to raise an army of five thousand and shut down the debtors' courts of Concord, Great Barrington, and Taunton.

Far from being an unlawful mob, the Regulators were impeccably organized and generally considerate enough to avoid causing any collateral damage to neighboring businesses and residences. There wasn't even a single casualty during the initial regulations since the many veterans involved were so skilled in military organization. Every detail had been worked out in advance at one of those "seditious" tavernkeepers' homes that Hampshire county militia leader William Shepard would, in 1787, call "the common rendezvous for the councils" of the so-named Shays Rebellion.[2] Despite the relatively peaceful nature of the insurrection, the new government was quick to respond to the all-too familiar tactics that it knew could easily be turned against it. Rumors spread that the Regulators were being manipulated or possibly paid by the British and, simultaneously, that they were radical reformers advocating the redistribution of property. A week after Taunton, the Massachusetts Supreme Judicial met in Worcester and indicted eleven "traitors" who were the supposed ringleaders of the Regulators, calling them "disorderly, riotous, and seditious persons."

Daniel Shays, himself a veteran of Bunker Hill and Ticonderoga who had fought with the Green Mountain Boys, was insulted by these accusations, which bore no resemblance to their extremely orderly direct action, organized by people behaving in greater harmony with patriots' original sentiments than those now in charge of formulating tax policy. Shays was the poster child for the movement. He had been discharged with no pay, despite early heroism and service to the cause, and twice been to debtors' court. Organizing out of Conkey's Tavern in Pelham, Shays led hundreds on a protest march to Springfield and, from that point, took on an even more prominent role in the rebellion. While other rebel groups were recruiting from the Upton Tavern in Fitchburg, the Old Goldsbury Inn in Warwick, and Fuller's Tavern in Ludlow, Conkey's remained the movement's symbolic home.

Everybody is saddened to see their heroes grow old and give up youthful revolutionary ideals. And none could be more disappointing to the tavern historian than publican Sam Adams. The one-time radical and tavern-frequenter pulled up the ladder, suggesting that martial law and the suspension of habeas corpus be declared in similar future cases. He made an additional modest proposal—in the new republic, traitors should be subject to capital punishment.

In January 1787, the Shaysites launched an attack on the Springfield armory but were handily defeated. After four of Shays's men were killed, the rest fled and two of the many captured were executed at the end of the year. While the political climate lightened the following year, when Shays was pardoned, the new republic, in its very first test, had failed its taverns and their rebellious patrons.

Writing to James Madison from Paris, Thomas Jefferson was unconcerned, commenting that "a little rebellion" was a necessary "medicine" for the "sound health of government." He added his hopes that "honest republican governors" would be "mild in their punishment of rebellions as not to discourage them too much." His views were not shared by many. Madison, for instance, unmoved by Jefferson's words, said of the Shays Rebellion that "Liberty may be endangered by the abuses of liberty as well as the abuses of power." This represents a fairly radical shift in political rhetoric and, along with that shift, we begin to see an attempt to curtail the tavern and the liberty it represented. In New York in 1788, all gaming in licensed establishments was declared illegal—a crackdown on some of the fun that was being had in taverns, which, along with theaters, had been identified as twin "evils" threatening both city and state.[3]

This tavern control was urged by no less a figure than Benjamin Rush, an early member of the Sons of Liberty, signer of the Declaration of Independence and Surgeon General, first of the Continental Army and later of the United States. Rush was also no stranger to stirring prose and the uses of propaganda, having helped Thomas Paine with *Common Sense*. After the victory, he was still taken with politics and wrote tracts that equated the health of the citizenry with the health of the republic. In 1790, Rush urged "good men of every class to besiege the general and state governments with petitions to limit the number of taverns" and to penalize drunkards with the temporary revocation of "some civil right." He was concerned primarily with spirits, cheap rum, and, increasingly, whiskey, all of which, he felt, helped put people in the poorhouse and distracted them from the task of building the great nation. Drunkards were of a weakened mind, easy prey for politicians seeking votes and what was at stake, according to Rush, was nothing less than the country's survival. Without measures curtailing "ardent" spirits and taverns, the country was reeling toward extinction; "bad legislators" would be chosen by "intemperate and corrupted voters," placing the "republic in danger."

While Rush may have slightly overstated the case between spirits and tyranny, there was a clear relationship between alcohol and electioneering. Indeed, its blatant nature shocked French traveler Ferdinand Bayard, when he made his way through the country in the early nineteenth century and noted how politicians offered "drunkenness openly to anyone who is willing to give them his vote." His countryman Alexis de Tocqueville would later write that "Electioneering in America" was the process by which politicians were forced to "haunt the taverns" and "drink and argue with the mob." When Washington Irving published *Salmagundi* in 1807, one of the many New York institutions he satirized was the Old Bull's Head Tavern, one of George Washington's stops on his way into New York on Evacuation Day. In Irving's work, the tavern is rechristened "Hogg's Porter House," and in it a patron would find the "same stories, the same jokes and the same songs every night and . . . some of the longest and thickest heads in the city" who come to "settle the nation."

However, those in both the federalist and antifederalist camps still needed the taverns to gain political support for their competing visions for the country. There was more than a touch of irony and hypocrisy involved in the federalist camp which was working to curtail taverns when used by its opponents, yet simultaneously using them to bolster its own political support. The fight to control the tavern was the fight to control what democracy—the world's most radical political experiment to date—actually meant.

The first major deliberations into the pending constitution took place in Philadelphia in the summer of 1787. Much of the decision-making at this Congress took place behind the scenes at the City Tavern, the very same taproom in which the Republic was conceived thirteen years earlier. And the Shays Rebellion was being used as a bogeyman by federalists to rally support for the "Virginia Plan," a model for the Constitution that favored a strong central government, in contrast with the "New Jersey Plan," which advocated State's rights.

The Virginia Plan prevailed and, that September, a constitution that favored the federalist vision was drafted and proposed to the states for ratification. This was going to require some serious campaigning. In New York, for instance, people were evenly divided over the proposed constitution, which was getting bad publicity in anti-federalist taverns. Nothing like a little "treating," though, to help steer the course. The federalists—Alexander Hamilton (the patriot, not the doctor) orchestrating—put together a massive parade, which swung by Old Dock Street (just in time to watch two boats, one named the *Hamilton*, salute one another), then ended up at Bayard's Tavern, where no fewer than five thousand were treated to a free dinner—and plenty of rum punch. Festivities lasted until sunrise. Soon after, in July 1788, New York ratified the Constitution.[4] New Hampshire's ratification a month earlier had actually guaranteed the success of the founding document but New York's approval was still crucial to the union.

This was not Hamilton's only coup in a New York bar, either. The following year, when the congressional election was to take place, he managed to get a thousand supporters to swarm an opposition meeting at City Tavern and turn it into a night of campaigning for his own candidate, a lawyer named John Lawrence. The election was soon Lawrence's and poor John Broome, the man he would defeat, was "left to solicit votes through the newspapers."[5] Perhaps Benjamin Rush had a point, after all.

Not all taverns and their clientele were so easily manipulated by the promise of a parade and a free dinner. They would continue to fill their role as unruly and independent institutions, where an active and political public still met to educate itself and to plan for change. For every easily bribed tavernkeeper, there were several more hosting the antifederalist opposition—Democratic Societies and Republican Clubs.

The very first one of these was established in Philadelphia in April 1793 by Peter Muhlenberg, a German American. As this club catered mainly to the German community, David Rittenhouse, along with Charles Biddle, George Logan, and Alexander Dallas, started another for English-speaking political activists, known as the Democratic Society of Philadelphia, which had its first meeting on July 4 of that same year. (Rittenhouse, incidentally, had also served as president of the American Philosophical Society, which had grown out of the Junto.) In any case, the two clubs were the first of many political organizations set on opposing the country's new federalist direction and supporting the political philosophy of Thomas Jefferson, which prioritized freedom of speech, limited federal government, and agrarian values. These societies and clubs were sometimes founded and/or headed up by elites but, primarily, were frequented and supported by farmers, craftsmen, and laborers.

The Democratic and Republican Societies were not only a reaction to the short shrift farmers were getting after the Revolution under the administration of industrialization-minded politicians, but also a manifestation of the concerns that individual liberties and ideals of egalitarianism were slipping away. Despite the institution of the Constitution and the strong new federal government in place after the Shays Rebellion, tavern talk was still divided. In addition, the new societies were openly supportive of contemporary struggles against aristocrats in Europe, viewing those rebellions and revolutions as kin to their own movement for independence. At the second meeting of the Democratic Society of Philadelphia, they toasted "allies and brethren, the Sans Culottes of France" and also the "Patriots of Poland."[6]

Sympathies such as these were shared and discussed in taverns all over America. In Dover, Massachusetts, a Federalist named David Waldron complained that "the grog shops of Esq. Williams and A. Pierce have been the rendezvouz of democracy (i.e., Jeffersonians)" and accused his opponents of the "grossest lying" while they "preached democracy."[7] In Philadelphia, a tavernkeeper named Israel Israel was an active leader of the local Democratic society; in Canaan, New York, the local chapter was led by tavern-owner Jonathan Walker; Patrick O'Flinn, another keeper, led the charge in Wilmington, Delaware.[8] In Massachusetts, as one might expect, there were many chapters: Asa Wood's in Poplin; Marshall's in Greenland; Pike's at Epping; and Emerson's at Amherst. In one instance, Federalists' attempts to take over a meeting at Emerson's were branded as "scandalous, outrageous and aggravating" in the *Concord Patriot*, presumably a Democrat-Republican newspaper.[9]

Even before the official Democratic-Republican clubs were initiated, a proto-Democratic society had been established in New York. First called the Cincinnati Society, it was later the Society of Saint Tammany (otherwise known as the "Wigwam"), and eventually came to be known as Tammany Hall, named after Indian Chief Tamanend, who was said to have helped William Penn in his initial settlement. Some say Tammany was formed in the Fraunces Tavern; others claim the society was initially housed in Bardin's. Whatever the case, it eventually moved to Martling's tavern at Nassau and Spruce Streets on what were then the outskirts of Manhattan, near where the entrance to the Brooklyn Bridge is today. It was a rundown old building that the locals called the "pig pen" or "pig-sty." Nonetheless, it was there that William Mooney and company drank, sang, told stories, celebrated Independence Day and Evacuation Day, toasted the French and "Citizen Jefferson," and denounced what they saw as the new Federalist values: "Ambition, Tyranny, Sophistry and Deception."[10] Tammany had substantial influence in the other major New York tavern institution, the Tontine Coffee House, a members-only private club at the intersection of Wall and Water Streets, replete with bar, ballroom, and a chamber where the majority of the city's financial transactions took place. (This would eventually become the New York Stock Exchange Board.) Opinion was often slightly divided in the Tontine, but a liberty cap flying from its roof declared its true colors. It, too, was Democrat-Republican.

On Independence Day in 1799, the Tammany Society recorded its traditional sixteen toasts, leading with: "*America!* Our Country! The mother of the doctrine of equal rights. May she refuse to nurse any other children, but the sons of freedom and may they be victorious," and winding up with a toast to the American mother: "May they teach their sons to love liberty, and their daughters to hate tyranny and virtue." Sixteen toasts may sound like a good many and one might conclude that this level of drinking was reserved for a special day, such as the Fourth of July. Actually, the number of toasts is nearly identical to those, not only at all Tammany meetings, but at all the other Democratic-Republican societies across the country—the symbolic sixteen referring to the number of states at the time. The Democratic Party was thus conceived in a tavern and spent many of its first years there—drinking and recording its traditional sixteen toasts at each meeting. Years later, some opponents would still call the Democrats the party of "Rum, Romanism, and Rebellion."

In Philadelphia, the mood was largely in sympathy with the revolutionary brothers and sisters in Europe and very few tavernkeepers would have dared to show any allegiance to French nobility. One of the few who did—by putting up a portrait of the Queen of France—was hectored into using red paint to indicate blood around her neck. Bastille Day anniversary celebrations were held at places such as Oellers' Tavern. When news of the beheading of Louis XVI reached Philadelphia, a reenactment was repeatedly performed throughout the evening at the Black Bear Tavern on Second at Callowhill to the delight of all patrons—particularly when the head was rolled down a ramp. Bastille Day and similar celebrations took place in all the American cities, but Philadelphia was particularly caught up in the fervor because of the unusual number of French immigrants who'd arrived as a result of a slave revolt in Haiti and, of course, the French Revolution. Naturally, many of these refugees, having been aristocrats themselves, weren't particularly delighted when Louis' head rolled. One of the more famous French refugees was gastronome Jean-Anthelme Brillat-Savarin, who, it seems, was a regular patron at a tavern owned by a man named Little. One evening, he was treated by a couple of confident Brits to a big dinner—highlighted by plenty of claret, Madeira, and a bowl of rum punch big enough to serve forty—solely for the purpose of drinking the Frenchman under the table. It was the British hosts who wound up under the table, however, thanks, in part, to Brillat-Savarin's grasp of the necessary balance between food and alcohol.

Support for the French revolutionaries was of little concern to the Federalists. What was of concern was the fact that the Democratic-Republican clubs were spreading so quickly. The Federalists also couldn't help notice a familiar pattern emerging with the publication of partisan newspapers and the establishment of partisan taverns and clubs formed for the sole purpose of debating the legality of the Constitution. Many of the clubs were, in fact, political machines which operated in the same way that the Boston Caucus had: selecting candidates for local representation and then ensuring their election—often as not through tavern politics and treating at the polls. Rather than tolerating tavern discourse as a part of a healthy and engaged public, Alexander Hamilton proposed the one thing sure to ignite the passions of the already grumbling progressive and radical factions—an excise tax. Worse, this one was to be placed on distilled liquors and became known as the Whiskey Tax. Obviously, some serious controversy would be in order here, given that the War for Independence had been largely fueled by a reaction to the direct levies on a variety of goods. Excise taxes had never been terribly popular outside of America, either. In England, there were riots from 1645 to 1647, again in 1733, and yet again in 1763, all stemming from direct taxes on food, wine, cider, and perry (pear cider). Land taxes were generally considered a more democratic method of taxation.

Hamilton knew an excise would be unpopular but he was doing more than simply trying to recover money to pay for war debts. He was also trying to reduce the consumption of whiskey that Benjamin Rush had recently written about in *Inquiry Into the Effects of Ardent Spirits Upon the Human Body and Mind*, the book that, in some editions, made the case for spirits being a threat to democracy. In his *Inquiry*, Rush consistently praised cider and ale but attacked the hard stuff, which he believed he had seen at work during a trip to the back country of Pennsylvania, when he was shocked by the disorder and lack of industry. He wrote of untended farms and livestock and broken-down structures and fences, all of which he attributed to the "quantity of rye destroyed and whiskey drunk." Excessive drinking, he concluded, had devastating "effects upon the industry, health and morals" of the people living on the frontier. There, he also may have witnessed some of the worst effects of drinking, also catalogued in *Inquiry*. Included were excessive talking or excessive silence; being in a disagreeable mood or in good humor; an inability to keep a secret; a willingness to tell others their faults; immodest behavior in women; "singing" and, of course, "ballooing." There was more, too: "imitating the noises of brute animals," "dancing naked," and "sometimes with such a relaxation of the muscles which confine bladder and the lower bowels, as to produce a symptom which delicacy forbids me to mention." For drunkards, he prescribed a combination of aversion therapy and medical treatments—shaming, whipping, blistering the ankles, and bleeding (which Rush prescribed, no matter the ailment, for every patient, of which he lost a scandalous number).

Hamilton, who wouldn't have been politically aligned with Rush on any other front, took the doctor's work on spirits very seriously. And Rush's empirical observations were essentially correct. People who drank more rum and whiskey typically did have more problems with their health. It takes a generation or two to adjust to the refinement of any drug—as was the case with the gin panic in eighteenth-century England. And, while spirits weren't exactly brand new, they were taken up in measures never previously seen in America—particularly on the ever-moving frontier, now western Pennsylvania, where portability and preservation were important considerations. Beer, cider, and wine last only so long. Any cask-conditioned ale aficionado will rail on about the importance of freshness. Cider has a similarly short life span and wine is extraordinarily temperamental in conditions of extreme heat or cold, both of which were a problem for about ten months of the year in Pennsylvania.

Hamilton used Rush's work to support his agenda for changing the nation's drinking habits—and raise a little coin at the same time. He wrote: "The consumption of ardent spirits particularly, no doubt very much on account of their cheapness, is carried to an extreme, which is truly to be regretted, as well in regard to the health and the morals, as to the economy of the community." Hamilton hoped the new sin tax would discourage the consumption of hard liquor and that people would instead consume "cyder and malt liquors," which would benefit drinkers' health, productivity, and the nation's agriculture. When small, rural producers objected to the burden (the tax was to be paid at the still), Hamilton countered that ultimately the excise would be passed on to the consumer. The best way to avoid the excise, therefore, was to drink less whiskey.

Few people on the frontier would have been happy to hear that news. Out there, they drank a lot and weren't about to change that practice. Whiskey was drunk by ministers and bishops—unabashedly—in public. In some cases, the minister's salary was even paid in "old Monongahela rye."[11] Whiskey was drunk at christenings and at wakes—in fact, on all occasions. Not that they needed an occasion to justify whiskey drinking, given that it was set "on the table as a beverage at mealtimes," "taken as a strengthener between meals," and used year-round to acclimatize or, as Davy Crockett once said, whiskey made a man warm in winter and cool in summer.[12] These were ingrained routines, not likely to be altered by a tax, and even Benjamin Rush didn't expect habits to change overnight. He prophesied that his efforts would take a century to pay off, predicting that, by 1915, "the use of spirits" would be "as uncommon in families as a drink made of a solution of arsenic or a decoction of hemlock." He was only five years off on the passage of the Eighteenth Amendment and the beginning of Prohibition.

Even had Pennsylvanians decided to drink less, they would still have had a problem with the new tax. Actual currency remained rare, particularly in rural areas. Business was depressed and traditionally done through the barter of goods and services. Paying the tax was a hardship on those who had small stills, which offered the average Pennsylvania farmer the only way to sell his grain. Although western Pennsylvania may not seem terribly remote, at the time, the areas on the outskirts of that state, as well as Virginia, North Carolina, and Georgia, were isolated and undeveloped, especially compared with the Eastern seaboard, which was gradually transforming into the Hamiltonian dream of urban centers thriving with commerce and industry. On the frontier, roads were primitive and transporting crops posed a tremendous challenge. As a result, many frontier farmers processed their rye into whiskey. A horse could carry four bushels of rye to market or, converted into two eight-gallon kegs of whiskey, the equivalent of twenty-four bushels.[13]

According to the tax legislation, large distillers were given the option of paying a flat tax on the maximum capacity of their still's annual production, which turned out to be about two-thirds the rate others paid per gallon. Small distillers (even the communally owned ones) couldn't run at maximum capacity and therefore couldn't take advantage of the reduced excise. George Washington was a large distiller, only subject to the lower flat tax. Furthermore, East Coast elites were partial to European wines and sherries, subject to only eight to fifteen cents tax per gallon, as opposed to whiskey's twenty-five, and thus paid less tax than whiskey drinkers. Hamilton had even argued that imported liquors were already too expensive.

Had the federal government promised to build infrastructure in these underdeveloped areas, local farmer-distillers might have been more open to the new tax. In their eyes, though, the government did next to nothing for them. Many also felt abandoned in their constant strife with the Indians consisting of chronic skirmishes, retaliations, and massacres of both sides. No military help was available to them and, besides, East-erners were generally horrified at the brutality of the Scots-Irish and sympathetic towards the Indians. Finally, as with the one-time federal promise to honor Continental notes just before the Shays Rebellion, most of the war debts Hamilton's federal government was generously willing to assume were already held by speculators. It was beginning to look like Shays all over again, especially to those sitting around taverns in frontier towns, discussing the state of the union.

Twice, the bill containing the whiskey tax failed to make it through Congress, largely because of strenuous objections from a few distillers in New England and Southerners such as North Carolina's John Steele, who estimated that residents of his state would pay ten times as much tax as those in Connecticut.[14] At first, Thomas Jefferson, known for his later oft-repeated gem "no nation is drunken where wine is cheap; and none sober, where the dearness of wine substitutes ardent spirits as the common beverage," was against the tax on the grounds that it was an excise. Under British colonial rule, patriots had called the excise the most "odious of taxes." For the young government to turn around and implement an excise of its own—and so quickly—seemed the ultimate hypocrisy.

Hamilton, however, was becoming known for getting exactly what he wanted and managed to negotiate with most of his opponents until, at the time of the bill's final passage, remaining objections came mainly from one man, Georgia's James Jackson, who pointed out that the South had "no breweries or orchards to furnish a substitute." Jackson also rejected the logic that spirits were in any way worse than soft liquors, arguing that the law might as well interdict the use of catsup, "because some ignorant persons had been poisoned eating mushrooms."[15] Jackson and his handful of allies were also unmoved by the prospect of a tax to pay off war debts, since, unlike the Northern states, they had none.

Nevertheless, in early March 1791, after substantial political maneu-vering, Hamilton got his bill passed. By summer, opponents of the tax sent delegates to a meeting in Pittsburgh—one of the first of many at-tempts at political organization against the excise. Once again, the pro-test process began within legal and acceptable channels and, once again, a tavern would do the honors—in this instance, the Green Tree Tavern at the corner of Wood and Fourth. Hugh Henry Brackenridge, an ambi-tious lawyer and writer who had moved west to become a big fish in a small pond, recorded the resolutions, which protested the tax on the grounds that it restricted liberty and hurt local economies. In attendance were groups of representatives from Democratic Societies and Republican Clubs, including three from Western Pennsylvania which were destined to become notorious: the Democratic Republican Society of the County of Washington, the Republican Society at the Mouth of the Youghiogheny, and the Society of United Freemen of Mingo Creek. Almost all of the societies and clubs were against the excise, but none more so than the Mingo Creek chapter, which Brackenridge later claimed was at the heart of the Whiskey Rebellion. David Bradford stood at the helm of Mingo Creek, which operated in an identical fashion to the prerevolutionary Boston Caucus—vetting candidates before they stood election and acting as the region's political machine.

Both moderates such as Brackenridge and rabble-rousers such as Bradford agreed that the whiskey tax was placing a disproportionate amount of the burden on farmers, especially those on the frontier. When attempts to rectify the injustice through legal channels failed, direct action began again, often employing the same tactics and rhetoric the patriots had used. In Lexington, Kentucky, a mob paraded an effigy of Colonel Thomas Marshall, the local excise collector. In Washington County, Pennsylvania, a group of about a hundred protested with an effigy of John Neville, the Pittsburgh excise man. On the extralegal side, in 1791, the "Whiskey Boys" disguised themselves as a group of women and caught collector Robert Johnson in Washington County. They cut off his hair, stripped, tarred, and feathered him, then stole his horse, leaving him stranded. Johnson not only resigned his post, he publicly announced it in the *Pittsburgh Gazette*—as per his captors' instructions.

Most of the early direct action, however, was aimed at the people who acquiesced and paid the tax, which was seen as akin to giving the federalists a mandate. Therefore, one of the first orders of business was to ensure that everyone boycott it. To this end, a group of Whiskey Boys, who organized in taverns and were probably led by a man named John Holcroft—a veteran of the Shays Rebellion—began a violent campaign to gain support among still-owners. Distillers caught complying with the law were strong-armed by local resisters who "mended" their stills by shooting them full of holes. The group became known as "Tom the Tinker's Men" and stills didn't function nearly as well once tinkered with. They also left notes on people's doors, strongly encouraging them to send letters denouncing the tax to the *Gazette*, in which pieces by Tom the Tinker himself (presumed to be Holcroft), were frequently published. Editors who turned down his submissions risked having their own possessions "mended."

By mid-1794, there were liberty poles in front of most of the region's taverns—,especially outside Pittsburgh city limits—to the south in Mingo Creek and Washington County—where the rebels were most active. One of the more famous of these was Jean Bonnet's, a public house in Bedford that had been licensed to Bonnet and his wife in 1780. Disgruntled farmers met there in the middle of 1794 to raise objections and, of course, a liberty pole. The Old Stone Tavern in Greentree, in Pittsburgh's west end, was another headquarters for the Whiskey Rebellion. There's a record of a John Woods having been served there on June 16, 1794. He obviously hadn't been welcomed, since next to his name is written "(spy)." Pittsburgh was apparently full of strangers at the time and there were numerous reports of people, reportedly "on business," whom nobody had ever seen before.[16]

When Old Stone Tavern owner Daniel Elliott died, his young children were cared for by none other than Brackenridge, who didn't confine his writing talents to drafting protests in taverns. He also wrote what is generally considered America's first novel, *Father Bombo's Pilgrimage to Mecca*, and was closely involved with the founding of both the Pittsburgh Academy (later, the University of Pittsburgh) and the *Pittsburgh Gazette*. Brackenridge wrote various political tracts for the *Gazette* meant to be read in taverns. He also authored several witty stanzas about the virtues of his whiskey-swilling countrymen, in comparison with the wine-drinking snobs: "Far better than the drink ca'd wine: Wi' me compar'd tis wash for swine." Brackenridge's oenophile-bashing was in particular response to the excise tax, of course, but also to the backlash against hard liquor, which had been started by Rush and was increasingly supported by East Coast elites.

At the Old Stone Tavern and other venues in western Pennsylvania, the Whiskey Boys and others expressed their outrage at the persistence with which the federal government was collecting taxes. Distillers were summoned to court and forced to travel three hundred miles to Philadelphia and back, a round-trip journey over bad roads that would have required at least a couple of weeks and forced farmers to leave their crops and property untended—a dangerous prospect on the frontier. Like the Salem Villagers, western Pennsylvanians resented having to trek the distance from their home to the state's political hub, particularly in order to pay taxes considered unjust.

What they did, then, was plan an attack on John Neville, former Revolutionary War general turned head tax-collector for the region. In taverns, Bradford mobilized five or six hundred men to attack Bower Hill, Neville's country house, located a few miles south of Pittsburgh. Neville and his family fled but rebels burned the mansion to the ground, then headed back to Jean Bonnet's Tavern. Knowing that the federal army would soon be dispatched to put their rebellion down, Bradford and company vowed that they wouldn't be "frightened by finely arranged lists of infantry, cavalry and artillery."[17] The *Gazette* weighed in, too, arguing that the government's main responsibility "should be the protection of the liberties of the people," not the reverse.

The next step for Bradford was to try to take Pittsburgh, where the region's remaining federalist supporters might still be found. Indeed, they had a list of men who had explicitly supported the excise and the plan was to throw those men out of town. This proved unnecessary since the men complied and left on their own accord and, as a result, the Whiskey Army's march through Pittsburgh was peaceful and even congenial, since townspeople and tavernkeepers provided the rebels with plentiful free food and drink. Many of the rebels were practically utopian philosophers, set on implementing what they saw as a "pure democracy" that some historians have referred to as the "epilogue" of the American Revolution.[18]

The politics that evolved out of taverns west of the Allegheny Mountains were as radical as those that had sparked the Revolution and perhaps even more so. Not even the Shaysites had been this radical. This is how Brackenridge articulated matters:

> July 31. The root of the trouble is far deeper than a mere quarrel over the excise. It is, as our people see it, a stand of the democratic, poverty-ridden West against the encroachments of the aristocratic Money Bags of the East; of a people who feel themselves taxed in order to fasten the yoke of Plutocrats about their necks, the Whiskey excise being but one in a step of a series of tyrannical measures. The crisis arises from an opposition to the fiscal policies of Government which they aver are for benefit of speculators in credits from the late war and bear hardly on the poor . . .[19]

George Washington recognized the threat posed by populist tavern politics and quickly led an army into rebel territory. It was a controversial move, since it marked the first time in America that an army had been raised against its own citizens. In the month that it took to cross Pennsylvania, Washington, as he had during the Revolutionary War, used the taverns as way-stations and military bases. In part, he was attempting to win them back to the federalist cause. On October 19, he installed many of his troops at the Bonnet Tavern, a deliberate choice. Washington's arrival was not, however, the cause for celebration it would have been in another era and, often, his troops were met with silence.

The Whiskey Rebellion collapsed without a fight. Bradford escaped to New Orleans but would later be pardoned. The whole series of events reflected badly on the new government, which seemed to have been perfectly happy to use the taverns for its own political ends, but wasn't about to extend the courtesy to those who disagreed with it. The right to oppose perceived tyranny, it seemed, was to be granted only to those in power.

But the tavern, as always, had a mind of its own, and now there was a new controversy: how to pay for the wages of the thirteen thousand men recruited to put down the Whiskey Rebellion. The answer was another new tax—this one, a direct land tax that was put into law on July 14, 1798, the very same day as the Sedition Act that prohibited saying malicious things about the government and further encroached upon state's rights. Jeffersonians (including Jefferson, himself) attacked these new developments as unconstitutional. It was the land tax that would lead to violent political action, again in Pennsylvania, this time in the southeast, where a settlement of German farmers with large properties would argue that the tax was disproportionate and therefore unconstitutional.

Led by men such as John Fries, who had actually been a member of the Continental Army's efforts to quash the Whiskey Rebellion, a small group of rebels began harassing the tax collectors in the area, sometimes soaking them with buckets of hot water. In an attempt to resolve the problem, two taxmen agreed to meet with area residents at Mitchell's Tavern in Bucks County. Once there, though, the crowd refused to give the collectors the floor. Officials responded by arresting those who refused an assessment. The prisoners were held captive at a temporary jail at the Sun Tavern in Bethlehem, Pennsylvania. On March 7, 1799, two meetings were held—one at Conrad Marks' tavern in Milford and another at Martin Ritter's tavern in Northampton. At Ritter's, it was decided that Fries and Andrew Shiffert would lead a charge of some one hundred and forty rebels to Bethlehem and demand the release of the prisoners. They were successful but securing the release represented the limit of their ambition for direct action. Shortly thereafter, two hundred people met at Conrad Marks' and decided to acquiesce to the tax. Fries was tried and convicted for treason under the new Sedition Act, but, like Bradford, would eventually be pardoned.

Although none were successful, the Fries, Shays, and Whiskey rebellions strengthened the resolve of the Democratic-Republican Societies, which grew more numerous and influential within the network of taverns across America and served as the backbone of the antifederalist movement. These societies also began shying away from open rebellion, which had proved unsuccessful in these three early test cases, and, instead, followed the Boston Caucus model for winning political support. Taverns would be used less to agitate a violent mob and more to consolidate power.

In Pittsburgh, for example, antifederalist supporters rallied at a number of taverns, the most prominent of which was Molly Murphy's General Butler Tavern. Their meetings grew into an association known as the Clapboard Row Junto and came to dominate the local political scene. Back at the Green Tree, meanwhile, tavern-owner Adamson Tannehill became known as one of the city's leading antifederalists and political leaders. The Clapboard Row group founded *The Tree of Liberty* newspaper, which was often read aloud in the General Butler. It was the same drill: members planned and wrote editorials for their paper, recruited supporters, selected candidates, and mobilized voters. The latter included naturalizing new residents so they could vote for Clapboard Row candidates.[20]

This pattern emerged in city after city, virtually guaranteeing the eventual election of Thomas Jefferson and the ousting of the Federalists. In fact, the aforementioned New York Democratic Society, known as the Society of Saint Tammany, is specifically credited with helping Aaron Burr win New York for the Democratic-Republicans, thus edging out John Adams in the 1800 election. This was the birth of nineteenth-century machine politics, which had taken its cue from the Boston Caucus and would refine it by weaning the rabble off direct action and, instead, channeling it into the polls.

The Democratic-Republicans would increasingly be critiqued for their treating tactics, but treating didn't always translate into victory. One fairly famous setback occurred in Hudson, New York, and was described on May 6, 1806, by editor Harry Croswell in his Whig newspaper, *The Balance and Columbian Repository*. Shortly after an election, Croswell published an editorial detailing a bar bill incurred by the Republican candidate in plying voters: "720 rum-grogs, 17 brandy, 32 gin-slings, 411 glasses of bitters and 25 dozen cocktails." Croswell couldn't resist juxtaposing the amount of alcohol bought with the end result of the election—a Republican loss. This list, incidentally, has been made famous as, for many years, it was thought to be the first reference to the word "cocktail." Although an earlier reference has since been found in an 1803 edition of a newspaper called *The Farmer's Cabinet*, where this appeared: "Drank a glass of *cocktail*—excellent for the head."[21]

A reader had written to *The Balance*, however, asking for clarification on the meaning of the word. He submitted that it might be a necessary concoction with which to warm and rouse Jefferson and Clinton supporters, who were "sunk into rigidity." Croswell wrote back to explain that it was a drink of spirits, sugar and bitters which was of great use "to a democratic candidate: because, a person having swallowed a glass of it, is ready to swallow any thing else." It wasn't only the proto-Democrat party that used taverns and treating for political gain, but it would always be thought of as the worst offender.

The very notion of what America was—why the Revolution had been fought and what it had meant—was being hashed out during the new country's first two decades. Born in a tavern, it was struggling to redefine itself in one, too. The results were not heartening. What wound up displacing the utopian democratic ideals embodied by the direct actions that had shaped America would be temporarily displaced by means-to-an-end politics, created and maintained through backroom manipulation.

6
KEEPING
TABS

BARROOM SCENE BY
WILLIAM SIDNEY MOUNT, 1835
Image courtesy of The Art Institute of Chicago.

Let's launch the second part of this book by taking a step back to show how the bar evolved from the seventeenth- and eighteenth-century tavern into its nineteenth-century incarnations—the grog shop, frontier saloon, urban saloon, American bar, and hotel bar.

Until the early nineteenth century, taverns were relatively uniform and uncomplicated. Most had a few bed-chambers (with feather beds) to accommodate out-of-towners and a taproom or two that catered to both locals and travelers and served food. None would have had long bars at which the customers stood and drank but, rather, a "cage" in which the tapster prepared drinks and tables where patrons sat to drink them. As we've seen, it was often the town's political, social, and economic center and, typically, the hostler of a town's preeminent tavern was a prominent figure, often holding another public office, such as that of postmaster or municipal representative. Even if political debates occasionally got out of control, the majority of taverns were still respectable public forums in which local and national affairs were vigorously discussed by out-of-towners, locals, and the landlord himself, often a veteran of the Continental Army.

Obviously, some taverns were better outfitted than others and it would be safe to say that the farther a person got from urban centers, the less likely he'd be able to find true comfort. The average nineteenth-century American country tavern was a log cabin, often identifiable by its display of patriotism, such as a picture hanging out front of George Washington or Thomas Jefferson (or, later, Andrew Jackson). Sometimes it was hard to know just which president was being depicted, however, and poor renderings meant that the president was largely "identifiable only by the name beneath." Dinner might have benefited from similar labels, since it was usually a massive spread of indifferent meats. Even in the earliest days, the priority was to provide diners with quantity, not quality, and European travelers consistently registered shock over the amount of food the average American put away at a single sitting. In 1833, Sir James Edward Alexander, another traveling memoirist, wrote that, in Tennessee, men ate plates heaped with steaks, fish, and apple tarts slopped together, then shoveled the whole disgusting mess down as if "it was their last meal, or as if they intended to choke themselves." After the cacophonous clang of plates and silverware, the men pushed back from their tables and immediately disappeared to the bar where they received a "stiff glass of sling from the bar-keeper."[1]

Vegetables rarely made the grade. Fruit was usually drunk by the glass, in the form of peach brandy and apple cider, except in urban areas where, on occasion, the upper classes indulged in West Indian tropical fruits. In the country, people ate corn bread, squirrel, chicken, potatoes, eggs, and a phenomenal quantity of pork. Breakfast was even advertised as "pig and coffee." At a more upscale establishment, a patron might find "chicken fixings," meaning all the things traditionally served to accompany fried chicken—typically, veal cutlets, sausage, and steaks. One tavern sign did away with the niceties of a name or the portrait of the president and advertised, quite simply: "Stranger, here's your chicken fixings."[2]

Nobody knew better than George Washington how bad the "common doings" could be at some of the country's taverns, thanks to the ambitious and grueling two-thousand-mile, thirteen-colony, hand-shaking-and-baby-kissing tour he undertook between 1789 and 1791—an attempt at keeping the country unified in purpose and the spirit of '76 alive. His reception was considerably more enthusiastic than the one he got in backcountry Pennsylvania on his Whiskey Rebellion–quashing tour. Washington was besieged with requests from admirers that he stay the night at their homes. This would not have done, politically, though, since Washington dared not ruffle feathers by choosing between invitations and favoring one local dignitary over another. He made a blanket rule that he would only stay in public accommodations, namely, taverns. And this is how Washington came to have "slept here" in so many places.[3]

Washington must have been pleased that judicial circuit riders had preceded him and legislated for a few feather beds and some other basics. However, in some of the smallest towns, the basics were about all he was going to get. In Connecticut, he stayed at Perkins' Tavern, which, he noted, was "not a good one." He complained of one lodging's entertainment as being "not very inviting," and of another in Virginia where they had "no rooms or beds which appeared tolerable," and "every thing else having a dirty appearance." That said, Washington must have had access to the crème de la crème, since other contemporary travel accounts brim with complaints about everything from swarms of flies to dirty sheets being used as tablecloths. On one striking occasion, a patron witnessed the landlady yank the dirty sheets from under her sick husband, throw them over a table, then lay out the evening meal.[4]

Historian A. K. Sandoval-Strauss links Washington's cross-country tour with the push for bettering public accommodations that followed. In larger cities, hotels (the word borrowed from the French, for host) were replacing taverns and architecturally distinct from their predecessors. A tavern could easily have been confused with a private dwelling; the new inns were larger and reflected a new style of "public house architecture." In Baltimore, the Fountain Inn was one of the better early examples of this new strain of accommodation. (Speaking of new strains, that's where Francis Scott Key would write the Star-Spangled Banner in 1814 to the tune of an old drinking song.) In Alexandria, Virginia, the famed Gadsby's Tavern was the city's preeminent inn and, nearby in Washington, DC, most agreed that the new Union Public Hotel was one of the very best in the country.[5] New York was not to be outdone by some upstarts on the swampland of the Potomac, however. A group of investors bought New York's City Tavern in 1793, tore it down and erected the City Hotel in its place. The City was a four-story red brick building occupying an entire city block on Broadway and boasted a bar, wine cellars, and high-ceilinged public spaces. The bar was full "from morn to dewy eve" with men drinking strong drinks while they "read newspapers and talk(ed) politics." The Madeira-tasting "Jolly Good Fellow" club met there, as did James Fenimore Cooper's Bread and Cheese Club. Cooper called it a tavern on the "grand scale," which had "the double character of a European and American house." And in the bars of these new establishments, especially in the middle of the nineteenth century, some of the more refined aspects of American drinking took shape.

Hotel bars were the alternative to the myriad places where, increasingly, all of America was getting drunk—saloons. The saloon seems to have come out of nowhere since, prior to 1820, the bar landscape of America was dominated by the tavern; yet, by 1850, it seems all anyone could talk about was the saloon and the evils it represented. Although there were some prominent figures interested in curtailing the tavern and its political power, it was still partially associated with the heroism of the Revolutionary War. In sharp contrast, the saloon was generally known as a hardcore, violent, and unheroic sphere that would come to be so hated and vilified that it nearly brought an end to drinking in public in America.

It's important to clarify that there are two fairly different entities referred to by "saloon"—the urban East coast, politically-oriented watering holes and the ones with the swinging doors that came to be inextricably associated with frontier culture. Generally, it's thought the word itself is an Anglicization of "salon," a reference to the intellectual gatherings in Paris, which, along with coffee-houses, were a part of the "public sphere" transforming European politics.

The frontier saloon needs little introduction. An image of it, replete with atmosphere, is easily conjured. In any of the lawless towns dotting the landscape all the way from St. Louis to California, those swinging doors open to reveal a long bar, a stern barkeep, spittoons, and barrels of whiskey set on top of a dusty floor. These were rough-and-tumble places where men drank whiskey, gambled, and got into gunfights—often an evening's trifecta. In addition, one might imagine a few tables for card-playing and, in the high-end saloons, a billiards table. There might be a few saloon-girls lingering about and, while these generally wouldn't have been considered suitable companions in polite society, they weren't always prostitutes, either. In all, this is the iconic image, reinforced by hundreds of movies—good, bad, and ugly—and the contemporary ersatz saloons trying to capitalize on the undeniably romantic aspects of such places.

As the frontier moved west, the saloon continued to fill a role similar to that of its tavern ancestors, standing in for nearly everything as towns were being assembled from scratch. Saloon historian Katherine Weiser identifies the first place to call itself a "saloon" as Brown's Hole, named for the town in which it was established in Utah in 1822.[6] Early frontier saloons were sometimes housed in tents and, from those rudimentary structures rose a whole range of drinking establishments, separated, among other things, by ethnicity and race. Their names helped lead prospective patrons in the right direction. The "Shamrock," say, would have something different going for it than one called the "Bismarck." Black men would likely not go looking for a drink in any of the many "White Elephant" saloons, and certainly not when there was an alternative "Black Elephant" in the vicinity. In more established settlements, there were also generally high-end saloons that tended to be exclusive. Often these instituted a relatively strict door policy that kept out both prostitutes and undesirable patrons known for especially violent behavior. This was particularly so—as was frequently the case—when they were owned by a town's alderman, judge, or sheriff.

The upscale saloons would have a few more options than the standard beer and whiskey—the latter known variously as "Coffin Varnish,"

"Tarantula Juice," "Cactus Juice," "Sheep-Dip," or, most simply, "Rotgut." One might run across one of the new whiskey-based proto-cocktails such as the "Mule Skinner," made with whiskey and blackberry liqueur.[7] If someone ever had his fill of Tarantula Juice for the night he might well get handed a saloon "token," good for a free first drink the following day. Saloon tokens were by no means confined to the frontier and were popular even in Benjamin Franklin's day, as evidenced by one of the era's euphemisms for being piffled: "He swallowed a tavern token." Saloon tokens became a veritable institution, although the gimmick was universally reviled by reformers who correctly identified it as a means to entice people back to the saloon the following day. Theoretically, a patron could come to cash in his token and leave but, given that this was perceived as poor etiquette, often as not, it led to another round of general debauchery. In one instance, saloon tokens led to a major innovation, which was obviously before its time—the latrine bar. According to bar historian Brian Rea, a barkeeper in San Francisco was livid about losing a constant trickle of patrons to a competitor, lured away from his bar by boys giving out tavern tokens by the outhouse. The owner devised a trough that ran the length of the bar so that drinkers need never leave the saloon for a pee.[8]

There *were* places where saloons operated as political headquarters in tavern-like fashion, such as in San Francisco. New York saloonkeep David C. Broderick emigrated there in 1849 during the Gold Rush, opening a saloon that marked his first step toward a rapid rise to the U.S. Senate. Mostly, though, the frontier saloon was an apolitical haven for individualism and vice, with no pretense to hominess or camaraderie. In the East, the urban saloon was profoundly different, having in common only alcohol and the occasional set of swinging doors. The Eastern urban saloon would become firmly associated with political organization.[9] Taverns had been centers for caucuses and Democratic-Republican societies; saloons took things up a notch and became the hub for gang-dominated machine politics. Later, they would also be firmly associated with radical anarchism, socialism, and labor unions. Their roots were the community grocery store.

This grocery/proto-urban saloon would have been similar to a Spanish bodega, in which the line between take-out and drink-in was slowly blurred until entirely indistinct. One of the earliest known of these proto-urban saloons was in New Orleans, at Bourbon and Bienville, where the Absinthe House now stands. Some claim that's where Andrew

Jackson and gentleman pirate Jean Lafitte aligned their interests and worked toward fighting off the British in the War of 1812. This may be true but, if it is, the meeting would have taken place not in a saloon but a grocery store, operated by the Juncadelia family, who hailed from Barcelona. The Juncadelias sold tobacco and Spanish liquor in addition to food, so their place was more than simply a "general store" but, in fact, a hybrid—a bodega or, as it was more commonly called in English-speaking America, a grog shop. Historian Luc Sante goes so far as to narrow down the origins of the urban saloon to one neighborhood of grog shops in New York, "the area of Five Points."[10]

Grog shops weren't a new phenomenon and the number of them that existed in Philadelphia's Helltown had been of great concern to Benjamin Franklin. Known also as "tippling houses," these unlicensed bars were subject to much (mostly futile) legislation. In Helltown, though, it wasn't a law that eventually rid the area of grog shops but the influx of French refugees, whose arrival after the French Revolution gentrified the neighborhood. Most grog shops had a back room in which liquor and tobacco were sold and, depending on the day—or time of day—one that turned into a makeshift, casual, and illegal barroom, appealing to those of slender means. The sale of liquor slowly outstripped the sale of food until the pretense of selling groceries was abandoned entirely.

One grog shop Sante identified in Five Points was Rosetta Peer's at the intersection of Centre and Anthony (now known as Worth) and home to Edward Coleman's legendary Forty Thieves of the Five Points. Rosetta Peer's was also merely one of about fifteen hundred grog shops in New York, in which *mainly* Irish proprietors sold wine and spirits. In later years, the Irish Kerryonians, the Roach Guards, the Plug Uglies, and the Shirt Tails (so named because they refused to tuck in their shirts) would terrorize New Yorkers, using various grog shops as their home bases. These grocery-turned-tippling houses served to facilitate new associations and acted as a headquarters for conspiratorial meetings.[11] They were the social centers for one of America's most dangerous neighborhoods, the so-called Bloody Ould Sixth Ward.

As grim and violent as grog shops like Rosetta Peer's were, they were actually respectable compared with some of the other drinking venues growing up in the vicinity by the mid-nineteenth century. In some places, called "shock houses" or "shock joints," customers imbibed punch mixed with liquid camphor and/or benzene. On the Bowery, some bars did away with the nicety of glasses and, instead, allowed customers to suck alcohol from the barrel through a rubber tube. For three cents, patrons could drink until they had to come up for air. This spawned an increasing number of Bowery boys with superhuman lung capacity and "circular breathing" techniques.[12] These were the sort of places reformers wanted to draw public attention to, but there can be no one characterization of public bar life in antebellum America. The range was beyond anything seen before or, perhaps, since.

Farther south, in New Orleans, other bar variations included the barrel-house and the concert saloon. Crime historian Herbert Asbury called the barrel-house the "lowest guzzle shop ever operated in the United States"; and Asbury would have been quite familiar with the Bowery grog shops, given that he wrote *The Gangs of New York*. Once a patron entered a barrel-house, says Asbury, there was one inevitable end: he would be robbed, virtually stripped down, and, quite frequently, beaten. Alcohol was manufactured on the premises from a neutral spirit base and usually doctored with knockout drops. The police were often in on the scam, as in New York, where barrel-houses devised another wrinkle for their "shock and block" patrons—so-called because they were never expected to make it more than a block before passing out. These poor sods would not only be drugged, robbed, and stripped, but later picked up and charged with public intoxication and indecency by police.

One level up from the barrel-house was the concert saloon. Some of these had full bar rails, but most were simply beer halls with a stage show of some kind—of can-can girls and other entertainment. Some can-can performances were more decorous than others, but the real debauchery was likely happening with the waiter girls employed by the establishment. The larger concert saloons would have hundreds of these women working for tips and a share of the profits from the beer they managed to coerce patrons into buying. Most concert saloons were really just fronts for prostitution and there was no doubt that more money was to be made upstairs.

Women were hardly the only entertainment. There were also wrestling and butting (boxing) matches, as well as dog and rat fights, one of the most popular activities in saloons across America. One evening at Bison Williams's Buffalo Bill House—the diviest of New Orleans' saloons—where goods were fenced in plain sight and robberies were routinely and openly planned—patrons were charged fifty cents (a dollar bought a ringside seat) to watch a champion rat-killing terrier, brought in from New York, dispatch sixty rats in five minutes. In the middle of this particular event, though, the headliner gave up after succumbing to a rat bite and a local rat-dog had to finish the job. The record, by the way, had been a hundred rats—but that took eleven and a half minutes. (A Mexican wild boar had been promised as part of the ticket, too, but failed to make an appearance.) Unsurprisingly, there were those who wanted the Buffalo Bill House shuttered. Williams said he couldn't understand why this was, since he had gone to great lengths to open his saloon where "decent people do not live."[13]

On a more positive note, there was a new community service that saloons across the country were beginning to provide in the nineteenth century—the free lunch. At saloons of all levels and in almost every region, patrons who bought a drink were allowed to help themselves to the fixings on the lunch table. This soon became a sine qua non for saloonkeepers but also created some new problems—customers who helped themselves to free food without buying a drink, or those who lingered over a drink in order to pile up huge portions of food. Increasingly, saloons had to employ a little muscle.

There are two oft-repeated origin stories for the free lunch. The first is from Chicago, where saloonkeeper/politician Joseph "Chesterfield Joe" Mackin was apparently trying to drum up business—not to mention votes for the Cook County Democratic Party—with the offer of a free oyster for every drink purchase. Known as the "Oyster" (when he wasn't being called "Chesterfield Joe"), Mackin was certainly involved in machine politics but was not the father of the free lunch. This honor, according to Herbert Asbury, belongs to New Orleans and La Bourse de Maspero, which is thought to have established the practice in 1838. The name translates into Maspero's Exchange, so named because it was the slave traders' bar and café of choice. It also has a solid claim as the location of Jackson and Lafitte's actual plotting of the Battle of New Orleans. The name "Exchange" incidentally, would become nearly interchangeable with the word saloon in the nineteenth century. The City Exchange, as Maspero's would come to be known, pioneered the custom of handing a plate to anyone who ordered a drink. Free food or lunch eventually became such a popular institution that it soon merited its own special table, typically stocked with soup, meat pie, and oyster patties—the very first lunch counter.

"Saloon" and "free lunch" soon became synonymous, even if the quality of the lunch provided was sometimes questionable. It was always, at its core, a ruse to get people to enter a saloon, order a drink, then drink more than they had intended. The salty food played a role in the scheme (saloon historian George Ade once referred to the sardines on the counter as "silent partners"), but so did human nature in that, once in a bar, it was hard to leave. Add to that the optics. Most men did not want to appear cheap, especially in a saloon, so often ordered a second, which could then lead to an entire afternoon.

There were several other distinguishing features of the saloon as it came of age. Typically, saloons vied for a corner location, taking advantage of both the greater visibility plus the fact that entrances could be installed on two sides. Often the entrances featured those iconic double-swinging doors to protect customers and owners from the prying eyes of fellow citizens and law enforcement officers, while still offering prospective patrons a tantalizing glimpse into the bar. Ade describes the exterior as often adorned by a gilded beer sign and the interior as having only a brass foot-rail for rest along a "long lengthwise bar counter," a saloon innovation. There was generally sawdust on the floor (good for absorbing spills, beer, blood, or fixings), a large mirror, prizefighter photos, pictures of large, half-naked ladies, and an "array of 'grape beverages,' like champagne, wine, brandy and assorted liquors, which grew dusty cause nobody drank them."[14]

Rituals and bar etiquette were considered extraordinarily important— just as drinking healths were in taverns. In many places, it was considered a nearly actionable offense for a stranger *not* to offer to buy the man next to him a drink and the long, if unspoken, list of acceptable behavior for clientele included not lingering at the free lunch table. While everyone likes getting a free drink or lunch, explicitly angling for it breaches barroom etiquette. Some link this to codes of masculinity and working-class pride, and this is certainly true. But it also speaks to a more fundamental joy of drinking—the pleasure of buying a round for someone else, without ulterior motive. A close second to that is being stood that next round. That feeling of camaraderie is one of the many ways we forge bonds and learn to cooperate as a group, which many have conjectured helps us as a species and, perhaps, has since the early days of brewing in Mesopotamia.

These rules extended to the better saloons of the era, too, many of which were increasingly located in hotel lobbies. New York's City Hotel, erected near the turn of the nineteenth century, managed to retain its prominence into the 1840s in the face of stiff competition. Partly this was a result of the remarkable service ethic at the hotel—especially in what was to become another great American institution, the hotel lobby bar. The City Hotel set the standard because of its barman, the immortal Orsamus Willard. Known throughout the city, Willard was also a legend abroad and sitting at his bar to enjoy one of his drinks was a priceless souvenir from a trip to New York. Willard was apparently *always* on shift, attending to guests "from sunrise to midnight." Despite chronic sleep deprivation, he never forgot a face or a name. In one instance, a first-time guest had to check out early because his son was ill. Five years later, he returned to the City and, to his amazement, Willard not only recognized and welcomed him but inquired after his son's health as he instructed the porter to take him up to his old room. Reading about Willard always puts us in mind of Murray Stenson of Seattle's Zig Zag cafe, one of our candidates for the best bartender in America today. Stenson's mixing and shaking is renowned but eclipsed by his spectacular customer service and his reputation for never forgetting a customer's name.

Willard apparently also never left the hotel, testified to by the fact that he supposedly didn't own a hat—a necessary accoutrement for stepping out. This became an issue one night when restaurateur Billy Niblo insisted that Willard come to the grand opening of a new venue.[15] Willard hoped his lack of a hat would get him off the hook, but someone ran across the street to Charles St. John's millinery shop to get him one. The hatter was most surprised of all—not because Willard didn't own a hat but because the barkeep was actually going to leave the hotel.

Besides his skill, Willard was also known for his wit. There's a story of a "Hoosher" from Indiana who sat down at Willard's bar and asked for a brandy and water. At the time, it was common practice to give a patron the bottle and let him pour his own. This particular guest, however, filled his glass to the brim, added a drop of water, then, as Willard watched on, proceeded to down it on one "draught." The guest was shocked to get change back when he paid for the drink and asked how it could be that it could cost so little. Replied Willard: "We retail it at a shilling a glass, but when we sell it at wholesale we make a discount."[16]

Customers could pour their own, but only when they wanted a straight, uncomplicated shot. For the fancier drinks, many of which he was responsible for inventing, Willard did the mixing, most likely touching off the Peach Brandy Punch craze of the early 1830s. He was also the go-to guy when newspapers wanted an authoritative recipe for an apple-toddy. The drink that truly propelled him to fame, though, was his signature mint julep. One travel diarist wrote that Willard was "allowed to be the first master of this art in the known world. . . . I have heard many calculations of the number of mint juleps that he has been known to compound in one day and of the immense profits resulting to the hotel from his celebrity."[17]

Willard's fame eventually would be eclipsed by the country's next celebrity bar star, Jerry Thomas (1830–1885), mainly because Thomas thought to do what nobody had before—collect and publish all his recipes, along with some bar-and-service philosophy, in the first dedicated bartender's recipe book (1862). To even a casual observer of bars and cocktails, Thomas will need no introduction. Much has been written about him (most recently in David Wondrich's *Imbibe* in 2007). Thomas opened his first saloon on Broadway in New York in 1851 and, although there were many professional bartenders in high-end saloons and gentlemen's clubs, he became famous for taking service up a notch and for his flair. He wore flashy jewelry; his bar tools custom-made out of silver and adorned with precious stones. He was not averse to juggling while mixologizing and patented the Blue Blazer technique, which involves pouring flaming Laphroaig whisky back and forth between two shakers to create an arc of flame.

Thomas's saloon was located directly below Barnum's American Museum on Broadway, which showcased Ned the learned seal, a loom run by a dog, and a monkey corpse with a fish tail (stage name, "the Feejee Mermaid"). At various times, it was known as Thomas' Saloon; Thomas' Gallery & Saloon; Thomas' Gallery; Thomas' Billiard Room; Thomas' Billiard Room, Bowling Alleys & Art Gallery; the Sportsmen's Rendezvous; and, finally, Thomas' Exchange—all told, one of New York's most famous and frequented drinking establishments. The bar was noted for having many drawings by caricaturist and editorial cartoonist Thomas Nast and funhouse mirrors; but the Barnum spirit of theatricality and showmanship was most noteworthy in Thomas's repertoire, which was clearly influenced by ventriloquists and other performers more than by the understated Willard.

Thomas also toured America and Europe, performing feats of bar for audiences to help promote and sell *Jerry Thomas Bartender's Guide,* in which he outlined the world's greatest bar recipes. By Wondrich's account, in the year 1863, Thomas was earning more than the Vice President of the United States. It's his bar and service credo, though, that are most pertinent to our story, since what Thomas represented was the professionalization of the industry. In the opening section of his Guide, "Hints and Rules for Bartenders," Thomas lays out twenty-seven laws of bartending, ranging from tips about mixing egg whites into hot liquors without cooking the egg, to dealing with customers. Thomas wasn't the only bartender working to improve the industry. By the mid-nineteenth century, there was a demand for high-end service in clubs, hotel bars, and better saloons. And many of these were working to perfect use of the latest cocktail ingredient to capture the public's imagination—ice.

Before refrigeration, ice was a rare commodity in a bar. It was still harvested from frozen lakes and rivers, stored, and imported to the city by men such as Frederic Tudor, the "Ice King" from Boston, or those responsible for "Concentrated Wenham" from Lake Wenham (in Massachusetts), a name that became synonymous in Europe and England for ice from America. While a refrigeration system for turning water into ice was first developed in 1842, it was decades before it became widely available and affordable. The Astor House in New York, the Fremont in Boston, the Union Public in Washington, and, later, New York's Saint Nicholas and Metropolitan were among the few places in early America to feature the innovation of cold, hand-crafted liquor concoctions.

Obviously, ice wasn't a new phenomenon, nor was it an entirely novel idea to cool drinks with it. However, in the period when Jerry Thomas was refining his craft, there was an explosion of ice harvesters. The resulting ice was of different grades and it was common for it to arrive mixed with snow, dirt, and other foreign matter that had to be cleaned off (but often wasn't). Thomas insisted bartenders apply due diligence in this area. With the proliferation of ice came an expanded repertoire of cocktails that quickly transformed the prevailing and crude combinations of whiskey, bitters, and sugar into a dazzling new array of concoctions. They also became an American standard. Albert Rhodes, writing of American mores and manners in *The Galaxy*, said that most men "insist on a cocktail before dinner and possibly one before breakfast." The appeal of the cocktail and the "American bar" became so widespread that it was exported to the Paris Exposition of 1867, where it was a headliner. The English journalist George Augustus Sala described the exhibit as spectacle: "At the bar, and from siphon tubes decorated with silvery figures of the American Eagle, were dispensed the delicious 'cream soda' so highly recommended by the faculty; 'cobblers,' 'noggs,' 'smashes,' 'cocktails,' 'eye-openers,' 'mustache-twisters,' and 'corpse-revivers,' were also on hand."

Sala also mentions an "exhilarating 'morning glory'" and something surely lost forever to history—"one of them things." He claims that he once had "two of them things" and was so hung over the following day, he had to cure it with some hair of the dog, which he calls "one of them *other* things." He was clearly enjoying his job as correspondent for *Harper's New Monthly Magazine* in April 1868, when an editor introduced this Sala piece with the following preface: "The great subject of alcoholic minglings is one that has occupied the mind of the American citizen in every walk of life. Alas! That this should have been thus! The peoples of other nationalities, however, are fast emulating us in this regard, and look with kindly as well as wondering eye on the bibulous triumphs of the Federal saloonist."

In 1873, it was clear that the gastronomic achievements of Jerry Thomas ("Professor" Jerry Thomas, as he was called) and his imitators were considered the apex of the alcohol world when the headliner of the Vienna Exposition was the *"Amerikanische"* bar serving its signature *"Amerikanische"* cocktails.[18] Aside from the novelty and genuine excellence of many pre-Prohibition drinks, the fact that Europe's vineyards were being devastated by phylloxera at the time—a vine-eating aphid—helped make American cocktails all the more popular. Within a few short years, better hotels across Europe adopted the New World style and installed American bars of their own. Distinct from the cafés and restaurants, the new bars, as well as selling spirits and cordials with flashy mixers, also mimicked the physical layout of American bars. They even started using ice.

Although the American bar was dominant in the media and the public's imagination, the old-fashioned tavern was still intact—particularly in rural areas but also in cities. To some, like Henry David Thoreau, these taverns still embodied all the same virtues they had when they (and their keepers) were regarded as revolutionary heroes. Thoreau praises the helmsman of taverns like the "Black Horse" or the "Spread Eagle" in his 1843 essay, *The Landlord*, as "a man of more open general sympathies, who possesses a spirit of hospitality which is its own reward, and feeds and shelters men from pure love of the creatures."[19] Thoreau concedes that not all barkeeps are perfect but that the best of them are none other than a "self-appointed brother of the race." He argues that they who welcomed strangers with open arms should be exempt from both taxes and military duty. "Surely, then," writes Thoreau, "the gods who are most interested in the human race preside over the Tavern."

Nathaniel Hawthorne also immortalized his own local, Parker's Tavern in Concord, Massachusetts. In 1850, Hawthorne writes in a May 7 diary entry that a screen at Parker's, conceals "the interior from the outside barbarian." Hawthorne sings the praises of the diverse crowd of lawyers, old men, flashy young men and rural visitors taking "gin, brandy, or whiskey, sometimes a Tom and Jerry, a gin cocktail, a brandy mash, and numerous other concoctions." He continues, "Nothing is so remarkable in these barrooms and drinking places as the perfect order that prevails; if a man gets drunk, it is no otherwise perceptible than by his going to sleep, or his inability to walk."[20]

Walt Whitman also sketches a loving account of his regular New York watering hole, Charles Pfaff's beer cellar on Broadway near Bleecker. Once a temperance advocate of sorts, Whitman claimed that he went mainly to observe the wild scene of bohemian writers, actors, and artists—women and men—who came to write, cavort, and drink. Congregating in Pfaff's were some of that generation's best known writers and artists: Horatio Alger Jr., Ada Clare, Ralph Waldo Emerson, Winslow Homer, William Dean Howells, Thomas Nast, and Artemus Ward—to name but a few. From that famed basement bar also emerged *The Saturday Press*, a weekly literary journal of great acclaim. Whitman writes that Pfaff's was where "the drinkers and laughers meet to eat and drink and carouse," while overhead rolls the "myriad rushing Broadway." Pfaff's is on an alternate plane in Whitman's universe—an underworld, but free from the gloom of both Hades' rule and the constraints of the streets above.

While Hawthorne, Thoreau, and Whitman praise the barroom as a nearly utopian model of decorum and an egalitarian gathering place (granted, tongue-in-cheek, on Hawthorne's part), and the tapster as a valuable public servant, feelings about the saloonkeeper varied wildly. To some, he was the front man for King Alcohol and, in his insatiable drive for profits, tricked customers into drinking more and was frequently associated with gambling, prostitution, violent crime, and political corruption. Those who followed Jerry Thomas would barely have recognized the sort of man who watered down his drinks or, worse, laced them with knockout drugs. As the negative connotations persisted, it was clear that Thomas and his profession faced an uphill battle toward legitimacy. For example, at almost precisely the same time that the American bar was being perceived as a cultural ambassador to Europe, the first chapter of the Knights of Labor was taking shape. One of America's most inclusive workers' groups, having opened its arms to both blacks and women, the Knights invited all who were gainfully employed to join, with one notable exception—saloonkeepers.

This disparity reflects the polarities that have accompanied drinking in America since the early days, when the tavernkeeper, despite being one of the most respected men in town, still had to suffer being policed to within an inch of his life by selectmen and nosy neighbors. As time passed, attitudes became more clearly marked by class. French sociologist Pierre Bourdieu was among the first to identify how class and taste work in tandem to create and reinforce hierarchies and power structures. Highbrow taste is defined by Bourdieu as "good taste" simply because it was what the upper classes were doing (watching, reading, eating, or drinking). In turn, those who couldn't partake in highbrow activities (or afford to) exhibited "poor" taste and were increasingly marginalized. Postcolonial drinking in America was one long demonstration of Bourdieu's theories, from the moment East Coast Madeira drinkers taxed the whiskey-swilling hill people. But in the ramp up to the Gilded Age, these differences became yet more pronounced. Those who catered to the immigrant and indigent were increasingly derided; those who served the elites were pronounced artists.

Reformers seemed able to ignore that the well-heeled were abetting and celebrating a new cocktail culture, such as that found in hotel bars. Beginning in the 1840s, they began establishing their own temperance hotels so that fellow-travelers could be free from temptation. This would have been a welcome find to English writer and travel diarist Frederick Marryat, who noted that travelers had nowhere to go but the bar. In his 1839 *Diary in America*, he characterized the country as being in a state of "national intoxication" where every occasion was marked with a drink: "If you meet, you drink; if you part, you drink; if you make acquaintance, you drink; if you close a bargain, you drink; they quarrel in drink, and they make it up with a drink."[21]

Marryat was more than a little cynical about American democracy, given that he had come to the United States principally to fight the rampant copyright infringements that were reducing his royalty payments. His friend Charles Dickens, who had complained that nearly every "low house" was a tavern, had done the same. While abroad, Marryat—a captain in the Royal British Navy—was called upon to help quell the

Lower and Upper Canada Rebellions, anticolonial uprisings in 1837 and 1838. Although unsuccessful, the Upper Canada Rebellion had been an American-style republican movement aimed at reforming banking and land grant systems that were considered unfair to farmers. Rebel William Lyon Mackenzie rallied a small army of a thousand people at Montgomery's Tavern just north of Toronto, but it was defeated by British soldiers who looted and leveled the place. To Marryat, no friend of republican-style tavern politics, the drunken state of America was an "appropriate tribute of gratitude for the rights of equality." Free from parental guidance, America seemed to be going through a drunken adolescence.

Marryat, of course, wasn't alone in his opinions. There was no shortage of religious reformers and, in fact, even some drinkers were beginning to wonder if the situation was out of control. Most notable among those drinkers who questioned the prevalence of alcohol was a small group that met regularly at Chase's Tavern in Baltimore and would wind up, in 1840, inventing America's first secular anti-drinking group.

Chase's was a regular haunt for skilled workers and craftsmen who used to like to drink every night until they were "Pidgeon Ey'd." On April 2, 1840, however, a couple of regulars at Chase's embarked on a "road trip" (another tradition of the American bar patron). In their drunken enthusiasm, they dropped in on Reverend Matthew Hale Smith, a temperance advocate visiting from New York who was at a nearby church. The drinkers expected little more than some new material for making toasts but, while listening to Smith, found themselves moved. When they returned to the bar, they began a conversation about the virtues of temperance and a rather heated discussion followed between the drinkers and owner Chase, who predicted that none could give up alcohol. This would backfire when it was pointed out that Chase had a vested interest in keeping them all drunk—a routine that was costing the craftsmen dearly, particularly as America happened to be in another deep recession at the time. Things went back and forth for a few days when, finally, during one night of particularly heavy drinking, six of the men decided they would sign a pledge to give up alcohol. Silversmith William K. Mitchell volunteered to draft it and, next day, hunted down the others to sign. Which they did, despite (or, perhaps, helped by) several members' crippling hangovers. They called themselves the Washington Temperance Society and, strangely enough, still met at

Chase's tavern—until Mrs. Chase decided she had had enough and asked them to leave.[22]

The six would quickly become seven and, before too long, seven hundred. As the Washingtonians grew, the group attracted media attention, most notably from Timothy Shay Arthur, who chronicled the growth of the novel temperance group in a series of articles that were later used for the compilation of his book, *Six Nights with the Washingtonians and Other Temperance Tales*. What was so unique about the group, Arthur realized, was its members' willingness to confess their tales of degradation, a practice that would prove so much more effective than the hellfire and brimstone rhetoric—so effective, in fact, that a version of it is still used today by members of Alcoholics Anonymous. Arthur collected what he felt were the most poignant confessionals, then retold them for the reading public, which helped both his career and the Washingtonians' membership rolls.

Arthur was then inspired to dramatize the tales in a book called *Ten Nights in a Bar-Room* (1854). It was wildly successful, both as a book and as inspiration for stage version after stage version. *Ten Nights* would become one of the most-staged plays in America's history. Its success was very jealously watched by his colleague, Edgar Allan Poe, who had spent many hours with Arthur in a barroom on Water Street in Baltimore called the Seven Stars Tavern—also home to the first official chapter of the benevolent organization, the Independent Order of Odd Fellows. That Poe drank heavily there is a certainty. Whether or not Arthur indulged or simply stuck to water, we may never know, but the two convened there with a few others who made up a small competitive literary circle named after the tavern. Of the Seven Stars literary coterie, Arthur was, by far, the most commercially successful. *Ten Nights in a Bar-Room* sold four hundred thousand copies, making it the nation's new all-time bestseller. *Ten Nights* was also only one of a staggering 150 novels Arthur wrote in his lifetime. Poe, a relatively obscure talent who was always struggling financially, was understandably envious of his friend who, it seemed, had achieved fame and fortune without having any particular talent for writing. Poe wasn't alone, either. Most contemporary literary critics have derided Arthur, who, despite having written one of the most important cultural artifacts of American social history, has fallen into literary obscurity.

This is no great loss to the literary canon. Even *Ten Nights*, which is considered one of his better efforts, is hackneyed. The story centers on

Simon Slade, a happy and successful miller who decides to get into the barkeeping business with his new venture, the Sickle and Sheaf—the best new tavern in the fictional town of Cedarville, USA. The narrator has some trepidation over Slade's new business, but gives him the benefit of the doubt and wishes him well. Over the course of ten years, the narrator has a chance to return to the town on various occasions and is witness to the degeneration of Slade, his wife, his children, his customers and, in fact, the entire town.

It doesn't take long for Slade to morph from the kind-hearted miller, father, husband, and upstanding community member into an abusive, neglectful, stingy, coarse man, who allows corrupt activities to take place on the premises, to the detriment of his family and community. In fact, it's only on "Night the Second" that drunken Slade throws a glass at his former best friend, Joe Morgan. He misses but hits and kills his friend's ten-year-old daughter instead. Slade manages to escape manslaughter charges thanks to his barroom connections.

Arthur's thesis, one he developed while listening to the confessionals of the Washingtonians, becomes clear: once a person starts drinking, the conclusion is inevitable and tragic, save for the few who see the light and quit drinking altogether. Other than the narrator, the only person whose life is (relatively) intact at the end of *Ten Nights* is Morgan, who had made a promise at his daughter's death-bed to stop drinking. The notion that habitual drinking only ever worsens, that moderate drinking can't exist, was being established with this type of temperance literature; and Arthur was a pioneer in propagating this view.

Arthur was breaking new ground in a couple of other ways, too, namely, in the invention of the new genre of "temperance weepies" and with his image of the tavernkeeper, embodied by Simon Slade.[23] Just a little over fifty years earlier, after the Revolutionary War, the tavern had ranked among the country's greatest heroes, cherished within the community and kept by the strongest and most patriotic of men. Slade represents the precise opposite. His only interest is in money-making and his forays into politics are attempts to corrupt court proceedings, protect his illicit activities, and rig elections, so that his backroom gambling can continue. He jeopardizes his community by bankrupting previously respectable men who come to his house to drink and gamble. By the end of the book, he is a hopeless drunk who is himself penniless—the tavern's final victim.

Although Arthur was the first to offer a complete portrait of this new image of the tavernkeeper, it was representative of shifting attitudes. A small but growing minority of Americans was turning toward temperance, influenced by evangelists such as Lyman Beecher and horrified by the sheer volume of alcohol consumed during the 1830s and 1840s, which had resulted from a corn glut that was turned into cheap whiskey. And the new villains, the ones responsible for the nation's bender, were the unscrupulous and irresponsible saloon and tavernkeepers.

To the reformers, there was no differentiation to be made between the bowery grog shop owners and the wizards of the toniest hotel bars. All were peddlers of the demon rum and, ultimately, would corrupt others—and be corrupted, themselves. Standardization of the industry was not only impossible, it was a contradiction; there were no standards.

This would only be worsened by the increasing association between the urban saloon and politics, both machine and radical, made even worse by the elements of racism and xenophobia. The remainder of the second part of this book will explore how various "undesirable" new immigrant groups and political movements came to be involved with the saloon and how those relationships were used against them in the nineteenth and early twentieth centuries, when the reformers, joined by reactionaries, gradually won over the country to the dry cause.

THE
POLITICAL
MACHINE
INVADES
A BAR

THE DRUNKARD'S PROGRESS, OR THE DIRECT ROAD
TO POVERTY, WRETCHEDNESS & RUIN

*Designed and published by J. W. Barber, New
Haven, Conn. In this 1826 engraving, the grog shop
is stage two in the Drunkard's Progress on the
"Direct Road to Poverty, Wretchedness and Ruin."
Image Courtesy of the Library of Congress.*

Of the many new hotel/tavern hybrids that were springing up around America, one of the most prominent was Gadsby's in Old Town, Alexandria, Virginia. Still standing, it boasts having housed and served many eminent guests, including George Washington—the first president to stay there, of course, but hardly the last. Gadsby's also hosted John Adams, Thomas Jefferson, James Madison, James Monroe, and Andrew Jackson. The latter did the hotel the honor of spending his first official night as president there, but this was no grand official visit. Jackson went to escape his inaugural party, which, by all contemporary accounts, was a riotous all-night affair—all the more so, given that he had actually invited the public.

Gadsby's wasn't Old Hickory's only sanctuary, either, and Jackson could often be found haunting another of the Eastern seaboard's more famous taverns, the Franklin House in Washington. One of the things Franklin House had going for it was the hostler's daughter, Peggy Timberlake, who, while husband John was away at sea, passed the time speaking frankly with the men in the taproom about politics and other serious matters, earning her the respect of many, including Jackson, who called her the "smartest little woman in America." It wasn't Jackson who fell for Peggy, but, instead, his Secretary of War, fellow Tennessean, John Henry Eaton. When husband John Timberlake was considerate enough to die at sea, Peggy soon became Mrs. Eaton. This was all a little too much for the public and the upper echelons of Washington society, which weren't convinced the whole business had been chaste. Before long, a rumor surfaced that Timberlake had killed himself in despair over his wife's affair with Eaton. Jealousy may be a silent killer, but pneumonia was the actual cause of death.

Nonetheless, no coroner's report was ever going to clear Peggy Eaton's name and get her accepted into good society. It was an enormous scandal and one that Lady Floride, wife of Vice President John Calhoun and ringleader of the anti-Peggy camp, just wouldn't let go of. Aside from the suspected infidelity (in what became known as the "Petticoat Affair") Peggy had three other things going against her: she was Irish, she was outspoken, and she had spent considerable time socializing with men in a tavern. Jackson, under tremendous pressure to censure his friend and revoke his position, not only refused to do so, but stubbornly supported Eaton. In the end, the Eatons couldn't overcome the stigma and would wind up taking foreign diplomatic posts.

The affair hurt Jackson, too. Allies abandoned him, including his Vice President. Running for his second term, Jackson shared the ticket with fellow Eaton supporter Martin Van Buren, who had been born in a tavern in Kinderhook, New York. Van Buren turned out to be a poor choice for the long-term prospects of the Democrats. They won the ticket and Van Buren even succeeded Jackson as president—but for a single term. The Democrats had been holding the reins of tavern politics since the Democratic-Republican Societies had been in the habit of buying twenty-five dozen cocktails, but were now losing popular support. This was because of both the poor economy caused by the Panic of 1837, (itself caused by the bursting of a bubble inflated by speculation), and the savvy tavern tactics of the ascendant Whig Party. The name "Whig" pays homage to the original British and revolutionary American Whigs, who were united in opposition to monarchical rule, a tyranny the new Whigs felt was being revisited upon the nation by the strong executive powers exerted by democrats like Jackson.

The new Whigs were formed in the early 1830s by John Quincy Adams and Henry Clay—the former the son of John Adams; the latter, a man widely known for having introduced the mint julep to Washington, DC, in the Round Robin Bar of the Willard Hotel.

Whig William Henry Harrison beat Van Buren in 1840, a victory that was wildly celebrated at Nutt's Tavern in Amherst, Massachusetts, as well as at many other Harrison tavern-campaign offices.[1] Although the Whigs were traditionally associated with early temperance movements, for Harrison's election, they rebranded themselves as the common drinking man's party, a winning strategy that had landed on their doorstep. In the *Baltimore Republican*, a Democrat newspaper, an opposing correspondent wrote of Harrison: "Give him a barrel of hard cider and settle a pension of $2,000 a year on him, and our word for it, he will sit the remainder of his days in the log cabin by the side of the 'sea-coal fire' and study moral philosophy."

The barb was meant to skewer Harrison's high-brow reading tastes but, instead, the "Tippecanoe and Tyler Too" people embraced the insult and featured the log cabin and hard cider as symbols for the political campaign—to represent Harrison's core values. Thousands of barrels of cider were ordered for the campaign and an enterprising glazier even designed log cabin–shaped bottles for it. For some time, it was even believed this was the origin of the slang "booze," since it was claimed that the glazier's name was E. G. Booz. This, unfortunately, is a false etymology (as so many of the best ones are). Boozy was even included in Benjamin Franklin's 1737 "Drinker's Dictionary," which catalogued all the contemporary slang for the state of intoxication.

Nearly overnight, Whig meetings went from relatively sober events to cider-soaked affairs. At the establishment of the Whig association at Alden's Hotel in Dedham, Massachusetts, a correspondent wrote that "a good feeling prevailed" and that several "good and spirited resolves" were passed. At the next Whig event at Alden's, customary Whig fare of "hard cider and crackers," and the "bountiful supply" of refreshments apparently was also enjoyed by the "Loco-focos," (an epithet applied to all Democrats, even though it had originally only described one radical faction) when opponents crashed the Whig celebration.[2]

After a rally in Salem, Ohio, the Whigs were forced to congregate at a Democrat tavern, where the tapster tried to spoil the celebrations by substituting a concoction of vinegar, rain water, and rot-gut whiskey for cider. The head Whig detected the switch and spontaneously altered his rallying toast:

Cold water may do for the Locos,
Or a little vinegar stew:
But give me hard cider and whiskey,
And hurrah for Old Tippecanoe

So, it wasn't only Democrats campaigning in taverns; everybody was getting in on the game. It was an era that marked the beginning of the "spoils system," in which political supporters were rewarded with political positions and favors. One of the more common manifestations of this system was the appointment of postmasters, a relatively lucrative sideline for a tavernkeeper, as we've seen. Postmaster jobs would bounce back and forth between partisan taverns with each election. In the public eye, however, it was the Democrats who were the most corrupt, in part because they had a longer record of electioneering in taverns, but also because they were beginning to dominate the newest (and seemingly most dangerous) innovation in watering holes—the urban saloon. In fact, the political machinations had begun back when the saloon was still a lowly grog shop.

Since grog shops were typically unlicensed and illegal, it was impossible to regulate them. In 1838 Boston, however, authorities came up with a creative solution to suppress them. They would make it illegal to sell spirits in any quantity *under* fifteen gallons. Advocates for the seemingly backward legislation, such as Boston lawyer and abolitionist Richard Hildreth, justified the measure by citing the "enormous" consumption of rum and other spirits as having led to the sorry state where "drunkenness [had become] a distinguishing characteristic of [the] commonwealth." Hildreth and legislators seemed driven as much by their resentment over the control grog shop owners had over the lucrative business—and, by extension, their political influence—as they were by concern over public health. Hildreth wrote that the city's "rumsellers . . . might be reckoned for wealth and influence, among the princes of the earth."[3]

It hardly seems temperate to encourage people to buy larger quantities of spirits, which was one of the principal objections to the law. But it was more a way of singling out the unseemly grog shops than an attack on actual spirits, which, for some, were still vaguely associated with patriotism, especially since whiskey was home-grown.

This was not the first full-fledged legislative attack on places where people congregated to drink. Throughout the 1830s, a number of municipalities, especially in Massachusetts, adopted "no license" campaigns, which put pressure on local authorities to place an early permanent moratorium on new licenses. Cautious legislators didn't want to seem to be attacking drinking, which was at the apex of its popularity and still seen as perfectly healthful, especially if it was confined to ale and cider. The new focus of antidrinking action was aimed at urban-dwelling idlers who spent their days in the grog shops. The farmer, who, of course, had a hand in producing the glut of cheap alcohol, had "property, self-respect, and a character to lose" and would not "be seen in such places." Instead of idling at the grog shop back counter, the farmer, the very model of productivity and temperance, would buy his "four or five gallons" and carry it home.

Despite serious opposition from the general population and from the manufacturers, who often supplied the grog shops spirits on credit, the law on a fifteen-gallon minimum was passed in July 1838. Grog shop patrons and those with a stake in the business weren't the only ones who objected, however. Notable legal minds such as Harrison Grey Otis (James Otis's nephew) argued that the law was tyrannical and reflected a clear prejudice against those who couldn't afford to buy fifteen gallons of rum at a time—which it did. The law would have had virtually no effect on the rich but cut off those who bought their drinks by the dram.

Hildreth's attempt to sober up the poor and shiftless both echoed the past and foreshadowed the future. The rhetoric behind the attack on the Boston dram shops in the 1830s was almost identical to the antisaloon discourse that would prevail in the years to come, building up to the passage of the Eighteenth Amendment. Hildreth asked the public to consider the poor alcoholic, his drinking increasing year after year, until he was reduced to pitiful poverty and, eventually, death, leaving behind an impoverished widow and orphaned children. This would become an enduring refrain.

The Boston grog shop laws were an overt early attempt to control Catholics, even if Hildreth wasn't as clearly motivated by bigotry as much as some of his contemporaries. He argued that explanations for immigrant criminality neglected to lay the blame at the grog shop's door, where it deserved to be laid: "Unfortunately it is too true, that numbers of immigrants, as well as a still greater number of native-born citizens, fall victims to the hundreds of grog shops, set like traps in every nook and corner of our great cities." Immigrants were "first seduced into drunkenness, and then betrayed into crime."[4] There was the deep concern that this moral decay would be spread in the grog shops and that even the country's most privileged youth might be contaminated. In 1838, noted anti-Catholic Leonard Bacon, pastor in New Haven and professor of theology at Yale, wrote that "a gentleman who visited the back room of a dram shop states that it is the complete vestibule of the pit." Concerned about Yale's reputation, he was aware students "congregated there in great numbers and the drinking and swearing was perfectly astounding." Parents who visited the campus and discovered such lowly activities would balk at leaving their sons in his care.[5]

Evasion of the fifteen-gallon law was widespread and immediate. Some stores allowed patrons to buy fifteen gallons and one dram and return all but the dram, which was, of course, drunk in the store. One enterprising Boston tavernkeeper got out of selling liquor altogether and into the entertainment business, charging patrons six cents to view his striped pig, which he had proudly painted himself. Customers got a free glass of rum to keep warm while they viewed the pig, which many did several times over the course of an evening. Who knew when they would ever see a striped pig again? Policing was made difficult by the fact that inspectors and informers were routinely harassed. By early 1839, though, widespread disregard was the least of the legislators' worries; direct political action had begun again. Crowds attempted to disrupt the trial of anyone convicted of selling liquor under the now illegal minimum. One trial was stopped by threatening witnesses for the prosecution; another cut short by no fewer than six thousand people massing outside the court. The law made it to February 1840, when it was repealed.

Whether at home, on the job, in an urban grog shop, or at Willard's counter in the City Hotel, a lot of alcohol was being consumed. In 1790, the average American drank five gallons of spirits per year; by 1830, it had almost doubled to nine and a half gallons. The amount of beer consumed had dropped slightly but not nearly enough to offset the jump in spirits consumption. America was "drunk as a beggar" and the reason it was drunk was because the average citizen practically couldn't afford *not* to buy whiskey. Corn juice was scandalously cheap, thanks to a number of factors, including a glut of corn stemming from increased agricultural production and a more efficient distillation process developed by the Scots-Irish immigrants on the frontier. The spirit of choice was, increasingly, whiskey, boosted by the repeal of the Whiskey Tax in 1802. Since then, it began dominating the market, squeezing out rum. Whiskey flowed from the backcountry at what, to some, was an alarming rate and the market was soon flooded with the cheapest bourbon ever made. By 1825, a day's wages for the average working poor could purchase two gallons of whiskey. Alexander Hamilton's attempt to cure the country of its dependence on ardent spirits had failed—spectacularly. Thirty to forty years after his controversial campaign to wean the country off whiskey, Americans were drinking more than ever.

While some of that whiskey was meant for home consumption, it also led to an inevitable and unprecedented proliferation of outlets selling the spirit; most of the new ones, as we've seen, were grog shops and saloons. In urban areas, those grog shops, saloons, and taverns were also home to the political machinery that, by the early to mid-nineteenth century, controlled many public offices. Nearly every urban saloon was home to a gang and nearly every Irish-American adult male was a member of one. The gangs and the patrons over whom they had sway in the saloons and grog shops acted as a voting bloc. The saloonkeeper or head of the gang (often the same man) would control the way his bloc voted and his "soldiers" were responsible for registering new immigrants so that they could vote for the right candidate. If consistently successful, the saloonkeeper would make his way up the political ladder to become ward boss, backed up by lieutenants and "heelers," who did most of the dirtiest work—rounding up drunken ringers to vote and intimidating those who might vote for the opposition. In some places, the intimidation was even more intense. In Baltimore, for instance, the practice of "cooping"—kidnapping voters, force-feeding them near-fatal quantities of alcohol, then making them cast their votes over and over again—was fairly common in the late 1840s. Some suggest that Edgar Allan Poe was a victim of cooping the night he died.

In New York, politics and liquor were more closely connected than almost anywhere else in the country. And the politicking went on everywhere, from high-end hotel bars, where members of the Tammany society met, down to the waterfront, where groceries sold liquor to drunken sailors at three cents a glass. This is where Fernando Wood's career began. After two years of hustling sailors, Wood had enough money to enter politics and become a congressman, Grand Sachem (head honcho) of Tammany Hall, and, eventually, mayor of New York City. Despite his success, allegations that Wood had run a "clip shop" and made his money through overcharging and tricking drunken customers, dogged him throughout his controversial and colorful political career. Wood embodied the "machine politics" against which reform candidates were beginning to rally. He exerted control over the voting populace and political candidates through a network of saloons, some of which he owned. His graduation to Tammany only reflected his ability to climb the ladder of success and was not an example of a clip shop owner going legit. Tammany was quickly becoming the most corrupt political machine in the country, thanks to men like Wood, of whom an opponent once said should have been "on the rolls of the State Prison." Others accused him of already owning the police force.

The person who closely managed that police force was Captain Isaiah Rynders, who owned most of the "groceries" around Paradise Square (roughly adjacent to today's Columbus Park), a few bowery saloons, and a tavern by the name of Sweeney's House of Refreshment. In 1843, the dashing Rynders, whose curriculum vitae bragged professional gambler and Bowie-knife fighter, opened up the Empire Club, a saloon at 28 Park Row. This became a major political center and marked the beginning of a new era of his influence over New York voters. In the tight presidential race of 1844, Rynders was credited with winning the city for James Polk through intimidation, extortion, and outright fraud. He ruled by having New York's finest psychotics under his thumb. One would-be lieutenant had introduced himself to Rynders by bursting into the Empire Club and offering to fight any man in the room. After he was pummeled, he was offered a position by Rynders, who'd been impressed by his utter recklessness. The Empire Club's gangs were known to break up rival Whig political meetings and, at one of the city's polling centers one Election Day, Rynders declared that his men would murder any Whig voters brought in from Philadelphia. The crowd dispersed. He was also credited for the success in New York of two subsequent Democratic presidents, Franklin Pierce and James Buchanan, and was considered so effective that New Orleans' politician John Slidell once hired Rynders's lieutenants to intimidate Louisiana voters.

Like many other saloon-based machine politicians, Rynders didn't end his politicking at election time. He was in the business of controlling government and agitated against the opposition year-round. One notable emotional political event orchestrated by Rynders was the Astor Place Riots of 1849, which grew out of a seemingly unlikely antipathy brewing among New Yorkers over two competing versions of *Macbeth* and the rival headliners. Patrons of the rum-selling groceries, clip shops, and Bowery saloons, alike, were all passionate about Shakespeare and partial to the stylings of American tragedian and matinee idol Edwin Forrest. Uptown at the recently opened Astor Opera House on Broadway, however, wealthy New Yorkers had invited British rival William Charles Macready to perform. Forrest and Macready had been enjoying a very public spat over the previous few years, stemming, in part, from their very different acting methods. Macready was staid and reserved; Forrest went over the top in a manner Macready denounced as vulgar.

While this may not sound like a recipe for a major urban riot, the atmosphere was highly charged. The Astor symbolized some of the last vestiges of English aristocracy in New York and Macready's insults were taken as a personal indictment of American tastes. This was enough to ignite the passions of Bowery dwellers, especially after Rynders got them properly mobilized—and lubricated. Rynders may or may not have had an opinion on acting styles, and was more likely attempting to make the Whig mayor, Caleb Woodhull, look bad, while also demonstrating his own power, which was threatened by a non-Democrat administration. Rynders wrote an incendiary handbill, reading, "Shall Americans or English rule in this city?" and distributed it—along with a large number of tickets to the Astor House performance—at his Empire Club and through a network of area saloons. Rowdy ticket-holders stopped the performance from the inside, while some ten thousand people rioted outside, smashing the Astors' windows. Twenty-two died; many more were injured. Woodhull called in the National Guard, a heavy-handed reaction that was widely seen as entirely appropriate. While Rynders didn't manage to do much damage to Woodhull, he certainly further hurt the reputation of that "Scottish play", since the riots added to the lore that *Macbeth* was cursed.

The Astor Place Riots are often regarded as the first real clash between urban immigrants and the so-called Nativists, an anti-immigrant group, also known as the American Party, which would come to dominate the political scene as the Whig Party imploded in the 1840s and 1850s. The Nativists weren't gunning for the Whigs, however. Their prime targets were the Democrats, often perceived as having a corrupting influence over America's major cities. The political control the Democrats exerted through Irish American gangs operating out of grog shops and saloons was one of the many reasons used to justify the early Nativist campaigns, which were buoyed by burgeoning anti-Irish and anti-Catholic sentiment. Aside from opposing further immigration and urban growth, the Nativists almost universally advocated for the institution of "blue laws," like Sunday closing ordinances, which interfered with the urban saloon's business.

Of course, the Irish weren't the only ones despised by the Nativists, who didn't much like German immigrants either. From 1830 to 1860, there had been a massive wave of Irish and German Catholic immigration, prompting a sea-tide of anti-immigrant, anti-papist feeling from those who saw both groups' arrival as a threat to Protestant values. Although they were lumped together by those who hated them, the Germans and Irish couldn't have been more different in their drinking habits. Where the Irish were ambibulous—happy to drink both spirits and beer—Germans generally stuck to lager, a lighter, bottom-fermenting beer that they began brewing in America as soon as they arrived. Lager, incidentally, would soon take off in nineteenth-century America. As soon as regular ice deliveries and refrigeration made cold lager readily available, it began replacing the traditional darker and heavier beers.

In addition, the Irish were known for drinking in saloons, standing at a rail while serving themselves shots of whiskey. In contrast, German beer gardens often welcomed entire families. They were well lit and relatively quiet and orderly, though the larger ones sometimes featured shooting galleries, live classical music, and bowling alleys. The term "beer garden" is slightly misleading; there was rarely any garden involved and was really just a large hall with tables for people to sit at. Occasionally, there might have been a large mural of some natural scenery but, where budgets were tight, the artwork was a luxury. Contemporary accounts of the behavior of the patrons are mixed. Some actually reported being unnerved by the quiet with which most Germans drank; others complained that, on special occasions, the patrons would go on a "dutch lager beer spree."

Lager or whiskey, saloons, grog shops, or beer halls, the sight of the working classes drinking anything, anywhere, was offensive to some, and they began lobbying for the first neoprohibitionist policies, many simply thinly veiled attacks on freedom of association for immigrants and the working poor. The Germans and Irish were singled out for having an insidious control over the liquor supply in America, and fearmongering began over the "liquor power" that Cincinnati temperance leader and Congressman Samuel Cary wrote was "unquestionably the mightiest power in the Republic. It can make or re-make officers, from President to constable."[6]

Given the gangs of the Bloody Ould Sixth Ward and other urban centers, there was almost certainly more than a grain of truth to the assumed association between crime and public drinking. However, what motivated some of the anti-Catholic bigotry was a series of inflammatory tracts. The first was a piece of fiction published in 1835 called *Six Months in a Convent* by Rebecca Reed, who gained advance publicity for her book by claiming to have been held captive at Boston's Ursuline Convent. Before the manuscript was even published, Boston townspeople began rioting, burning down the convent on the grounds that another young woman was allegedly being held captive there. This turned out to be false but, nonetheless, helped the novel sell two hundred thousand copies, then surpassing both Cotton Mather and Thomas Paine for all-time American bestseller status. On its heels came Maria Monk's *The Hidden Secrets of a Nun's Life in a Convent Exposed*. This book turned out to be completely fraudulent, a crass attempt to cash in on the wave of anti-Catholicism—some of which can be attributed to Lyman Beecher, one of the most important figures of the Second Great Enlightenment—which would bring evangelism to new heights. Beecher is also seen as having helped to incite the riot which resulted in the burning of the Ursuline Convent, since he delivered his incendiary anti-Catholic sermon, "A Plea for the West," in Boston shortly before the incident.

Beecher was developing an argument that he fervently believed would change the American psyche forever, namely, that if too much drink is a sin, none at all must bring a soul even closer to perfection. Beecher was the first to promote abstinence as a lifestyle choice.[7]

Ironically, the very same democratic and egalitarian ideals that stemmed originally from the taverns were key to the success of the populist evangelical movement that swept America during the Second Great Awakening. Beecher and other religious leaders rejected the negativity of Calvinism (predestination, meaning that no matter how well you behave, you can never be certain you're getting into heaven) and adopted the more hopeful promise of eternal salvation for everybody (a very democratic notion) so long as they reformed thoroughly. Part of the new optimism involved devotion to social activism and reform. Human society was theoretically perfectible, according to reformers, and it was their duty to be part of the drive toward that ideal. Members were actively working on improving social conditions, establishing women's rights, and ending slavery.

Alongside those laudable and high-minded goals, however, was a dogged commitment to abstinence. Temperance movements, like the one Benjamin Rush had advocated, became more radical. Adherents rejected even mild alcoholic beverages, caffeine, medicinal drugs, meat, hot food (because it led to appetites of the flesh), leisure, masturbation, and more than once-monthly sex for married couples. Proponents of this new extremism, such as Sylvester Graham (of the cracker fame), espoused waking before dawn, hearty exercise, prayer, cold cereal, contemplation, hard work, vegetables for dinner, and an early bedtime.

But, while Graham expanded the repertoire of things to abstain from, Beecher concentrated on alcohol. It was during his career as minister in East Hampton, Long Island (an area which now has one of the greatest bar-to-human ratios in all of America), that Beecher came to realize he would devote his life to the eradication of liquor. In his parish, complained Beecher, was a "grog seller" who "drank himself, and corrupted others." The grog seller, Beecher noted, kept a jug right under his bed to slake midnight or early-morning thirsts. In the course of working toward eliminating intemperance, it became clear to Beecher that calling for moderation was no longer enough. This extremism earned him followers but also enemies and, when his Boston church caught fire in 1830, the volunteer firefighters, who spent their watch-time in taverns, didn't even attempt to put it out.

It wasn't difficult for Beecher and others to connect the hated grog sellers to the hated Catholics, making life increasingly difficult for urban immigrants. Although they were victims of a growing discrimination, the German and Irish Catholics didn't always passively accept vilification and marginalization. In the 1830s, for example, many Irish-Catholic immigrants in Rhode Island still didn't have the right to vote, a result of the original charter for the colony that granted the rights to vote, sue, and serve on juries only to men with property. Recent Irish immigrants, many of whom lived in cities and worked in textile mills, were lobbying to change the qualifications for full citizenship. Theirs was an uphill battle against the Protestant, land-owning, agrarian citizenry, which, despite representing less than half the population, controlled almost the whole political scene.

Lawyer Thomas Wilson Dorr campaigned for suffrage for Rhode Island's largely Catholic workers. After trying to introduce a new constitution through legal channels and failing, he staged an extralegal election in which he was elected governor in 1842. The actual governor, Samuel Ward King, refused to give up power or introduce electoral reform, which prompted Dorr and his supporters to organize a general assembly at Sprague's Tavern in Chepachet to discuss further action.

King's men, however, launched a preemptive attack on the rebel tavern, occupying it over a period of several months, during which time they ran up a tab that amounted to thirty-seven gallons of brandy, twenty-nine gallons of rum, and smaller quantities of cider, Madeira, champagne, and various liquors. When not drinking, the troops ate and smoked cigars, too—all at Jedediah Sprague's expense. King and his men made an example of Sprague but also of Dorr, who was tried for treason, then sentenced to hard labor and solitary confinement. Although harsh punishment took a toll on him before his eventual early release, Dorr's legacy was electoral reform—a law that allowed any man who could pay a one-dollar poll tax to vote, instituted in 1843. This would make Rhode Island the first state to allow blacks to vote.

Most of the anti-Irish and anti-German prejudice elsewhere was more insidious than that found in Rhode Island, however. Instead of explicitly denying political and legal rights to Catholic immigrants, Nativists typically launched campaigns that tightened the regulations around the public spaces the Catholics used for political organizing. They had their work cut out for them, though. By 1850, Boston, for example, had at least twelve hundred licensed liquor sellers, most of whom were Irish. In

New York, the *Tribune* editor complained that three-quarters of the city's saloons were operated by Catholics, even though they represented only a quarter of the population. The number of *shebeens* (illegal bars run mainly by Irish women out of their private homes), dram shops, and grog shops is impossible to guess, but there were many.

It was clear that policing unlicensed bars was going to be almost impossible, so in 1851, inspired in part by Beecher, one state, Maine, decided upon a radical solution—instituting a prohibition on alcohol, thanks to the perseverance of the crusading Neal S. Dow, Portland mayor and "Father of Prohibition." Eleven states would follow with their own "Maine Laws" and, where there wasn't political will for state-wide abstinence, local municipalities often voted to go dry. Inspired by the Maine Law, Stephen Miller, a Nativist who was at the helm of two "non-partisan" newspapers in Harrisburg, Pennsylvania, campaigned for the adoption of a local dry law. After temperance, Miller's second-greatest cause célèbre in his papers was "Americanism." Coupled with the editorial policy of announcing all arrests for public drunkenness that involved Irishmen, the message in both the *Harrisburg Telegraph* and the *Morning Herald* was clear. "Patrick O'Gutter" was characterized as a drunken wife beater who passed out in ditches and belonged to the lowest "class of Irish paupers who are daily thrust upon our shore by the thousands, to subsist upon the bounty of American citizens."

Not far away, in Wayne County, Pennsylvania, a letter to the editor voiced the complaint that Americans had been "humbugged long enough by tavern keepers, and their groggeries, and naturalized citizens." The author then proceeded to declare his intention to join the "Know-Nothing Party" (the other party name for the Nativists, in addition to the American Party). In the *New York Herald*, an editor wrote the following in support of the Nativists: "The Know Nothing Order is the sign of the first movement against these rum hole conventions and grog shop politicians." *The New York Tribune*, owned by Horace Greeley, was in another political camp. Greeley was a Whig—the last of a dying breed—and fiercely anti-Nativist. It had been Greeley, in fact, who had come up with the epithet "Know-Nothing"—a jab at the party's secretive meetings, at which all members were counseled to say they knew nothing if questioned. Strangely, the Nativists embraced this nickname. Greeley's anti-Nativism didn't translate into a radically progressive editorial line, however, since the *Tribune* blamed liquor for the prisons being full of Irish "culprits" and the gallows "hideous" with Catholic murderers. Still, his sentiment was a degree more moderate than that of the Nativists. To quote one editorial: "The fact that the Catholics of this country keep a great many more grog shops and sell more liquor in proportion to their number than any other denomination creates and keeps alive a strong prejudice against them."

The collapse of the Whig party left a void, making it possible for the Know-Nothings to gain power in many municipalities nearly overnight, especially in the Northern states, where they capitalized on a burgeoning anti-immigrant sentiment. As the Democrats increasingly became known for "Rum, Romanism and Rebellion," the Know-Nothings rode anti-Catholic sentiment to victory across Massachusetts, in Philadelphia and in Washington, DC, in some cases with candidates running on a Whig ticket but secretly representing the Know-Nothings. The key to identifying a candidate's political bent lay in his pledging three campaign promises: a crackdown on crime, barring immigrants from holding any government job at any level, and enforcing or instituting Sunday closing laws for bars.

These were common to almost all Know-Nothing candidates. Although they claimed to be motivated by Sabbatarianism, a Puritan legacy that encouraged the shuttering of all businesses on Sundays, the motives behind the movement were readily apparent. In 1849, the *Irish American*, a New York newspaper, laid them out clearly: "Whilst wines and brandies are imported, sold and consumed by the rich; whilst the 'upper ten' guzzle, and swill, and get drunk with impunity, the working man's lips are to be padlocked, the liquor stores shut up." The editorial ended with a call for legislators to stop making separate laws for rich and poor.

Other than Catholicism and being feared and hated by Nativists, the main thing the Germans and Irish shared was Sundays. That is, drinking on Sundays. Since many of these recent immigrants were working in the worst possible hard-labor jobs with exploitative practices, Sunday was the only day off most had and drinking at the saloon or beer garden represented the only recreation many immigrants enjoyed. In addition, the housing many lived in was so inadequate that even the most meager of these public spaces would have seemed palatial.

While waiting on the institution of state laws, a number of municipalities, most notably Chicago, considered following Stephen Miller's Harrisburg example and adopting local "blue laws" (so named, some say, for the blue paper on which the laws were written in New Haven in

1665; others maintaining "blue" is a reference to "true blue," implying a rigid adherence to principle).[8] Stirred by a combination of racial and religious intolerance and a desire to shut down the "machine politics" of the immigrant taverns, and emboldened by the prohibition movements of the era, Chicago "Know-Nothing" Mayor Levi Boone (grandnephew of Daniel Boone) decided to enforce an existing Sunday closing law. This was actually a state law, enacted in 1843 and universally ignored. According to a *Chicago Times* article that recounted the incident a few decades later in 1877, Boone also raised the fee for a liquor license from fifty dollars a year to three hundred in an attempt to force out "all the lower classes of dives and leave the business in the hands of the better class of saloon-keepers, who, when the temperance law should go into force, could be rationally dealt with."[9] At the time, Illinois was facing the introduction of a "Maine Law," which would be voted upon in June 1855.

That same year, Boone made good on his campaign promise and had the police begin enforcing the old state law—although only in the sections of town where immigrants lived, who represented more than half of Chicago's population in the 1850s. Taverns frequented by Protestants were overlooked in the attempt to clean up the city, whereas two hundred German immigrant owners were arrested for keeping their establishments open on Sundays or neglecting to pay the higher license fees. When the first of the cases went to court in May 1855, five hundred Germans and Irish descended on the Cook County Court House to protest the trial. "After making themselves understood that the decision of the court must be in their favor if the town didn't want a taste of war," they blocked traffic at Clark and Randolph Streets, gathering strength until Boone instructed the police to arm themselves with clubs and break up the riot.[10]

Boone declared martial law, but the mob only grew bigger and immigrants joined in from all corners of the city. After an hour-long battle, the rioters fled, and while many were injured, only one was killed. A few were arrested and only two were convicted (Irishmen, of course). Nonetheless, the protest, dubbed the "Chicago Lager Beer Riot," mobilized immigrant voters, who rejected Boone in his run for office the following year. The Illinois "Maine Law" was also rejected by the voters.

When voting, moderates who hoped to avoid more unrest were mindful of the 1857 New York riots, in which large parts of the Five Points and Bowery had been turned into veritable war zones. This had been the unintended result of a New York State initiative to clean up the city, despite the attempts by Mayor Fernando Wood and Captain Isaiah Rynders to thwart reform. At stake were "dead letter" Sunday closing state laws, brought back to life by Nativism, that Wood had promised would never be enforced by his police, who answered to Rynders. What neither Rynders nor Wood could control, however, was the state legislature's plan to discharge the entire city police force because of its widespread reputation for corruption and replace it with state agents. Ex-policemen, joined by German and Irish immigrants motivated by Sunday closing laws, and by the established Bowery and Five Points gangs such as the Dead Rabbits, Roach Guards, and Bowery Boys, erupted onto the streets in May and again in July. In the midst of this chaos, which Rynders typically reveled in, he somehow lost control. Perhaps he had lost his edge before the 1857 riots. In the 1850s, he went Native himself for a few years, despite the fact that he was half-Irish, half-German, and the chief string-puller of the saloon politics in the immigrant quarters of New York City—an exemplar of the very brand of politics the Nativists were campaigning to dismantle.

The Nativists weren't going to last long either and the American Party was replaced by the Grand Old Party, the Republicans. All this came about in 1854, when President Pierce (son of a tavernkeeper, by the way) introduced the Kansas-Nebraska Act, which divided the Nativists into proslavery and antislavery camps. The Act, which allowed the residents of the new states to determine for themselves whether or not they would permit slavery, was a clear affront to abolitionists, since it reversed the Missouri Compromise of 1820 that prohibited slavery in Kansas. The fracture was too much for the Nativists to bear and they would disappear in a few years. The Republicans, however progressive they were regarding slavery, shared many of the same reactionary and bigoted values as their predecessors. In 1855, the Chicago chapter of Republicans announced in the *Tribune* that it would not court the "grog shops, foreign vote, and Catholic brethren," unlike those who catered to the "lowest class of foreign citizens." Chicago Democrats, its Republican opponents claimed, were "the Irish Roman Catholic and Whiskey Party of the city."

Regardless of the rhetoric, voters were shying away from any kind of extreme measures, for these always seemed to lead to violence in the streets, not to mention a new proliferation of establishments designed to evade the law—shebeens, blind pigs, and blind tigers. Of course, illegal and unlicensed establishments had always existed but, anywhere there was a Sunday closing law, you could expect new "resorts," which weren't bars at all but places where you paid admission to view a blind pig or tiger. Looking at blind pigs can be thirsty work and so a drink was supplied to the patron—gratis.

Voters were beginning to see the cracks in Maine Laws, too, although they had been billed as unmitigated successes. In Maine, itself, Reverend Theodore L. Cuyler insisted that the law was responsible for the shuttering of three hundred grog shops in one day and, accordingly, greatly reduced arrests for public intoxication. With alcohol banned and police with more time on their hands, went the logic, it wouldn't take long for the force to bring the remaining outlaws who insisted on running rum shops to justice.

In reality, though, there were tavernkeepers all over Maine who had refused to close up shop simply because of a little law prohibiting the sale of alcohol and, right from the get-go, had been devising creative ways around it. Importing liquor from other states, they simply gave alcohol away to customers with the purchase of, for example, a stale cracker, which cost, coincidentally, about the same price as a beer had before the state prohibition.

Worse than this widespread defiance, however, was the public image problem with which reformer Neal Dow would eventually have to contend. His nickname, the "Napoleon of Temperance," would start to take on prophetic dimensions, when, in 1855, he was caught with $1,600 worth of liquor intended, he maintained, for "medicinal purposes." Dow's opponents, led by a man named Royal Williams, went to the Portland court and demanded that a warrant be issued for a search of Dow's property. The massive cache of liquor couldn't possibly have been for personal use but, rather, for eventual illegal sale. Dow's law contained a clause stating that, should three men accuse any other of illegal alcohol-selling, a warrant had to be issued. Meanwhile, a mob of somewhere between five hundred to three thousand (many of them Irish, apparently) were protesting outside the building where Dow's secret stash of liquor was held. As the situation grew more and more tense throughout the night, Dow ordered police to open fire on the crowd and, in the skirmish, John Robbins, the alleged ringleader, was killed.

This turned out to be the Napoleon of Temperance's Waterloo. He was not reelected on his secret Know-Nothing Party ticket and the Maine Law was repealed in 1856. The first round had gone to the tavernkeepers, but the fight had only really just begun.

THE
CRUSADER
WALKS
INTO
A BAR

JUDGE ROY BEAN TRYING A HORSE THIEF

Judge Roy Bean, the "Law West of the Pecos,"
holding court at the town of Langtry, Texas, trying
a horse thief. This building was the courthouse and
the saloon. 1900. Image donated by Corbis.

Abraham Lincoln had been an unlikely choice as the Republican's second presidential candidate in 1860, since the party was poised to do battle with the Rum, Romanism, and Rebellion of the Democrats, yet its leader was, himself, accused of having been steeped in the tavern business.

Most bourbon aficionados will be aware that Lincoln's father had once been a distillery hand in Kentucky, but the connection is even more extensive than that. As a young man, Honest Abe had operated three grocery stores in New Salem, Indiana, and, as his contemporaries well knew, a grocery store was often just a euphemism for a grog shop. There's no doubt that the first Republican president sold whiskey; the only question involves the quantities, and whether or not he sold any actual groceries.

One-time saloonkeeper or not, Lincoln was firm in his commitment to sever the connection between liquor and politics. He gave up his grocery stores as soon as he became politically active and worked hard to remove the taint. In one contest in Springfield, Illinois, a Democratic foe attacked him for hypocrisy, bringing up his having drawn "liquor for a profit" and arguing that this rendered him unqualified to critique the campaign habits of Democrats.

Still, Lincoln prevailed, and concerns over his connection to drinking establishments faded into the background. Mainly this was because most progressive reform energies were diverted to the abolition of slavery. Even the Washingtonians gave up, disbanding permanently in 1860. Indeed, temperance, abstinence, and anti-immigrant causes were now of secondary concern to the crises of slavery, secession, and state's rights. These had become the only political issues of any serious note since the Kansas-Nebraska Act. Also in the mix was the wild popularity of Harriet Beecher Stowe's *Uncle Tom's Cabin*, which sold three hundred thousand copies, a new record. Lyman Beecher's daughter, Stowe is the perfect symbol of this shift in reformers' priorities from abstinence to abolition and *Uncle Tom's Cabin* illustrated some of the era's ambivalence about tavernkeepers. In the book, taverns are used by both slave hunters and those who promise freedom. A hero is killed in a New Orleans saloon, a victim of the drunken violence that Second-Wave evangelists were committed to eradicating; but there are benevolent tavernkeepers, too, maintaining stops along the Underground Railroad.

Some of Stowe's sources were questionable and it's often alleged that she didn't quite do as much research as claimed when creating her account of the network that aided slaves in their flight north. The Spread Eagle Tavern, in West Chester, Ohio, owned by abolitionist James D. Conrey, however, has been confirmed as the model for Stowe's stagecoach stop on the underground. The Spread Eagle was only one of a number of abolitionist taverns that provided food and shelter to refugees. Proprietors of the Old Tavern in Unionville, Ohio; the Springhouse Tavern in Gettysburg, Pennsylvania; and the Old Brick Tavern in Will County, Illinois, were others who followed in the great tradition of the rebellious tavernkeeper, this time by providing refuge for runaway slaves.

The legendary Indian King in Haddonfield, New Jersey, instrumental during the Revolutionary War, was rumored to have had tunnels for escaped slaves, as did Gerhart's Tavern in Telford, Pennsylvania. Nathan Philbrick's tavern in Farmington, Michigan, had small sleeping rooms adjacent to the taproom for use by those on the trek northward. Often the arrangements were a natural fit, since so many taverns already had everything in place to hide smugglers and contraband. New Hampshire was a well-established stop for escaped slaves on their way to Canada. They hid at the Beal tavern in Dorchester and in several public houses in Lyme. Once they got to Canada, they were often initially accommodated in taverns like the Life Henry tavern in Simcoe, Ontario. Canadian taverns, like their American counterparts, played crucial roles in the transport of the nearly thirty thousand slaves who escaped between the years 1810 and 1850.

Still, the relationship between abolitionists and tavernkeepers was strained. At meetings and in the popular anti-slavery literature, it was agreed that "a slave-holder (was) better than a tavern-keeper," a common resolution at progressive meetings. After one such meeting, Levi Foster, an escaped slave and tavernkeeper who was residing in Amherstburg, Ontario, was so moved that he closed his business immediately.[1] That said, abolishing slavery was still the more urgent business and, as a result, the war against drink was shelved. Even the lowest of saloonkeepers experienced a period of relaxed enforcement and started taking advantage of it, particularly after the Civil War broke out in 1861.

In Chicago, where vice had previously been ghettoized into an area called "the Sands" (where the Magnificent Mile runs today), it expanded into nearly every corner of the city. Groggeries, saloons and brothels were soon found everywhere. The most infamous, by far, was a place called Under the Willow, a name that may have promised rural tranquility but, instead, delivered prostitution, pick-pocketing, and excessive drinking. Owner Roger Plant couldn't keep all the vice under one roof and the Willow wound up spreading to a row of houses known, to some, as Roger's Barracks; to others, as "one of the wickedest places on the continent."[2] During the war, Plant paid off the skeleton police force and was left free to conduct business as he liked.

Civil War saloons were therefore largely left to their own devices and degenerated during the war, instead of rising to the occasion and playing valiant roles as they had in previous conflicts. The telegraph rendered the tavern communication network obsolete and, while there were occasional stories of battles named after nearby taverns or of saloons that had provided soldiers with refreshment or sustenance en route to the front, their role as de facto military checkpoints was greatly reduced. In Philadelphia, the Union Volunteer and Cooper Shop Volunteer Refreshment Saloons, which gave free food, drink, and shelter to Union soldiers, weren't really even saloons. They'd been set up in boathouses or in coopershops and didn't dispense liquor but, instead, coffee.

Confederate sympathizers in the North used saloons to some degree. In New York, for instance, where citizens were resisting the draft in 1863, saloons were one of the few gathering places for those leaning toward the Democrat "Copperhead" side, which was in favor of negotiating peace with the South. While the majority of New Yorkers supported Lincoln at the outset, backroom politics were turning some immigrants away from the cause. Copperheads were opposed to any national draft to help the war effort but seized on one discriminatory aspect of the draft policy to stir up dissent among Irish laborers—the one allowing the wealthy to buy themselves out of service for $300. That the New York City Draft Riots were connected to saloon politics is suggested by the involvement of Captain Isaiah Rynders, who, although considerably less influential than he had been ten years prior, was still capable of pulling a few strings. Other major players in the riots were the Black Joke Engine Company 33, a volunteer fire company with deep connections to Tammany boss "Honest" John Kelly, and the Ivy Green Tavern on Elm Street (now Lafayette, below Canal), where many Democrat politicians and Copperheads mixed with the firemen.

After one drawing of names in mid-July, 1863, the Black Joke Engine Company led an angry mob to the draft office and burned it down, then proceeded to the Bull's Head Hotel and demanded refreshments. When they were refused, they burned it down, too. Now stoked, the pack then launched attacks on the offices of *New York Tribune* publisher Horace Greeley, the mayor's house, and several other buildings, including a black orphanage. All the while, it attacked any blacks it encountered. In the end, up to two thousand people were injured and perhaps as many as 120 killed. The draft continued but Tammany Hall emerged with an even stronger grasp on Irish voters, particularly after it offered to help pay fees for those who were drafted and couldn't afford to buy their way out.

By the end of the Civil War, machine politics and saloons were thriving, but a serious backlash was ahead. Even Roger Plant of Chicago retired and took up a respectable lifestyle, sensing a dramatic change in the country's attitude towards drinking. Saloons couldn't claim to have played any particularly patriotic role in the war as they had in the past and it certainly didn't help that the nation's next most traumatic event— Lincoln's assassination on Good Friday, 1865—was linked to a tavern.

One of the most controversial aspects of the ensuing trial was the execution for conspiracy of Mary Surratt, whose involvement was traced back to 1852, the year in which she and husband John bought a plot of land in what is now known as Clinton, Maryland (previously Surratt-ville), southeast of Washington, DC. The Surratts started out fairly industriously, developing the land and opening the area's most note-worthy tavern, which doubled, incidentally, as the area's polling center and post office. Despite the promising beginning, just as *Ten Nights in a Barroom* author T. S. Arthur might have predicted, things soon degener-ated for John Surratt, who took to drinking and gambling and, accord-ing to some reports, spousal abuse. In addition, the tavern had become part of an underground network for Confederate forces. The Surratts were known Southern sympathizers in Maryland, which remained in the Union despite torn allegiances, and their tavern was one of many in the "border states" used to hide and transport Confederate spies and activists.

It's thought that John Wilkes Booth made his way to the Surratt Tavern in the fall of 1864, accompanied by Mary's son, John. And while there's no hard evidence to prove the conspiracy was hatched at the Surratt, (given that it was known as a center of Confederate resistance and that Booth, a good friend of Mary's son) was in Surrattville at the time, it seems like a better than even bet.

After months of planning—plus a foiled attempt to kidnap Lincoln and hold him hostage for the release of Confederate soldiers—the con-spirators turned to the idea of assassination. On the day Lincoln planned to go to the Ford Theatre for a performance of *Our American Cousin*, Mary Surratt rode out to the tavern and left a package containing guns for Booth, so that he'd be armed during his escape. After killing Lincoln, Booth's first stop was the tavern, where he picked up field glasses, a rifle, pistols, and, of course, whiskey.

Mary Surratt's actions in furnishing the escapee with supplies was a key piece of evidence in her conviction. She was sentenced to hang, which some thought extreme on account of her gender, her age (at forty, was considered too old for such a cruel fate), the fact that she didn't directly physically harm anyone, and the widely held belief that her trial was mainly an attempt to smoke out son, John, who was still in hiding. Lincoln's successor, Andrew Johnson, however, defended the sentence on the grounds that she had kept "the nest which hatched the egg." Later, when antisaloonist John Marshall Barker wrote about "Wilkey's Booth's gang," he claimed that they "always met in a saloon." He further added that Booth (shot and killed by federal agents after a two-week manhunt) was a "heavy drinker" and that three other conspirators sentenced to hang—Lewis Powell (also known as Payne), David Herold, and George A. Atzerodt—were "common drunkards." "Mrs. Surratt was herself a rum-seller," he added.

One of the earliest indications that alcohol was going to resurface as a major issue after the war was the establishment of the National Temperance Society and Publishing House in 1865. The Society would publish over a *billion* pages of antialcohol propaganda over the next sixty years. Another sign was the jump in membership of the International Order of the Good Templars, which increased almost sevenfold—from sixty thousand to four hundred thousand—in the four years after the war.

Then there were those who were making a good living off sermonizing about temperance. John Gough, for example, had been relentless about getting the abstinence message out during his lecture circuit before the war, but found his career soaring after it, especially as more Americans began spending more time attending public lectures for entertainment and edification. The one-time actor took full advantage of the new medium of the lecture circuit and delivered talks about the "Dangers of Moderate Drinking." Gough did well for himself, far better than he had as an actor, delivering almost ten thousand lectures before his death in 1886. His stage career had been less than auspicious and, in one theatrical run, he collected wages only in the form of whiskey.

One of Gough's earliest public appearances was also connected with alcohol–but for the other side. He played the keeper of a temperance hotel in a play called *Departed Spirits: The Temperance Hoax*. Gough's character, like that of the other temperance leaders depicted in the play, was sent up for his stupidity and hypocrisy. There may have been something prophetic about his early stage role, given that Gough fell off the wagon several times. Once in New York, he went missing for six days before being found in a brothel in seedy Walker Street, under the influence of opium or alcohol, "one or both." He claimed to have been drugged and held against his will, *French Connection* style. However, before he left his hotel that first day, he told the desk clerk not to expect him back that night, since he was going to Brooklyn. Many suspected that he planned a binge which turned into a bender. Gough's occasional missteps didn't seem to interfere with his success, however. On his death, the *New York Times* ventured that he was "probably better known to old and young in this country and Great Britain than any other public speaker."

The strategies used by early temperance figures such as Gough consisted of a combination of Christian sermon, sordid tales, and heart-string pulling. Another reformer, Henry Willis Hawkins, spoke of the day of his rebirth as a sober man. It had been prompted by his daughter, who pleaded: "Papa, please don't send me after whiskey today." At the end of temperance lectures, many would take the pledge of abstinence on the spot. Given how many Americans went to these events (Gough is said to have spoken to nearly ten million over the course of his career), we might expect a considerably dryer country to have resulted. However, the fervor that Gough, Hawkins, and others whipped up was often fleeting. There was even a joke about the phenomenon: "He was so excited about taking the pledge, he had to go celebrate by having a drink."

One popular temperance lecturer, Dr. Dio Lewis, had a profound effect on his audience and wound up with a group who weren't content to simply pay lip-service to the virtues of temperance. Diocletian Lewis (who wasn't, strictly speaking, a doctor, since he had dropped out of Harvard), was one of America's earliest fitness advocates and his antialcohol lectures also promoted the "new gymnastics" and their health benefits. One December night in Fredonia, New York, he met with his dream audience, a group of women who decided to take direct action against the saloon. After two days of meetings, the women, "in the name of God and humanity," wrote an appeal to saloonkeepers: "Knowing, as we do, that the sale of intoxicating liquors is the parent of every misery, prolific of all woe in this life and the next, potent alone in evil, blighting every fair hope, desolating families, the chief incentive to crime, we . . . earnestly request that you will pledge yourself to cease the traffic here in these drinks, forthwith and forever." They added to this a plea for the end of gaming tables and then proceeded directly to the Taylor House Saloon, marched in, and read their plea to the proprietor.[3]

From all accounts, Mr. Taylor was fairly receptive to the women, although his response (which apparently was: "If the rest will close their places, I'll close mine") may strike many as an empty promise. Taylor's brother, it seems, was not so open to the notion and refused to negotiate with what was essentially one of the earliest chapters of the Women's Christian Temperance Union (WCTU). While the Taylors waffled, the women had more success with a Fredonian drugstore and hotel, both of which agreed to comply.[4]

This marked the beginning of what was called the Women's Crusade—a massive direct-action campaign of small groups of women who, inspired by Lewis's lectures in New York and Ohio, formed chapters and pleaded with tavernkeepers in the winter of 1873–1874. Undeterred by freezing weather, camps of women protested outside saloons with their appeals, sang hymns, held prayer vigils for the lost souls inside, and read religious tracts. Some of the more unnerving demonstrations involved women knitting or sitting in complete silence outside the tavern.

What made the campaign so effective was that the presence of the women—whether silent or vocal—proved bad for business. The crusaders wrote down the names of any patron entering the saloons and established vigils, taking turns warming up in "tabernacles" (makeshift shacks with small stoves inside). That year's winter was a particularly bitter one and especially harsh in the regions where the women were most active. The pressure tactics were often successful—maybe not *quite* as successful as Lewis's claim of seventeen thousand saloon closures in Ohio alone—but the Crusade definitely thrived there and, to a lesser extent, in New York, Michigan, Illinois, and in at least twenty-five other states. The WCTU was on the map.

The early WCTU's actual success in eliminating saloons was routinely exaggerated by those publicizing its efforts. A number of saloons merely closed for a few days and, reopened as soon as the women had moved on to their next target. Some, however, resisted the women, who were often subjected to significant verbal abuse from both patrons and saloonkeepers, and were sometimes, as historian Herbert Asbury put it, "kicked, pummelled, spat upon, deluged with beer and slops, bombarded with eggs, vegetables, and even stones." One saloonkeeper threatened to fire a canon at the crusaders. A Mrs. Wagner, who operated the Holly Tree Coffee and Lunch Rooms of Columbus, Ohio, was accused of nearly choking a reformer to death. It was quite common for the women to receive a "baptism" of either cold water or beer suds if they entered the saloon. Some of the more militant and vengeful saloonkeepers rigged up pumps to spray the women outside, again in Asbury's words, "so that a line of praying crusaders resembled a row of icicles." One keeper's wife went in the other direction, threatening to scald any protestors.[5] None of these tactics did much to enhance the image of the saloonkeeper and those who fought back against the "broken-hearted mothers and wives" lost an important battle in the public relations war.

There were other losses for the "whiskey apologists" in that era, too. In 1881 in Garrettsville, Ohio, a church was blown up. Nobody was hurt in this instance but, in other bouts of anti-reform violence, there were casualties. One of the more famous victims was Reverend George Haddock. Known as the "fighting preacher," Haddock had earned a reputation for being able to clean up a town and was brought in to help rid Sioux City, Iowa, of its numerous saloons, particularly those in an area known as Hell's Half Acre—operating in spite of the fact that the state was officially dry.

Haddock's method was simple enough. He'd visit the offending illegal saloons, observe and document the sale of liquor, then bring injunctions against the offenders in court. Neither the police nor court officials in Sioux City had much interest in proceeding with the trials. In fact, the illegal saloons and myriad "resorts" that catered to gamblers and to those seeking female companionship essentially enjoyed the protection of the local law—one of the recurring challenges reformers faced during that era. While the majority of Iowans had voted for the "Clark Law," which instituted prohibition for the entire state, Sioux City contained a large enclave of opponents—a discrepancy common in larger urban centers. While the state had gone dry in a new wave of fervency that resulted in similar state options (beginning with Kansas in 1881 and spreading to North Dakota, South Dakota, Rhode Island, and Maine) there was considerable resistance from small pockets such as those in Sioux City. Resistors could be found on both sides of the issue.

In states that chose to stay wet, individual municipalities frequently implemented high license fees, which, on average, doubled over the 1880s.

Sioux City wasn't especially cosmopolitan. It was on the frontier, practically in Nebraska, but many of its residents weren't interested in the civilizing influence of prohibitionists from Des Moines, and simply ignored a law they didn't believe applied to them. There was, however, a vocal minority of churchgoers and others who decried the violence and crime that thrived in Hell's Half Acre, where, besides the gambling and prostitution, there had been two violent and sensational murders in 1884 that were attributed to excessive drink. This vocal minority recruited Haddock.

Haddock's approach began working, too. Saloons were shut down one at a time as he brought indictments against those illegally selling liquor and prosecuting them himself before reluctant judges. In August 1886, some saloonkeepers formed their own association and apparently decided that its first order of business should be to hire thugs to threaten those testifying against them. Their primary target, obviously, was Haddock. One of the leaders, George Treiber, suggested that Sylvester Granda, also known as Steamboat Charlie, and Albert "Bismarck" Koschnitski, might be up for the job, which was supposed to involve simply "punching" Haddock "once or twice" and not "too hard."

What happened next is nearly impossible to sort out, since those accused offered so many conflicting stories that even contemporaries had trouble sorting truth from fiction. It seems that while Reverend Haddock was out investigating a saloon on the edge of town, a few of the association's biggest agitators were hanging out at a bar called Jung's, along with the foreman of a brewing company, John Arensdorf, and his delivery man, Henry Peters. When Haddock returned to town, he immediately sensed danger but, armed with a slingshot, went out to confront it. Unfortunately for the fighting preacher, it wasn't just Bismarck and Steamboat Charlie waiting for him. Somebody—quite likely Arensdorf—decided to improve upon the plan to merely scare Haddock and, perhaps spontaneously, shot and killed him. Haddock became a martyr almost the moment his body hit the ground—killed while spreading the word of God.

For saloonkeeps in Sioux City—or anywhere, for that matter—the options weren't good. Most packed up shop and moved across the river to Covington (South Sioux City), which was conveniently located in

Nebraska, where, under what was known as the Slocumb Law, alcohol was still legal (although discouraged by high licensing fees and a clause that made owners responsible for any damage caused by drunk patrons). Despite unfavorable laws, however, Covington saloonkeepers had a thriving business, since thirsty Iowans could easily cross a foot-bridge into wet Nebraska.

Haddock's death left more than just a local legacy of a border town with a pronounced wrong side of the tracks. The story of his murder became a national topic of conversation. The convoluted trial, which led to a hung jury, was reported in dailies nationwide and temperance advocates invoked his name at every opportunity in their lectures and sermons. According to one account, his "life was laid down at the command of duty," and his death "in such a cowardly way" would "give his sermons undying life and his lectures a perpetual force." Indeed, the term "Haddock" quickly became shorthand for the evils of the saloon and a rallying point for dry advocates across America.

Haddock's experiences reconfirmed people's notions that the West and its saloons were lawless places (which, on the whole, they were). Even West-going advocate Horace Greeley observed that saloon denizens had a "careless way, when drunk, of firing revolvers, sometimes at each other, and other times quite miscellaneously." And if a person needed to be brought to trial for firing his weapon into a crowd or at the wrong person, the case was often heard back in the saloon (before official courthouses and police stations were established).

At those trials, it would seem, drinking etiquette and rituals still applied. Saloon historian Madelon Powers uncovered a trial in a Sioux City saloon tent in which a man was being tried for the murder of the town's "trouble-maker"—a man no one was particularly unhappy to see go. When the trial adjourned for lunch, the accused said, "Well, Judge, I guess the drinks are on me this time." Powers surmises that the gesture was meant as an apology to his jury of peers, who were inconvenienced with having to go through the formality of a trial in which the outcome was predetermined.[6]

The further west you went, the blurrier the line between lawman and outlaw became. James Butler (Wild Bill) Hickok, for example, was a constable in Monticello, Kansas, but nevertheless was charged with the murder of one David McCanles. "Duck Bill" (as Hickok was known at the time) was acquitted, but it wouldn't be the last of the lawman's brushes with the law. In August 1865, despite widespread popular opinion that he ought to have been found guilty, Hickok was acquitted for the murder of a fellow professional gambler in Springfield, Missouri, and still managed to finish runner-up in that September's election for city marshal.

Later, as city marshal in Abilene, Texas, Hickok got into one of his more famous gunfights, this one with gambling gunfighter Phil Coe, over a painting on the exterior wall of the Bull's Head Saloon. The painting was of a bull—not at all unusual, except that Coe had it painted in all its glory, with a large, erect penis. Hickok had the offending parts painted over and, this, added to the news that he was courting Coe's woman, led to a street brawl. Coe took a shot at Hickok—but missed. A fatal mistake.

Ultimately, Hickok's fate would be sealed in a saloon, too, at Nuttal and Mann's Saloon Number 10 in Deadwood, South Dakota, when Jack McCall sought revenge over the previous night's gambling losses. Hickok, uncharacteristically, was sitting with his back to the door when McCall burst in. Hickok had been holding aces and eights.

For desperado and lawman alike, frontier life was lived largely in the saloon, where drinking, gambling, and brawling prevailed. The Earps, for example, were all equally at home in this environment, both as lawmen and barmen. James, one of the lesser known of the six Earp brothers, had been a successful bartender at a saloon in Wichita, Kansas, before becoming a deputy marshal in Dodge City. And when Wyatt was named city marshal of Dodge, he picked up a second salary dealing cards out of Chalk Beeson's Long Branch Saloon, which would go on to host Bat Masterson, Doc Holliday, and Luke Short—the latter's attempt to buy into the saloon eventually sparking the Dodge City War.

Wyatt would move on to greener pastures and came to own four saloons in San Diego, including an Oyster Bar on Fifth Avenue, and, was once part-owner of the Oriental Saloon in Tombstone, Arizona, where he continued dealing cards, often earning as much as a thousand dollars a week. His brother, Virgil, deputy United States Marshal at the time, was ambushed and wounded as he left the Oriental on December 28, 1881—fallout from the Gunfight at the O.K. Corral and a precursor to the legendary Earp Vendetta Ride.

The most famous figure to law with whiskey, however, is Judge Roy Bean, who doled out both from his saloon, the Jersey Lilly in Langtry, Texas. Bean claimed to be "The Law West of the Pecos"—no idle boast, since the closest court was two hundred miles away and there was really no official law in the region. The Jersey hadn't been Bean's first watering hole, either. In the 1850s, he worked in (and later inherited) his brother's place, the Headquarters Saloon in San Gabriel, California. In the 1860s, he operated a saloon with another brother near Silver City, New Mexico, and, in the 1870s, yet another saloon in a slum in San Antonio, Texas.

From these inauspicious beginnings, Bean managed to carve out a prominent space for himself in west Texas in the early 1880s. He began with a tent saloon and ten fifty-five-gallon barrels of whiskey, which he set up near a tent city housing thousands of railroad workers. The first to open shop there, he enjoyed his monopoly. Once, when a "Jewish gentleman" threatened to open up a competing saloon, Bean warned him to leave. When the newcomer failed to heed this sage advice and built it anyway (a shack, really), Bean, after reportedly saying, "Watch me make a Jew leave the country," began shooting indiscriminately at the new saloon. The would-be competition fled and Bean scooped all his alcohol for his own.

Bean's version of justice was eccentric at best and criminal at worst. The story circulated that he had received a book of Texas law on his very first appointment, then refused to consult any new editions—when he bothered to refer to any at all. In that there was no jail, punishments were meted out in the form of either fines or hangings. Fines were often set at the amount of money criminal offenders happened to have on them, coincidentally, the exact amount needed to cover court costs. Objections to the severity of a fine meant bumping it from $30 to $50—with the caution that any further argument would warrant a further bump to a hundred. One of the most frequently repeated stories about Bean is his acquittal of an Irishman who had murdered a Chinese railway worker. Bean's ruling: "Gentlemen, I find the law very explicit on murdering your fellow man, but there's nothing here about killing a Chinaman. Case dismissed."

Bean *did* have to run for reelection every other year, but would stop at nothing to ensure that, west of the Pecos, he remained "The Law." One year, the polling station was situated right behind his saloon, where he also happened to keep his pet bear. As if the bear wasn't intimidation enough, Bean paced the area with a shotgun in hand. Another time, a hundred more ballots were cast than there were Langtry residents. Despite the fraud and electioneering, Bean's sometime rival, Jesus P. Torres, would occasionally win an election and be declared Justice of the Peace for a two-year period. Typically, Bean ignored this inconvenient fact and held trials in his saloon regardless.

His bar wasn't run with any greater integrity than his courtroom. Bean was said to take a twenty-dollar gold piece off a tourist for a thirty-five-cent pint of beer, then refuse change on the grounds that anyone paying for a beer with such a large sum didn't have enough sense to hold onto his money. If the customer complained, Bean would simply put on his other hat and, as judge, fine the tourist something like $19.65 for disturbing the peace. Despite the corruption and threats, the Jersey Lilly became a destination spot after Bean's reputation for shameless and unapologetic eccentricity had spread.

Bean's bizarre persona may have helped his billing as a tourist attraction but, in the big picture, none of these colorful tales of recklessness was helping saloonists in the face of the countrywide antisaloon sentiment that was riding the new wave of Methodism that preached abstinence as next to godliness. The crusading women and preachers also made the most of the myriad violent incidents, especially the ones which made martyrs of men like Haddock. Add to these isolated incidents a new threat facing saloons on the East Coast and in the mid-West—the socialist and anarchist politics beginning to emerge in Irish and German saloons and beer halls. The saloon's opponents were about to find all the ammunition they needed to shut it down.

9

THE
RADICALS
TAKE
OVER
A BAR

LAGER BIER

*An advertisement circa 1879. Lager beer gains
ground in America and advertisements like this one
try to frame it as a patriotic drink. Image courtesy
of the Library of Congress.*

LAGER BIER IS EVERYWHERE: CHARACTERISTIC
SCENE IN A NEW YORK LAGER BIER SALOON
Lager bier, though, is still very much associated
with German beer halls. Image donated by Corbis.

Although the Nativists had long faded into the scenery, anti-immigrant
feelings had not, and saloons and taverns, still the primary organizing
hubs for many immigrant groups, were to resurface as targets in the
1870s, especially when it became clear that nascent labor groups were
using them for airing grievances and forging solidarity.

The fifty years following the Civil War were particularly potent
ones for labor activism for a number of reasons: a wild and unregulated boom-and-bust economy; an influx of European immigrants far
greater than America could handle; and competition for industrial
and manufacturing jobs caused by the great migration of blacks
northward after the war. On top of this, large companies were implementing a management structure brutally exploitative of this glut of
labor.

The "Molly Maguire" incident in Pennsylvania was one of the earliest
and most sensational episodes to emerge from this perfect storm of circumstances. The name refers to a group of Catholic rebels in Ireland
who were purported to have organized in a Donegal shebeen to protest
being exploited by Protestants. Over in the anthracite coal region of

Pennsylvania, where large numbers of Irish immigrants were being taken advantage of, railroad and mining executives—and their security forces—blamed unusually militant labor unrest in the 1870s on a secret sister society of the Maguires. Executives believed Irish ruffians had infiltrated the union and were encouraging members to wage a campaign of terrorism against management. This was probably something of an exaggeration and some historians doubt the very existence of an American branch of the Maguires.

The incident that triggered the hysteria over "Molly Maguirism" was the murder of a policeman named Benjamin Yost in 1875, the culmination of years of conflict and hostility. Irish laborers had won themselves few friends when they protested Civil War conscription, for many of the same reasons that had caused the New York Draft Riots. Miners were deeply resentful of being forced to participate in any endeavor that would result in the liberation of tens of thousands of slaves who might ultimately migrate and take their jobs. Even before that, staunch prohibitionist and anti-Catholic Benjamin Bannan, owner of the *The Miners' Journal*, the mouthpiece of the coal industry, suspected Molly Maguirism existed among the immigrant workers, blaming his candidates' losses in Schuylkill County on Irish bloc-voting. Bannan also claimed that his inflexible antitavern stance had been formed out of concern for the Irish. As he wrote in 1854, "There is no class in all our wide land which so much need [sic] the blessing of a Prohibitory Liquor law as the Irish. Coming into this country from the ignorance and poverty of the old world, they enter into any avocation which will yield a livelihood, and thoughtlessly plunge into vice and drunkenness."

As with all secret societies, no registrar took minutes of whatever meetings took place and, as such, there's no evidence of an actual Molly Maguire group in Pennsylvania. There was, however, a chapter of the Ancient Order of Hibernians, an Irish fraternal and charitable organization dedicated to helping Irish immigrants and operating out of saloons in the region. Critics charged that the Hibernians were merely a front for the Molly Maguires. Franklin B. Gowen, president of the Philadelphia and Reading Railroad, which, controversially, owned a large percentage of the Pennsylvania mining industry as well, certainly thought so. To him, this was justification enough to banish the Hibernians altogether, a move strongly supported by Bannan. Whether or not the Maguires existed, there was certainly organized labor resistance that took place not long after the establishment of the Hibernians—unsurprising, perhaps, given that many worked twelve-hour shifts every day but Sunday for about $10–$13 per week (roughly $200 by today's measure). The danger posed to miners by unsafe working conditions, however, was more alarming. In the fifty years that preceded 1870, more than thirty thousand miners lost their lives in Pennsylvania alone.[1]

Using the recession caused by the Panic of 1873 as justification (a crisis resulting from a chain reaction of bank failures), Gowen cut miners' wages 20 percent, forcing them into strike mode. He hoped to divide the union and thus weaken its political clout. When the union finally broke down in 1875, there were violent incidents, including the murder of night patrolman Yost, supposedly prompted by his earlier arrest of two union members.

Gowen wasted no time publicizing the alleged Irish Catholic conspiracy, claiming to have evidence gathered by Pinkerton detectives, a private security service that would be hired increasingly by management in labor disputes. The Pinkertons, founded in Chicago in the mid-1850s and as infamous as they were famous, were said to have infiltrated upper levels of the secret society. The truth is almost impossible to ascertain now, given both modern historians' assertions that the Pinkertons were fairly incompetent and that there was serious judicial misconduct, starting with Gowen's getting himself named special prosecutor. Virtually all of his evidence came from among his own employees and his Pinkerton detectives. The only testimony from outside the company rolls was provided by an alleged conspirator who turned state's witness but whose credibility was eroded by the many who denounced him, his wife included.

In the end, nineteen men were hanged for Molly Maguirism, including Alexander Campbell, a tavernkeeper and alleged leader of the Carbon County chapter of Irish radicals, and James Carroll, secretary of the Hibernian Society and owner of the Columbia House tavern in Tamaqua, which played host to numerous meetings. Also sent to the gallows were Hugh McGehan and Thomas Fisher, both Summit Hill tavernkeepers; Patrick Hester, owner of the Locust Gap Junction tavern; and, most famously, John "Black Jack" Kehoe, owner of The Hibernian House in Girardville, still operated by his greatgrandson. Carroll and McGehan were convicted of the murder of patrolman Yost.

Historian Kevin Kenny notes that, of the alleged "top brass" of the Maguires, these six were all involved in tavernkeeping, which might lead one to the conclusion that their activities were merely criminal and unrelated to labor strife. Kenny establishes that most of the nineteen had close connections to the mining community and that four of the six tavernkeepers had actually been miners. Newspapers covering the trials made much of the fact that Yost's murder had apparently been hatched in Carroll's Columbia House tavern and that saloonkeepers were involved in the plot.

So begins a murky chapter in the American bar's history. Although it's extremely difficult to separate the strands of events in Pennsylvania in the 1870s, it's probable that machine politics had infiltrated the Irish saloons of the era. Yet it's also true that the uprising against inhumane conditions in the mines was legitimate and, in all likelihood, took shape in the drinking establishments in which miners gathered and commiserated after a day's dangerous toil. Corrupt saloon politics and legitimate labor organizations were tarred with the same brush by their adversaries and, in some cases, do seem to have been interrelated.

Add to this the radical politics of the day, namely anarchism, and the picture becomes blurrier. This is especially so since anarchism and the labor movements of the late nineteenth century can seem almost indistinguishable from one another. They share many of the same roots and participants' involvement overlapped. In addition, much of the strife of the era can be traced to hostilities between Protestants and Irish and German Catholics. And everybody frequented urban saloons.

Anarchism and labor movements are philosophically distinct, however. Anarchists were often vehemently opposed to the philosophies of Social-Democrats and other radicals of the day. Anarchism, itself, is a complex and varied philosophical and political movement, which was (and is) open to a wide spectrum of interpretation and debate, even within its own circles. Its major theorists flip-flopped between "adjective-free" anarchism (meaning a rejection of modifiers like "communist anarchist"), individualism, philosophies that bordered on libertarianism, socialism, trade unionism, and strategies that included armed direct action.

Only two things united most of the anarchists. First, they were generally well versed in the writings of Western liberal thought, including that of Thomas Paine and the founding fathers. Second, they were sympathetic to the plight of abused and exploited working poor. That a majority of American anarchists in the late nineteenth century were German did not necessarily make them Marxist, although many would have considered Marx an important thinker. The Boston Tea Party, some of the ideals expressed in the American Constitution, and the eloquent *The Rights of Man*, however, were almost universally admired.

The German Americans of New York and Chicago had brought the tradition of using taverns for politicizing from their homeland, where the tavern was a *lokalfrage*—a safe haven for revolutionary politics and labor organization, particularly after German authorities imposed especially repressive restrictions following an attempted workers' revolt in 1848.[2] In addition, in the New World, most immigrants already frequented the saloon, just as they had in the 1850s. The first stop after Ellis Island had been the saloon, where they found people who spoke the same language and shared common reference points. Often as not, the saloonkeeper himself was instrumental in helping a new arrival with employment and housing, either through making specific arrangements or through an introduction to a network of people.

Necessity turned into habit. Religious leaders and newspaper editors criticized the use of the saloon, framing the association between immigrants and saloons in increasingly racist terms and portraying the relationship between saloonkeeper and immigrant as a predatory one. Many of these critics, however, failed to note the abject poverty and abhorrent conditions most immigrants faced and that they were often exploited in their quest for work and housing. In the vilified saloons, immigrants found something they were unable to find elsewhere—community.

In New York, Chicago, and smaller urban areas, these saloons turned effortlessly from social hubs and employment agencies into political headquarters. Between the marginalization of the immigrant communities, the safe-haven tradition of the tavern in both America and Germany, and the budding activism, symbolized, for example, by German saloonkeepers defying Sunday closing laws, the saloons, almost inevitably, became homes for anarchists.

While working and living conditions were atrocious for the German and Scandinavian immigrants all over America, those in Chicago, which underwent wild growth over the nineteenth century, were among the worst. It's almost impossible to process how Chicago went from a frontier town in the 1830s, when settlers had only barely managed to stake a claim, to its turn-of-the-century population of two million and a city whose underbelly Upton Sinclair would chronicle in his muckraking 1906 book *The Jungle*. As a result, Chicago was a place of contrast and unchecked individualism. The crime, vice and corruption there seemed to have no equal and, by the end of the 1800s, it was considered one of the most dangerous cities in America, surpassed only by New York, which had experienced immigration in almost inconceivable numbers.

In the 1870s, the combination of the Panic and the Great Fire, which, while responsible for only a few hundred deaths, left nearly a hundred thousand homeless and made life intolerable. Many victims of the fire were German and Scandinavian immigrants who lived on the northwest side. Soon after, when starving homeless and their aid workers assembled to protest living conditions in a city where often as much as 50 percent of a worker's income went toward food, the police proved merciless, cornering rioters in a tunnel and clubbing them. The next fifteen years saw further incidents of protest and resulting police brutality and an increased militancy among poor and working-class immigrants. When the Great Railroad Strike began in West Virginia in 1877, Chicago's radicals quickly joined in, effectively bringing the city's business and traffic to a standstill. The front page of the *Tribune* read: "Terrors Reign, The Streets of Chicago Given Over to Howling Mobs of Thieves and Cutthroats."

Later that year, a chapter of the "Society for the Prevention of Crime" (SPC) was established in Chicago, following New York's lead, where the inaugural chapter had been formed under the stewardship of Dr. Howard Crosby, a prominent teacher and minister who became chancellor of the University of the City of New York, later New York University. In Chicago, the chapter was active in the effort to close individual saloons, motivated, in part, by reports that many rioters were, in fact, drunken youths who'd been served in dodgy establishments. Some estimated that as many as thirty thousand underage boys regularly frequented the city's saloons. Community leader Andrew Paxton made "suppression of the sale of liquor to minors" the Society's top priority and took it upon himself to personally inspect Chicago saloons.[3] When he and his team of helpers discovered a violation, they would immediately report it to police who would then charge the saloonkeeper. Paxton believed that his efforts nearly eradicated the problem locally and, within ten years, there were some seven to eight hundred SPC chapters across the country and nearly a hundred thousand adherents. In Boston, SPC members claimed their vigilance was responsible for the closure of over six hundred saloons and the sobering up of some fifteen thousand underage drinkers.

The quelling of riots and shutting of saloons was championed as a victory by Chicago newspapers but, before long, two newspapers were disputing the dominant discourse: Albert Parsons's *The Alarm* and August Spies' *Arbeiter-Zeitung*. These papers were instrumental in getting the word out to Chicagoans about a nationwide strike for an eight-hour day, planned for May 1, 1886. Of the three hundred and forty thousand people in America who walked out of their jobs to protest inhuman conditions, eighty thousand were in Chicago, where, despite alarmist worries, the day was very peaceful. Joined by his wife and children, Parsons led the workers down Michigan Avenue in what amounted to America's largest strike to that point.

Things got more volatile a couple of days later, though. A preexisting labor dispute at the McCormick Reaper Works, a plant run by the notorious union-busting Cyrus H. McCormick, was revisited by those whose spirits had been buoyed at the show of solidarity. The Pinkerton men hired to protect the non-union, replacement workers clashed with the protestors and, in the end, six strikers were killed.

August Spies was incensed. He printed bills urging a mass rally in Haymarket Square for the fourth of May. The flyers turned up in a West Lake Street saloon called Greif's, a regular meeting place for German anarchists, who, it so happened, were planning a meeting for that very evening—perhaps to orchestrate their own response to the day's killings, or perhaps on entirely different business. Greif's was the hottest labor activist site in Chicago, where a number of union leaders congregated. It came out later that the Haymarket planners meeting had been relegated to the basement, since the bar was packed with those discussing the recent Pinkerton clash.[4] Many who were at Greif's that night, despite having nothing to do with plotting the next day's demonstration, wound up implicated in what would be called the "Monday Night Conspiracy," an alleged cabal that plotted the use of dynamite at the rally. There was also supposed to have been a secret meeting held at Liberty Hall, one of many beer halls in the German, Bohemian and Scandinavian neighborhoods that sold beer at a discount to union members. The bombs themselves were said to be at Neff's, yet another beer hall. Between the penchant by activists for using saloons for meetings and the saloons' labor clientele, it wasn't difficult to conclude conspiracy was afoot in the Chicago *lokalfrage*.

For all the planning, things didn't go smoothly at the Haymarket rally. The turnout was decent—some two to three thousand—but no speakers had been lined up. At the last minute, Spies recruited Parsons and socialist Samuel Fielden from a meeting of the American Group faction of the International Working Person's Association. Neither, apparently, had even been aware of the rally until late in the afternoon.

Parsons attempted to rise to the occasion but delivered an uncharacteristically mild speech, urging people to resist the urge for violence. Sensing rain, Parsons kept it short and invited the crowd to join him at Zepf's saloon, the home of the Lumbershovers Union of Chicago, where he was headed with his wife and children. There, he would join comrade Adolph Fischer, who, it seems, had skipped the rally altogether to go drinking.

Over at Haymarket Square, the stage had been left to Fielden and Spies. Fielden was in the middle of his speech—"A million men hold all the property in this country [and the] law has no use for the other fifty-four millions," he thundered, adding that those disenfranchised ought to "lay hands on [the law] and throttle it until it makes its last kick"— when the riot squad moved in. Fielden protested that the assembly was peaceful but the police insisted that he and Spies step down from the podium.

At the very moment they were desisting, somebody launched a bomb into the delegation of police. Between the initial explosion and the ensuing chaos, eight policemen and an unknown number of civilians were killed. In the midst of the mayhem, Spies somehow managed to make his way to Zepf's, where he filled in Parsons and Fischer.

Despite the fact that it would have been physically impossible for Parsons or Fischer, who were raising a glass, or Fielden or Spies, who were on stage, to have actually lobbed the bomb, all four were charged with accessory to murder, along with four others—toystore owner George Engel, bookbinder Michael Schwab, carpenter Louis Lingg, and yeast company owner Oscar Neebe. Fielder, Fischer, and Engel all had the misfortune of having been at Greif's the previous night, and became part of the so-called Monday Night Conspiracy. Fielden was reportedly there on other business and may never even have seen his "co-conspirators."

Neebe was sentenced to fifteen years in prison; the other seven were sentenced to death. Lingg hanged himself in prison before his scheduled execution and Fielden and Schwab had their sentences commuted to life in prison. Spies, Parsons, Fischer, and Engel were hanged on November 11, 1887, after one of the most skewed judicial proceedings of the era.

The jury had consisted exclusively of conservative businessmen, one of whom was a relative of one of the policemen who had been killed. It was soon made clear that, despite the fact that none of the men on trial had anything to do directly with the bomb, they were deemed guilty for having spouted anarchist rhetoric in their newspapers, at rallies and in the saloons. What had been on trial, in fact, was the men's politics. More absurd was the prosecution's case. It didn't contend that the accused had explicitly encouraged the bombing but, rather, that they hadn't *discouraged* Rudolph Schnaubelt, Schwab's brother-in-law, from throwing it (as was suspected). Most scholars dispute the Schnaubelt theory; there is little evidence to review, given that Schnaubelt fled the country and never took the stand.

There was a massive campaign to protest the verdicts. Parsons wrote "An Appeal to the People of America," outlining his case with a fair bit of incredulous sarcasm at the notion that, on the "day of miracles," he managed to be in two places at once—the Haymarket rally and Zepf's saloon, drinking a schooner of beer.

The public was divided. When the sentences were lessened for Fielden and Schwab, many disapproved of the leniency. Labor leaders, social activists, and sympathizers in Chicago and across the country, by contrast, were horrified at the sham justice and the silencing of dissent. More than a half million people attended the funerals of the hanged martyrs, which served to strengthen the resolve of the many who would soon become involved in radical politics. Supporters erected a statue symbolizing corrupt justice crushing a man and August Spies's last words were inscribed into the base: "The day will come when our silence will be more powerful than the voices you are throttling today."

The truth in Spies's prediction soon became apparent. New York saloons were abuzz with fervent revolutionary talk and, according to the *New York Sun*, were "draped in mourning." Doorposts were covered in black muslin and one on Mercer Street had its shroud "interwoven with blood-red cambric." At Frederic Krämer's beer hall, home to the machinists' union, there was a meeting of at least a hundred people in the back room and when anarchist newspaper publisher Johann Most arrived (his office, incidentally, was above a saloon at 167 William Street), the crowd broke into wild applause.

Back in Chicago, police kept a close watch on roughly ten beer halls, including Zepf's, Greif's, Emma Street Hall, Northwestern Hall and Thalia Hall—the latter of which was said to sell "Union Beer"—plus seventeen unnamed saloons where, according to Chicago police captain Michael Schaack, anarchists met "night and day." The captain was particularly incensed by the saloons, whose keepers, he noted, were often the loudest to cry "Anarchy!" Schaack suspected that their motives were more mercenary than political. He maintained that he knew of one saloonkeeper who began his morning with a drink and a toast that consisted of a hope that Captain Schaack would die by the end of day. And at the end of day, he'd close up with a similar ritual, this time pouring himself two drinks and announcing to all present: "I hope I will find Schaack hanging to a lamp-post in the morning when I get up."

Similar toasts were probably taking place all across the country, influencing future anarchists such as Voltairine de Cleyre, who shifted from mere so-called free thinking to anarchism immediately after the Haymarket executions and had her first outright anarchist essay published in 1888. She wasn't alone. Journalist Kate Austin would be moved to champion anarchism after the tragedy, as would labor leader William "Big Bill" Haywood and, most famously, Emma Goldman who, after the execution, "devoured every line on anarchism" she could get. Goldman wrote that she "saw a new world opening before (her)" and called November 11, 1887—the day of the four hangings—her "spiritual" birthday, adding that the day had the "same effect on hundreds, perhaps thousands, of people."[5]

Zepf's Saloon would continue to be home to anarchist meetings for years after the Haymarket tragedy, as would a number of establishments in urban centers across America. The fact that anarchism was increasingly being organized in saloons was not lost on anyone. In fact, in 1887, there was a veritable explosion of attacks that characterized the saloon as "the church of the gospel of anarchy." Retired Senator William Windom from Minnesota wrote in the *Boston Journal* on July 4, "The home and the ballot are the very cornerstones on which our free institutions rest . . . the liquor saloon aims its deadly blows at both." He continued to argue that, without the saloon, the anarchist and socialist would have nowhere to "teach his treason" or "rally his forces."

In addition, many critics were now forging a connection between the saloon and dynamite. Historian Paul Avrich describes how some anarchists were accused of being devotees to a "cult of dynamite," spurred on by the recent Nobel invention, Emile Zola's dynamite-using protagonist in the novel *Germinal,* and the tireless efforts of the aforementioned Johann Most, who, in 1885, published *Revolutionary War Science: A Little*

Handbook of Instruction in the Use and Preparation of Nitroglycerine, Dynamite, Gun-Cotton, Fulminating Mercury, Bombs, Fuses, Poisons, etc., etc. "Dynamost," as he was known, considered bombs a leveling force on an unequal playing field.

Dynamite had been used in a few labor disputes before Haymarket and was associated with the anarchists, many of whom indeed saw it as the revolutionary's natural weapon. Reformers, however, took matters a step further and linked it to the saloon. At the General Christian Conference of the Evangelical Alliance in 1887, Reverend R. S. MacArthur said, "But for the inspiration of hell breathed in the saloon, it is probable that bombs would never have been manufactured, and, if manufactured, would never have been exploded. In the saloon, the seeds are sown which blossom into bombs and ripen into murders." He continued: "Sow atheism and alcoholism, and you reap universal dynamite, national destruction and eternal death." In 1888, commentary from Pontiac, Illinois, resident A. E. Johnston emphasized the foreign nature of the violent anarchist movement and its saloons in a tract in *The American Magazine*: "The citizen-born American is not an anarchist. Anarchy is the product of foreign soil." Johnston went on to describe the (presumably German) immigrant who "lands in Castle Garden, meets a friend, and while tossing off his beer, is instructed to promote the interests of anarchy." New York's Castle Garden, located on the Battery, had been one of the city's most famous beer gardens since the 1820s. Through the connections the immigrant made at the beer hall, Johnston continued, "He secures a position as 'hustler' in a lumber yard at a dollar and a-half a day, spends his evenings in a saloon, wastes his mental energies in brooding, and makes bombs by which he hopes to gain the identical height he so bitterly hates—wealth."

Critics often managed to have it both ways: on the one hand, the anarchists were lazy idlers who sat in the pub wasting time; on the other, they were an industrious hive of conspirators plotting to blow up the nation and undermine its core values. Even when acknowledging the controversial nature of the decision to convict and hang the Haymarket martyrs, critics such as Johnston laid all blame at the saloon's door. It had "created the bombs that gave Haymarket Square a place in history and its subsequent horrors upon the scaffold."

The late-nineteenth-century working-class saloon was unquestionably a step up from many of the urban saloons described thus far—the ones that did without glassware and often featured rat and terrier headliners. It continued to provide welcome relief from substandard housing and grim working conditions but was hardly a paragon of virtue. It rose in response to changes in the workplace, especially the elimination of daytime tippling in factories. At the same time, wages were gradually rising and working hours shortened and standardized. Factory employees began to have fairly regular hours for recreation which, naturally, could be spent making up for all those sober hours spent at the plant. This didn't endear the saloon to businessmen, who increasingly blamed it for workplace accidents and absenteeism on "Blue Mondays." Management felt that hangovers and lunch breaks spent at saloons—remember the "free lunch"—were responsible for decreased productivity.

And since so much of the time spent away from the factory was spent in saloons, it was only natural that they became centers of dissent, rising from workers commiserating over a drink—or two. Even when there wasn't an official union meeting taking place in the saloon's back room, there was a constant airing of grievances in bar-rooms across America. The camaraderie often evolved into political organization. As a small but telling sample, saloon historian Madelon Powers reports that, at one point in the 1890s, sixty-three out of sixty-nine unions in Buffalo, New York, used saloons for their meetings. Furthermore, she notes that, nationwide, 30 percent of the Brotherhood of Boiler Makers and Iron Shipbuilders, 50 percent of the Wood Carver's Association, 70 percent of the Amalgamated Wood Workers, and virtually 100 percent of the United Brewery Workers used saloons for union activity.[6]

Determined to fight the costs of absenteeism and the political dissent stirring in the saloons, some, such as George Pullman, inventor and manufacturer of the railways' luxury sleeping and dining cars, took drastic measures. Pullman once moved all his workers out of Chicago, where temptations lay, and forced them to live and work in his new, dry company town named . . . Pullman, Illinois. There was one option for public drinking in Pullman—the Florence, a high-end hotel with a small pricey bar open only to business travelers. Business travel required drinks, of course, and Pullman was happy to make money off that, both at the Florence and in his saloon cars, which were called "marvels of skill, taste, and ingenuity." The Delmonico dining car, for example, launched in 1868, boasted a proper wine cellar. But Pullman required absolute sobriety from his workers.

Dry towns weren't novel. Many municipalities had exercised the "local option" to prohibit the sale of alcohol over the second half of the nineteenth century. Utopian dry towns were established during the strongest surges of the temperance movement. Harriman, Tennessee, for example, was founded in 1890 by a group that included National Prohibition Party candidate Clinton Fisk with the express goal of creating an alcohol-free community. The American Temperance University was founded there soon after, attracting students from around the country wishing to get a degree in Temperance Studies.

Company towns weren't Pullman's brainchild. In England, the Cadbury brothers, dissatisfied with their employees' living conditions in Birmingham, established Bournville, a factory town that was also dry. The main impetus for the town was deeply paternalistic—to improve workers' lives and get them out of cramped and unhygienic urban housing. Several more British factory towns were developed in the late 1800s; even Guinness considered establishing one (although presumably that one wouldn't have been dry).

When the company town made its way to America, many adopted the heavy-handed paternalism but neglected to actually improve living circumstances. Pullman, for instance, may have built better housing for his employees but failed to make it affordable. After the Panic of 1893, Pullman's company hit hard times and passed the hardship on to employees, slashing wages yet continuing to charge exorbitant rents. In May 1894, several worker representatives presented a complaint to management, outlining how the workers were being squeezed at both ends. Organizing even at this rudimentary level was a feat in Pullman where, in addition to saloons, newspapers, public meetings and speeches were also prohibited.

The worker reps were immediately fired, which led to one of the worst strikes in American history. When Pullman workers headed for the pickets, employees of the American Railways Union, under the stewardship of Eugene V. Debs, expressed solidarity by refusing to handle Pullman cars until the company settled the dispute. Both sides dug in and worked to control media and public opinion. On July 9, 1894, the *New York Times* reported that clergymen were denouncing Debs as a "dangerous demagogue" who was holding the railways and the public hostage in a time of economic crisis. Four days later, New York Methodist minister and antisaloonist Reverend Dr. John A. B. Wilson gave a sermon in which he explained how Pullman was paying the workers the best wage it could possibly afford—any less and everybody would be out of work. He also accused Debs of being power-hungry. "What is behind all of this?" Reverend Wilson asked. "It is the will of Eugene V. Debs, son of a saloon keeper, a man reared and educated upon the proceeds of human ruin." Wilson went on to characterize the new leadership of the unions as "saloon-trained men of the Debs pattern" and lamented the fact that, "when the wicked bear rule, the people mourn." Apparently, Wilson hadn't wanted the fact that Debs' father was not a saloon-owner at all but, rather, the owner of a meat market and a textile mill, to get in the way of a good sermon.

Not that Wilson was entirely off the mark, though. Debs had gained some of his admiration for the working man in the saloons of his youth, where he had listened to men who worked the railroads exchange their stories. This, of course, was an easy shot. If you looked at any labor movement closely enough, it would almost certainly have a connection to a saloon somewhere. As journalist and labor sympathizer Hutchins Hapgood would later write, the saloon was the "principal place in which ideas underlying the labor movement originate, or at any rate become consciously held . . . It is there where men talk over, think, and exchange feelings and ideas relating to their labor and their lives."[7]

The strike would turn out to be a life-changing one for Debs, given that President Grover Cleveland interfered on behalf of management and sent in armed forces to get the trains running again. Debs was arrested for interfering with the delivery of the federal mail and wound up being represented by Clarence Darrow, who'd started out as a lawyer for the railroad company but "crossed the tracks" and quit his corporate job to defend Debs's right to organize a strike. Although they lost the case, this would mark the beginning of two remarkable careers—Darrow as a defender of civil liberties and Debs, who would read Karl Marx in prison and reorient his politics from labor to "red."

There was at least one positive outcome, namely, that the town of Pullman was deemed un-American by the Supreme Court of Illinois in 1898, the year after George Pullman's death. The company was ordered to sell off its interests in the town and open up to free-market competition.

All the same, the saloon would continue to be associated with radicals and reform movements and, increasingly, antisaloonists were quick to connect the dots between violent incidents and barrooms. In a diatribe against the saloon published in 1905, Boston University sociologist and theologian John Marshall Barker would write that "the history of the great Hay Market Riot in Chicago and the mob violence in Cincinnati, Pittsburgh and other cities, show conclusively that the saloons were the headquarters of the plots and schemes of the leaders."[8]

At least Barker applied his argument evenly to all saloon patrons, and not simply to foreign radicals. The Cincinnati incident was a reference to the 1884 courthouse riots that were sparked by the trial of William Berner and Joe Palmer, a German-American and a mulatto, respectively. The defendants were accused of beating their employer to death on Christmas Eve 1883. When a jury returned a verdict of manslaughter rather than first-degree murder in this high-profile case, Cincinnati citizens were outraged. A rumor spread through the saloons of an area on Upper Vine Street that their defense attorney, a Democrat, had bribed the jury with a view to courting the black vote. Two thousand men took to the streets and attacked the courthouse, intending to lynch the accused. The prisoners had already been whisked off to Columbus by prescient authorities, but the riots that ensued, nevertheless, lasted for two days and resulted in a hundred deaths.

As for the Pittsburgh riots, those were overtly political. These were the Homestead Riots of 1892, in which Pinkerton security forces hired by management clashed with striking steel workers at Andrew Carnegie's mill. The union had been locked out by manager Henry Clay Frick, who had been aiming for nothing less than the total destruction of the laborers' organization. When the union asked for a pay increase, Frick countered with a proposed wage cut by nearly a quarter and a number of other concessions. Homestead was a landmark event, representing the first modern strike in the sense that the union had clear goals and demands and was exceptionally well organized. Strikers had shut down the plant with twenty-four-hour pickets and barred access by both land and water, using boats on the Monongahela River. Vigilant patrol of the river was key to keeping the plant closed and, when Frick advertised for non-union labor to reopen the plant, he hired three hundred Pinkertons to ensure that the "scabs" he had hired could cross the line, by barge off the Monongahela, at four in the morning. The strikers had been tipped off and the barge never got to unload.

The standoff between the Pinkertons and the strikers, who soon numbered five thousand and had broad local support, was long and violent with several on both sides killed. The strikers eventually managed to force Frick's security officers to surrender. Unfortunately, the taste for violence got the better of some union members and when it was learned that several Pinkertons were clubbed and beaten *after* their surrender, public support for the strikers began to wane.

John Barker's allegation that the violence was generated in saloons is hard to corroborate. Early union activity and organization almost certainly originated there, but strike leaders had actually solicited the support of tavern- and saloon-owners by asking them to limit excessive drinking during their action. Then again, there were certainly also some owners present at the riots, with one, Mother Finch, achieving a little notoriety. Finch owned the Rolling Mill House and was out "standing guard" with her "black-jack" a full two days before the Pinkertons even came to Homestead. When the attempt at the barge landing of scabs and the reopening of the mill took place, the "white-haired old beldam," as the *New York Herald* put it, took to the streets along with throngs of people—many of them women—"brandishing the hand billy she always kept around the house for just such emergencies."[9] This hardly seems enough to place the blame for the violence on Homestead saloon-keepers, but Barker may have been referring to the final act of violence attached to Homestead—the attempted assassination of Henry Clay Frick, who many called "the most hated man in America."

While much of the public stopped supporting the union after the violence, many still blamed the security forces for the escalation, as well as the deaths of ten striking workers. Frick became the focus of that blame, not helped by the fact that he apparently had as much personality as a steel rod. Although he hailed from a Western Pennsylvania family of distillers, Frick didn't seem to have inherited any of the rebelliousness that characterized so many of the men and women who worked in the whiskey business along the Monongahela.

Frick's grandfather, Abraham Overholt, had been the first distiller of Old Overholt rye whiskey, a concern he had started not long after the repeal of the whiskey tax in 1803. Unlike many of the area's rebels, however, Overholt managed to turn his operation into a major commercial enterprise. As a young man, Frick worked for the family while studying business and preparing for world domination—or, at least, that of Western Pennsylvania. He was unrelentingly hard-working, rejecting idle entertainments and socializing. No tavern-loafer was he.

Frick amassed wealth at a staggering pace, continuing to grow the distillery but also branching out into a new business, coke, the fuel derived from coal. Frick's coke business was eventually acquired by steel magnate Andrew Carnegie and, as part of the buy, Frick negotiated a deal to become chairman of Carnegie's company. This was a good bit of luck for Carnegie, a generous philanthropist who publicly supported workers' rights to collectively bargain through a union but who needed a fall guy to bust up those same unions to keep the industry profitable. With Frick absorbing most of the bad publicity, Carnegie generally managed to hold onto his image as a thoughtful, self-made benefactor.

Frick, then, became a lightning rod and a special target in radical circles, many of which were meeting in urban saloons. In one of the main gathering places for German anarchists in New York, Alexander Berkman, Emma Goldman, and colleagues were discussing the horrific events at Homestead and the media's biased account of the affair—perhaps even referring to the *New York Herald*'s characterization of Mother Finch as a "beldam"—when Goldman suggested they blow up the newspaper offices. Berkman dismissed this, suggesting that, instead, they strike at the root of the problem, namely Henry Clay Frick. Berkman was no idle talker. Three weeks after the Homestead riots, Berkman gained access to Frick's office and shot at him, hitting him twice and stabbing him in the leg as well. A carpenter working in a nearby office managed to save Frick by hitting Berkman in the head with a hammer. Frick was back at the office in a week; Berkman was sentenced to twenty-two years in prison.

The anarchist saloon scene in New York may have been slightly less active than in Chicago but it was nonetheless a seriously radical landscape. German saloons all over Brooklyn, Staten Island, Queens, Newark, the Bronx, the Upper East Side neighborhood of Yorkville, and the Lower East Side, were rife with heated political debate and plans of action. In part, the saloons became politicized, as we've seen, because many recent German immigrants had little or no adequate private space in tenements and therefore spent the precious few evenings and days off they had in the beer gardens and saloons, commiserating and talking politics. This was not unlike any of the other political movements that were birthed in bars. The saloon, however, was particularly suited to anarchism, since anarchism was, in part, a rejection of mainstream politics.

Saloon historian Tom Goyens has argued that traditional political organizational structures were "anathema to the anarchist movement" and that adherents prized community organization and decision making. For many, in fact, it was the foundation of their philosophy, evidenced by the constant meetings in anarchist communities. It was not uncommon for activists such as Alexander Parsons to be committed to speak at two different meetings at once. The two hundred anarchist saloons and beer halls in the New York City area embodied an idealized vision of social anarchism—a "decentralized network" of centers for communal discussion and nonhierarchical decision making. Anarchists of all shades consistently warned against consolidation of power in any institution. And, since anarchism was partially defined as small communities of people who supported each others' endeavors, denizens of the saloon were, in a sense, practicing and living anarchism at each meeting—formal or informal. Goyens refers to the saloons as "islands of anarchism" where the dissidents' political philosophies were both "lived" and "expressed."[10]

Furthermore, throughout the end of the nineteenth century, as Goyens points out, the small-scale brewing and serving of "craft beer" was a vanishing Bohemian art in an age when saloons were increasingly becoming mere fronts for major breweries. In fact, many seemingly independent saloons were essentially merely franchise outlets—and the saloonkeepers desperate franchisees. Not so for saloons like Justus Schwab's on First Street, which became the center for radical dissent in New York by the early 1890s. When Emma Goldman was released from a one-year stint in prison for inciting to riot in 1894, comrades gathered at Schwab's to welcome her. It would be her first stop and she entered through the same door as the men. Schwab's was one of the very few places in New York that would allow that—women coming through the front door and stepping into the barroom to drink and mingle with the men. Journalist Nellie Bly noted this anomaly when she visited the saloon, pointing out that Schwab's was further distinguished from its competitors by the absence of a free lunch counter.

Although Bly didn't mention it, Schwab's also had paintings of scenes from the French Revolution, portraits of revolutionaries, and a sizeable collection of books. Many anarchist saloons doubled as lending libraries, just as the Revolutionary-era taverns had. Along with recreation and artistic endeavor, radicals encouraged one another to read everything from the classics to modern political tracts published by people such as Spies, Parsons, and Most. Saloons also doubled as distribution centers for theater handbills, periodicals and alternative newspapers. Chicago police captain Schaack had once complained that saloonkeepers always "looked to it, first thing in the morning, that plenty of Anarchist literature and a dozen or so copies of the *Arbeiter-Zeitung* were duly on the tables of their places, and in some saloons, beer-bloated bums, who could manage to read fairly, were engaged to read aloud such articles as were particularly calculated to stir up the passions of the benighted patrons."[11]

With over six hundred volumes, Schwab's was a particularly well-endowed lending library. Goldman credited her familiarity with American writers such as Whitman, Emerson, Thoreau, and Hawthorne to Schwab, who extended her lending privileges by having books delivered to her in prison. Anarchists typically took a broad view of education, indicated by both the books and their homage to great writers. There was a bust of Shakespeare in Schwab's near the portraits of other revolutionaries.

When anarchists first began making the papers in the 1880s, they were generally considered a small, albeit highly undesirable, element of modern urban society. They were perceived as marginal and not likely to effect any major changes. Mainstream papers such as the *Chicago Tribune* considered Schwab and his ilk nuisances that had to be endured, thanks to the First Amendment. In 1881, the *Tribune* ran this editorial aside after an interview with "American Communist" Justus Schwab: "He may sit in his saloon among his frowsy followers and bark as loudly and as long as he pleases, but if he ever attempts to bite he will suffer the fate of a mangy cur." Fifteen years later, by the time of Goldman's release—post-Haymarket, post-Homestead—Schwab's could no longer be so easily dismissed; it would be known as a "headquarters of international infamies."

Schwab's was nothing if not politically cosmopolitan. Unlike many anarchist saloons, which were loosely segregated between different immigrant groups, Schwab's back room was notable for being, in Goldman's words, "A Mecca for French Communards, Spanish and Italian refugees, Russian politicals, and German socialists and anarchists." Schwab intended the bar to be a haven for outcasts of all sorts, many of whom were drawn to the tall, broad-chested, red-headed, jovial, and charismatic Schwab, whom Goldman described as having a "deep and tender" voice. He was known to sing frequently (notably *La Marseillaise*) in his bar, in concert with other patrons and members of the International Workers' Choral Society, which, Goyens points out, was the "best-known anarchist singing society."

Goldman dropped by Schwab's fairly regularly—almost every weekend when she wasn't lecturing. There, she'd converse and celebrate with

Schwab and lock horns with others, such as James Huneker, literary and music critic and one of a handful of writers, including John Swinton and Ambrose Bierce, who made Schwab's their regular watering hole. The proprietor had the remarkable ability to create an atmosphere in which all were welcome, especially those considered exiles from mainstream society. When Schwab died in December 1900, the *New York Times* ran an article on the funeral with the subhead, "Anarchists Forget Their Differences At His Funeral"—since the entire radical subculture attended, even those who had disagreed with him. Johann Most, who had argued with Schwab about almost everything, "gave way to his grief completely several times," and "bitter enemies" of Schwab's "cried like children." Goldman, it was reported, remained composed.

Goldman's stoic self-control would serve her well over the years, especially in Chicago in 1901, when she was facing persecution for crimes to which she had not, in any way, been connected. She held her own while in the Cook County jail—the same place in which the Haymarket martyrs had been held—on charges of conspiracy to murder in the assassination of President William McKinley. Her alleged coconspirator was Leon Czolgosz, who, it turned out, had no official affiliation with the anarchists but, in what was perhaps a capricious whim in a moment of disillusionment with his own Republican party, had started to become quite taken with the idea of anarchism. He had approached Goldman after one of her speeches and, it seems, on one other occasion, but that was the extent of their relationship. In fact, although she only met him briefly, Goldman was uneasy about Czolgosz. He seemed to know absolutely nothing about anarchist philosophy and was asking about meeting places and plans for violent action. Some thought he was a spy but, in all likelihood, Czolgosz, Michigan-born and probably of Polish descent, had been infatuated by the idea of assassination after the sensational killing of Italy's King Umberto by Italian American anarchist Gaetano Bresci.

On September 6, 1901, when McKinley was attending a Pan-American Exposition in Buffalo, Czolgosz managed to shoot the president twice before being apprehended by the crowd. McKinley died eight days later; less than two months after that, Czolgosz was electrocuted in the chair.

During the trial, many had been quick to make the connection between Czolgosz, anarchism, Goldman, and saloons, even though the associations were nearly all in the assassin's mind. Even after it had been shown that Czolgosz had been turned away from anarchist meetings, critics continued to try to make an association between Czolgosz and the saloon. John Marshall Barker said that he was "a product of the saloon," and had "received his early education in his father's saloon." Barker was taking a bit of a liberty; although Polish radicals *did* meet in his father's bar, Leon was already twenty-two years old when his father bought it.

The saloon's evil influence on Czolgosz continued, argued Barker, right up to the eve of McKinley's assassination and "for three days preceding his deed of violence, made his home a saloon in Buffalo." Czolgosz had indeed checked into John Nowak's saloon on Broadway in Buffalo, a "hotel" which probably only had rooms as a result of the Raines Law, a statute established in New York State in 1896 which limited legal Sunday drinking to hotels. As a result, many "Raines Hotels" immediately came into being, with saloonkeepers dividing their space into small drinking "closets," which were called "guest rooms." The legislation quickly turned into a farce and had the unintended consequence of providing more convenient spaces for solicitation and prostitution. Nonetheless, Barker continued his assault with a reference to Charles Guiteau, James Garfield's assassin, who had spent time in a saloon and been emboldened by heavy drink on the day he shot the president in 1881. Since Guiteau was known to be a moderate drinker, more damning was Barker's allegation that anarchists toasted Leon Czolgosz's actions in saloons across the country as news reached them that McKinley had been shot.

Barker wasn't the only one drawing the connection. In 1902, the first book-length tract denouncing the saloon and its ties to anarchy was released, partly in response to the McKinley assassination—*The Saloon and Anarchy, the Two Worst Things in the World, Versus the United States of America* by Hugh Vaughan Crozier. The hysteria surrounding immigrant saloons was mounting in all parts of America and, in many places, this led to increased surveillance and even crackdowns, especially on bars frequented by Germans and Eastern Europeans. In Portland, Oregon, the White Eagle, a Polish saloon, was raided by the Secret Service on the grounds that it was home to a conspiracy to assassinate McKinley's successor, Theodore Roosevelt. Archivists have since uncovered documents from these "secret radical meetings" in Portland and, it turns out, they involved plans for the construction of a Polish-speaking Catholic church.[12]

In truth, though, most saloons were not—or not only—making plans for churches. And antisaloonists such as Wilson, Barker, and Crozier generally had the facts on their side when they argued that saloons had become almost inextricably linked to labor and anarchist politics. This, however, was only half of the picture. Reformers were still battling machine politics, which were also housed in saloons and which had become more corrupt and powerful than ever. Between the machines and the racial politics being played out in saloons throughout the south, reformers were going to get all the ammunition they needed to effect the most radical legislation since the Civil War—Prohibition.

10

THE
MACHINE
POLITICIAN
GETS
BEHIND
THE BAR

THE VOTING-PLACE, NO. 488 PEARL STREET, IN THE SIXTH WARD, NEW YORK CITY.

THE VOTING PLACE, 1858

The Political Machine is dependent on the saloon,
as indicated by this cartoon depicting a saloon
located at 488 Pearl in the Sixth Ward. Image
donated by Corbis.

When campaigning to represent New York in the Albany state legislature in 1881, Theodore Roosevelt was taken around by his handlers to meet some influential New Yorkers. One of the first stops was a German saloon on Sixth Avenue, where saloonkeeper Carl Fischer complained to the young politician about the cost of license fees. Fischer suggested that, in exchange for his support, Roosevelt might see what he could do about an amendment to the law. Roosevelt countered with his opinion that saloon license fees weren't nearly high enough.[1]

Roosevelt somehow managed to forge a successful political career in New York, despite his candor and his unwillingness to play saloon politics. But he was one of the few—Republican or Democrat—to do that. By the 1890s, both parties were firmly entrenched in the back rooms in nearly every municipality and county that didn't reside in a dry state, or hadn't voted itself dry via "local option"—and some that had. And, since the level of corruption only escalated with the consolidation of power, nineteenth-century political practices made the Boston Caucus look like a bunch of choirboys and Captain Isaiah Rynders look like an amateur thug. Doctor of Divinity Daniel Dorchester warned in his sermons that the "fountain-head of justice is sometimes submissive to 'the gang' and roughs are discharged because they 'stand well' with 'the boss,' usually a saloon-keeper."[2] There's no question about the veracity of Dorchester's claim. Ruffians and saloonists still ruled.

Not only in New York, either. In San Francisco, "Blind Boss" Buckley's Alhambra Saloon was known as Buckley's City Hall. Thirteen of Milwaukee's forty-six-seat council in 1902 were saloonkeepers. In 1904 in St. Louis, it was said that an aldermen's meeting emptied in a stampede when a prankster yelled out, "Mister, your saloon is on fire!"[3] And in Boston, Patrick Joseph Kennedy would become one of the city's most influential ward bosses, consolidating his power as everyone else did—with the saloon. Kennedy, a teetotaler (and whose son Joseph Patrick would, one day, father Jack, Bobby, and Ted), bought his first saloon in Haymarket Square at the age of twenty-two. In short order, he was at least part-owner of two more on the east side of Boston—one by the docks on Border Street and another in the Maverick House, a high-class hotel in a much better neighborhood. By the time Kennedy officially went into politics, he had a good handle on his constituents—at all socioeconomic levels.

Chicago's political scene was one of the more extreme—a reflection of the city's wild social contrasts and income disparities. On Clark Street near City Hall, Michael Cassius McDonald ran a sordid "resort," catering to politicians—the foundation of a small empire. His four-story saloon and gambling hall was known as the "Old Store" and had a reputation for rigged tables and a proliferation of confidence men working for the house. Although "there's a sucker born every minute" is often attributed to P. T. Barnum, among others, many claim that it was actually McDonald who invented and popularized the phrase. (Same thing for "never give a sucker an even break.") McDonald would parlay his saloon into a real estate empire and, by the end of his life, was said to be worth between two and three million dollars (roughly the equivalent of fifty million dollars today).

"King Mike" established himself as a major political force in 1873 when Democrat Henry Colvin was elected mayor of Chicago. Other than a brief blip, "Mike McDonald's Democrats" remained in office until 1887. Herbert Asbury wrote that McDonald "named the men who were to be candidates for election," got them elected, and then controlled City Hall, since those in office were "merely his puppets." McDonald was Chicago's most powerful crime and political boss until his 1907 death, which, some thought, had been brought on prematurely by his young wife Flora's arrest for murder earlier that year. Flora would be acquitted of the murder of Walter Guerin, her lover who was apparently black-mailing her.[4]

Chicago's reputation as a wild town in the late nineteenth century was well deserved. Historian George Ade said that, when "a drink parlor was opened anywhere in the loop, the proprietor went over and threw the key into the lake," since nearly every saloon in Chicago was open twenty-four hours. A certain "Mushmouth" Johnson apparently opened a place on State Street that was never closed, even for a minute, until it was shuttered in 1907. Mushmouth's joint was the heart of "Whiskey Row," home to bars owned and patronized by gamblers, petty thieves, con men, and political saloon-owners such as Al Connolly, the perennial Democratic Committeeman. There was also Michael "Hinky Dink" Kenna and his partner "Bath-house" John Coughlin, who owned a bar called the Workingman's Exchange, which contributed to the Irish-Democrat stranglehold over the laboring poor. Lansing and McGarigle's "Round Bar" on Clark Street, operated by a duo hailing from the Chicago police force, Edward Lansing and William J. McGarigle (the latter had risen as high as General Superintendent before venturing into barkeeping) was a legendary political hangout. Raymond Calkins, saloon chronicler,

Harvard faculty member and author of the book *Substitutes for the Saloon* (1901), wrote that one Chicago saloon was referred to by all as the "Democratic Headquarters of the Eighteenth Ward" and crowded with "members of the political fraternity," especially around election time. And, although Calkins—part of the "Committee of Fifty," a self-appointed taskforce of doctors and professors that established itself in 1893 with a view to examine alcohol in America through an impartial lens—was looking for alternatives to the proliferation of the saloon, he noted that the men who hung out at "Headquarters" were educated in a "practical if not academic" sense and had "real insight into the cause of present evils, even if the remedies they propose are wide of the mark." Calkins also acknowledged that the saloonkeeper provided real services to their constituents, such as employment, legal and charitable help. Bosses gave the needy turkeys at Thanksgiving and Christmas and tickets to baseball games or dances and, on occasion, even helped out with funeral costs.[5]

It also helped that the boss of the ward typically hung out at the bar with constituents and was willing to stand a round or two. Sociologist Robert A. Woods observed that the boss would often stop in and relay a little political gossip from downtown. If the "racy, pugilistic talk" were "washed down with a drink," it made the boss "a good fellow, 'one of our kind.'" Some ward bosses had arrangements with bartenders so that they could appear to be drinking even when they weren't. Saloon patrons would hardly have trusted a teetotaler to represent their interests in office. To not drink with one's fellows would have violated an unwritten bar code, developed over two hundred years of toasting and treating. In any case, turning up to see one's constituents at the saloon was an integral part of keeping up the relationship.[6]

A boss feigning to drink with the boys became a fairly well-known trope and was parodied by Finley Peter Dunne in his "Mr. Dooley" articles in the *Chicago Post* during the 1890s. Dooley was a semifictional, Irish American saloonkeeper modeled after James McGarry, whose Dearborn Street saloon catered to politicians, journalists, and high-level public officials, including Police Chief John Shea. Unlike the sober politicians he served, McGarry was known for taking a swig and becoming "unusually oracular." Dooley, one of Roosevelt's favorite writers, claimed that politicians "pretended a vice if they had it not." He continued that a "politician was a baten man if th' story went around that he was seldom dhrunk in public." One politician "always ordered gin 'an I always give him wather" and "Sinitor O'Brien . . . used to dump th' stuff on th' flure whin no wan was lookin' an go home with a light foot while I swept out his constitooents."

In 1890, there were nine saloonkeepers on the Board of Aldermen in Chicago. In New York, eleven of twenty-four elected were saloonists, including Timothy "Dry Dollar" Sullivan, Charles Francis Murphy and "Big Tom" Foley.[7] Corruption had long been institutionalized in New York, ever since the Tammany Hall machine established its grip in the early days of the Republic with the election of Aaron Burr. By the 1880s, however, its power was nearly absolute. Destitute New York immigrants had always counted on Tammanites' social welfare for emergency provisions in times of hardship and employment leads—much of which was doled out through the saloons. Theodore Roosevelt would sum this process up in his 1906 postscript to his 1901 book on New York, in which he described the role of the district leaders, who "try to get them work when they are idle; they provide amusement for them in the shape of picnics and steamboat excursions; and, in exceptional cases, they care for them when suffering from want or sickness; and they are always ready to help them when they have fallen into trouble with the representatives of the law." Roosevelt conceded that many of those helped by Tammany saloonkeepers were "fairly decent men," but decried the vast numbers of "semi-criminals" who came from the "poorest" and most "ignorant" classes of New Yorkers.[8]

Scandals such as the "Boodle Board" affair, in which businessman Jake Sharp paid the New York Board of Aldermen to secure a Broadway railway franchise, were rampant. This type of corruption was also conducted in a cavalier fashion by aldermen like Patrick Farley, who, according to the *New York Times*, was the most "picturesque saloon-keeper" of the Bowery. Farley's also had a reputation for being the Bowery's "cleanest place" and he won the hearts of New Yorkers by employing Joe Brady, the city's most popular bartender, for some thirty-three years. Simultaneously, though, Farley's was the "council room of the most powerful politicians of the east side." There, New York representative Tim Campbell—known for having famously asked Grover Cleveland, "What's the Constitution between friends?"—schemed with Democratic cronies for graft opportunities to maintain their political and economic stronghold on the city. Jacob Riis, the writer and photographer who chronicled the poverty of the tenements in his groundbreaking, muckraking photo essay and diatribe, *How the Other Half Lives*, pointed out that the "successive Boards of Aldermen" were "composed in a measure, if not a majority, of dive-keepers." The term "dive," incidentally, a relatively new term in the lexicon of drinking terminology, surfaced in the early 1870s and referred to disreputable basement bars into which a patron could dive quickly, sight unseen. Riis argued that the Aldermen had given the city a taste of what he called "rum politics," taking aim at the saloon's role in the systemic poverty and dysfunction of New York. He counted 4,065 saloons below Fourteenth Street, compared with three places of worship. The saying, "Where God builds a church the devil builds next door—a saloon," Riis wrote, "had lost its point in New York."

As much as Riis despised the saloon's role, however, he knew that larger forces were to blame. In most tenement neighborhoods, the saloon was the "one bright and cheery and humanly decent spot to be found." Riis was not alone in understanding that, while the saloon represented the first step toward eternal damnation to the reformers, it also represented earthly salvation and charity to its patrons. Nobel Peace Prize winner and Settlement House founder Jane Addams noted in *The Subtle Problems of Charity* that missionary workers arrived at the doors of households full of platitudes, including a firm belief in the "horrors of the saloon." Workers would then be shocked to discover that the head of the family they were visiting shared no such feelings. Instead, he knew the saloon very well, and did "not connect with the 'horrors' at all." He remembered "all the kindnesses he has received there, the free lunch and treating which goes on, even when a man is out of work and not able to pay up." Addams knew that the most destitute found refuge in a saloon, not only to seek fellow patrons who spread cheer around, but also the keeper, who, in his capacity as the poor man's banker, was often good for a small loan. She noted that, while the charity worker's beneficiary might listen without comment to references of saloon "horrors," he would often consider it merely "temperance talk."[9]

Where as Addams was nearly sympathetic to saloon charity, Riis argued that the brief respite from misery that saloons provided and the short-term charitable gifts bestowed by Tammany Hall—often through the saloonkeeper—were essentially bribes to keep the constituency loyal to a machine that would never implement any real long-term reform. "The rum-shop turns the political crank in New York," posited Riis, who argued that machine politics operated through the saloon subverted democracy. Of the many telling statistics that can be found to support

Riis's claim, fully one-third of Greenwich Village saloon owners pursued a political career during that era.[10]

As a pioneering muckraker, Riis inspired people to demand reform. His photographs helped move New Yorkers to action, and attempts to improve living conditions in the tenements and clean up city politics were begun. One of the more striking reform measures was the Lexow Committee, an inquiry into New York City's corruption headed up by the state senate. A key target was Alexander S. Williams, a police captain who had also picked up the charming monikers of "Clubber Williams" and the "Czar of the Tenderloin"—the neighborhood of New York from 23rd to 42nd Streets and between 5th and 7th Avenues. Williams was infamous for profiting from the gambling and prostitution in what was the most notorious district in New York in the late 1800s. He was also credited with christening the red light area the "Tenderloin" when interviewed by a reporter for the *New York Sun* about his new precinct. "I have been living on rump steak in the Fourth Precinct," he responded, "I will have some tenderloin now."

The article was used against him at the Lexow hearings, where he played the naïf—rather unconvincingly. When asked to clarify his rump steak statement, he responded that it was due to the "better saloons" and "better hotels" and the fact that they "don't charge very high prices there." When asked how he had managed to accumulate his property— a country house and a yacht, among other things—he claimed that he had made some savvy investments in Japanese real estate. Ultimately, Williams was forced to retire early in a compromise settlement negotiated by reforming New York State assemblyman Theodore Roosevelt.

The fact that the Democrats had nearly perfected rum politics hardly meant that all Republicans were sober reformers who abstained from "swilling the planters with bumbo." As Herbert Asbury points out in his history of Prohibition, *The Great Illusion*, both Republicans and Democrats were electioneering in saloons and neither party took pains to hide this relationship: "Sometimes, indeed, they seemed to flaunt it, as in 1884, when six hundred and thirty-three out of the one thousand and two party conventions and primaries were held in saloons."

Corruption had become firmly institutionalized and mixing politics with alcohol was the norm at almost every level of office. The term "lobbying," in fact, was even said to have come from the Willard Hotel in Washington, where Ulysses S. Grant could often be found in the lobby, drinking, smoking, and willing to entertain political requests. This is another false etymology, but still speaks to the persistent connection between politicking and drinking. Contemporary accounts indicate that cocktails and politics were aligned at a slightly lower level of government, too. Writing for the *Atlantic Monthly* in 1873, Virginia-born diplomat A. S. Nadal accused higher-ups in the Texas government of discussing politics over "slings and cocktails, with knives and revolvers half-hidden in their belts." The following year, writer and diplomat Albert Rhodes charged those who were supposed to be in opposing political camps with "later clinking glasses over oyster stew." In Sacramento, politicians apparently didn't even wait for the end of the session to adjourn to a saloon and, according to J. Ross Browne, writing in *Harper's New Monthly Magazine* in 1861, during sittings of the legislature, "measures of the most vital importance are first introduced in rum-cocktails, then steeped in whisky, after which they are engrossed in gin for a third reading."

The veneer of charm that coated the marriage between drinking and politics at the higher levels was not applied to that at lower levels. Saloon opponents often ignored the refined drinking of congressmen and mayors but lambasted the practice when it took place in working-class, ethnic, and, perhaps worst of all, black saloons.

In some circles during the latter half of the nineteenth century, the Irish and Germans were arguably more despised than anyone. By the beginning of the twentieth century, however, some of that hatred was being re-directed toward black communities, thanks, in part, to a reimagining of Irish drinking. Increasingly, Patrick O'Gutter was no longer regarded a menace but, instead, as a harmless and occasionally even charming drunk. Figures such as Mr. Dooley helped soften the image of the Irishman as did reams of literature and stage plays which depicted him as a hopeless and hapless drinker—a stereotype that eclipsed most of the previous associations with criminality.[11]

The redirected racist animosity turned to others as well. In Illinois, Ohio, and Pennsylvania, millions of Slavs and other Eastern European immigrants who came and worked in coal mines and industrial sweatshops, were also being vilified, and their saloons, therefore, were soon deemed some of the most degenerate in America. The main protagonist of Upton Sinclair's *The Jungle* is a Lithuanian who initially finds warmth and "more food and better food than he could buy in any restaurant for the same money" in the local saloon, as well as "a drink in the bargain to warm him up." And the Chinese suffered an even lower status than blacks (Judge Roy Bean certainly thought so) throughout the late 1800s and early 1900s, though little of the blame for their horrific treatment can be placed at the saloon's door. Chinese immigrants were associated with different vices, namely prostitution and opium.

Black Americans—specifically those who frequented saloons—were increasingly identified as a problem after the Civil War. Concern built gradually, eventually hitting a fevered pitch in the South in the early twentieth century.

Even if segregation wasn't yet the law, in the majority of the saloons in the South and the West it was commonly the practice. The previously mentioned White Elephant saloons were merely an articulation of the whites-only policy in force nearly everywhere. In response to the dearth of hospitality in white saloons, black saloons sprung up to fill the void. Not every urban area—South or North—was segregated into black and white neighborhoods, at least not until after an intense flurry of Jim Crow laws was enacted around the turn of the century. In San Francisco, for example, black-owned saloons and gambling resorts were scattered throughout the city. Indeed, there was greater demographic diversity in most urban areas in the nineteenth century than there would be in the century to come. In some cities, though—Denver, for one—neighborhoods with concentrations of black-owned saloons were emerging.

Saloon historian Thomas Jacob Noel describes the "Deep South" of Denver (near today's Coors Field), a row of black-owned and frequented saloons. One on Larimer Street was informally known as the "G.A.R." (the "Great African Resort") and, when it came out at the trial of a particularly notorious criminal that he frequented the G.A.R., the prosecutor argued it would be best to "hang every man that ever entered" the place. The prosecutor couldn't manage this, but he did secure the execution of this one defendant. After the hanging, the media portrayed black bars as "promoters of defiance and violence."[12]

The means by which people were beginning to distinguish white from black drinking establishments becomes clear when we consider the White Elephant Saloon, located just outside the Hell's Half-Acre district of Fort Worth, Texas. The Elephant didn't allow prostitution, stocked high-end liquors, and reputedly boasted the area's best free lunch. It was also the town's gambling center—poker, faro (another card game, generally a con), and/or some illegal cockfighting. Although it was the classiest saloon in the city and violence was uncommon, it is still remembered for one legendary gunfight, in which saloon-owner Luke Short annihilated ex-marshal Jim Courtright with at least five bullets.[13]

On the other side of the tracks in Fort Worth was the Black Elephant and, while it's not clear what exactly might have gone on there, a local historian once cautioned that if you went in, "you were going to hell."[14]

Jim Crow laws, which bestowed black Americans with that so-called separate but equal status, segregated urban populations into progressively worse neighborhoods. As these areas emerged, so did a new fear—a fear of concentrated "blackness" in the very neighborhoods that violence, social pressure, and legislation had forced into existence. Black-owned businesses began to produce black "red light districts"—like the South Side of Chicago, Hardieville in Miami's "Colored Town," the Levee area of the Badlands of Springfield, Illinois, and Hell's Bottom in Washington, DC. Of greater concern was that saloons in these areas often served as headquarters for black politicians *and* the means for some entrepreneurs to rise into the middle class, which threatened some white elites who feared a loss of control.

Saloons seemed partly responsible for the toe-holds of power and the incremental gains black communities were making, simply because the saloon represented "one of the few opportunities" available for entrepreneurship. Historian Sundiata Cha-Jua describes saloon ownership as the "pillar of the nascent Black petty bourgeoisie" and outlined several political parties and affiliations that were born in the saloons in Brooklyn, Illinois, which he calls "America's first black town."[15] To many members of the community, the saloon was a political and social hub, rivaling other "third place" institutions, such as barber shops. This was not lost on those who feared black saloons. Frances Willard, longtime founding leader of the Women's Christian Temperance Union, had this to say in *The Voice* in 1890: "They rule our cities to-day; the saloon is their palace, and the toddy stick their sceptre . . . the grog-shop is its centre of power."

Evansville, Indiana, however, was one of the first cities in which the fear of black ascendancy erupted into violence. Unsurprisingly, the event began in a saloon—Ossenberg's, where an individual named Robert Lee was drinking one July evening in 1903. Lee reportedly got into a fight with the bartender, Thomas Berry, who ejected him from the premises. When an armed and angry Lee returned for vengeance, policeman Louis Massey tried to stop him and was fatally shot. The townspeople wanted to dispense with the usual channels of justice and, instead, treat Lee to a "necktie party." Lynching was increasingly used as a terror technique to enforce segregation. When Lee wasn't released to the angry mob, they took it out on black-owned businesses, in particular, on neighborhood saloons, many of which were burnt down. With the mob "inflamed by strong drink," as saloon critic John Marshall Barker would describe it in his book published shortly thereafter, authorities ordered every saloon closed down. Unfortunately, as Barker wrote, "they had locked the door after the horse was stolen." The riot continued for several days and at least ten were killed.

Barker and other reformers criticized the "wide-open" privileges bars in Evansville enjoyed. Its saloons had been associated with gambling, drunkenness, and prostitution ever since the Germans had established a saloon culture several decades prior. The black community had stepped into that saloon culture, through both ownership and patronage and, as a result, Evansville's vice was now firmly associated with it. Barker said that the town was full of "roughs" and "beer-drinking and carousing individuals" and that the saloon was the source of "the explosion of bad passions." While Barker makes no particular slur against black saloons and, indeed, places equal blame on the one saloon where it all started and on the many white saloons that fueled the mob, most framed the saloon problem as especially out of control in the black community.

Critics claimed that slaves had effectively lived under a form of prohibition on the plantations (even though there were a number of grog shops and ordinaries frequented by slaves) and that their newfound freedom had left them unprepared for the responsibility of drinking and thus was causing a "relapse into animalism."[16] Like most of the ethnic groups encountered over four hundred years of public drinking in America, blacks had not yet mastered the "art of drinking well." Worse, with their supposed animal natures, they were especially susceptible to the temptations of alcohol and, since they were also said to have had no sexual self-control, far more dangerous under its influence.

Lurking not too terribly far beneath the surface was a fear of miscegenation. Jacob Riis complained that the worst of the New York saloons were the "black and tans," which catered to both white and black clientele. Herbert Asbury was scandalized by what might have been America's first multiracial gay bar, run by a man named Miss Big Nellie in 1890, in New Orleans. Nor was this entirely new. Some of the most damning evidence about John Hughson's Oswego in 1741 involved prostitute Peggy Sorubiero's relations with black men. A hundred years later, when the grog shop concerns were at their height, Southern critics drew attention to the mixing of the races in these unregulated and unlicensed spaces. But around the turn of the century, the notion that black men were simply incapable of controlling their base sexual instincts reemerged—with a vengeance. Newspapers that thrived on yellow journalism sensationalized (and, in some cases, actually invented) cases of white women being assaulted by black men, adding to the culture of fear and the sentiment that the black race was more animalistic than the white. Individual incidents were continually linked to these larger themes. For example, in 1908, when a white teenaged girl was raped in Shreveport, Louisiana, after walking by a "negro saloon," the incident was blamed on Devil's Island Endurance Gin.

Before long, on behalf of vulnerable white women everywhere, attempts were made to limit black saloons and to redefine drinking as a privilege for white men only. In 1904—a year after rioting in Evansville—residents of Springfield, Illinois, followed suit, attacking black establishments in the aforementioned area known as the Levee. Two years after that, it was Atlanta's turn. At the time, there was a row of black-owned saloons on Decatur Street that troubled white Atlantans, who fretted over how a mainly black clientele was being served cheap gin (allegedly straight from the bottle) in an environment that was said to be decorated with pin-ups of white women. White leaders claimed that the gin produced a "toxic heat" in black men and that the "Decatur Street Dives" were a "breeding place of lust and animal insanity." While gin was simply shorthand for all the spirits blacks drank, it became particularly closely associated with black saloons and problem drinking. A St. Louis liquor company, for instance, was charged by Tennessee antisaloon forces with having "abetted sexual assaults against white women," since the labels on its gin bottles featured pictures of "half-clad white women." The name of one brand: Black Cock Vigor Gin.

The association between "nigger gin" and the threat to white women would be played up significantly by antisaloon advocates such as Ohio Prohibition Party candidate George M. Hammel, who claimed that "black man, made drunken by unscrupulous white men engaged in the liquor trade, had become a peril to the womanhood of the dominant race."[17] Here, take "unscrupulous" to mean Jewish, the group increasingly vilified as opportunists dominating the liquor market. Even without the threat of black-on-white sexual violence, the mixing of the races at the Decatur Street dives was offensive to racial purists. While the majority of customers were black, the saloons also catered to whites, causing concern over the mixing of the races and rumors that white men were employing the services of black prostitutes.

The drinking habits of black men had been a concern since emancipation. Historian Charles Crowe writes that the slogan, "Keep whiskey from the black man" had been popular since Reconstruction. While it wasn't possible for agitators to close the black saloons, they frequently harassed and raided them. Its patrons were often arrested on vagrancy charges, which brought particularly severe consequences in that era—prohibitively high fines or jail time, which was generally served in convict camps devoted to hard labor, occasionally as scab workers who were used to bust unions, often in coal mines. Gainfully employed black men with fixed addresses were arrested for vagrancy if they were found to be "loafing and loitering around pool halls, bar rooms, dives, lewd houses and similar places," even if they could demonstrate that it was their day off. On August 25, 1906, the *Atlanta Constitution* sent two reporters out to count the black men on Decatur. They discovered 376 men "idling" or "loafing" inside or outside bars. Most were also "tipsy," claimed reporters. Readers inferred that the men must be stealing if they could afford to both loiter and drink—a rationale similar to one that had been used to ban slaves from New York taverns two hundred years earlier. Articles were accompanied by editorials that argued that "idleness breeds viciousness" and that the "loafing vagrants are the class that are assaulting the white women."

The following month, September 1906, saw an upping of the ante in yellow journalism. Atlanta papers tried to outdo each other in proving themselves tougher on black ascendancy, carrying more editorials and reports of vagrancy, drinking, and sexual violence. Both gubernatorial candidates, Hoke Smith and Clark Howell, made promises to reform the situation. And both had close links to rival Atlanta newspapers—Smith as ex-publisher of the *Atlanta Journal*; Howell, as editor of the *Atlanta Constitution*, the paper devoted to loiterer-counting. In the vicious political race, the papers waged a war to see which could be the most Negrophobic, each publishing yet more sensationalist accounts along with reassurances that its particular candidate would be toughest on black crime. This issue was key to some members of the white population of Atlanta, many of whom actually defended lynchings as a humane alternative to drawn-out trials. Some considered lynchings "too good" for black rapists.[18]

Add to all this the publication of *The Clansman: An Historical Romance of the Ku Klux Klan*, which author Thomas F. Dixon Jr. adapted into a play for maximum dissemination. *The Clansman* inspired many to revive the Ku Klux Klan (KKK) by giving the movement a mythological backbone— a post–Civil War history in which heroic white supremacist leaders saved the South from black dominance and its women from rape. Dixon juxtaposed strong, religious Scottish descendants, revitalizing ancestral clans, with monkey-like black men with an uncontrollable appetite for white women and drink.

The fear of black ascendancy was largely related to political power, now threatened by legally eligible black voters, of whom there were nearly a quarter million in Georgia alone. Hoke Smith was explicitly advocating disenfranchisement of these voters by whatever means necessary, to arrest the seemingly inevitable "black dominance" that the "barbaric inferiors" would rise to if left unchecked. Smith also charged that the black vote was especially corruptible and could be easily bought by Northern politicians, particularly in a saloon. While Clark Howell could hardly be defined as a progressive, he was perceived as soft on the issue, particularly compared to Smith, who endorsed schemes designed to circumvent black voters' rights, including instituting poll taxes and tests for voter eligibility. A minimum education requirement was bandied about but ultimately rejected, since it might encourage the black community to pursue education. The preferred alternative was to require prospective voters to take a test. In reality, though, there were two tests—a simple one written in plain English for white voters and a convoluted one for blacks.

To reassert himself as a viable candidate, Howell had to continually ramp up his campaign by portraying himself as tough on black crime. His paper stepped up rhetoric against the combined threat of black dominance and rape—the two themes Dixon emphasized in *The Clansman* as the means of Yankee and black revenge on the South. Nothing embodied the two fears better than the black saloon. It was the site of black ascendancy, community and political power, and, simultaneously, the venue where black men relapsed into animalism while staring at pictures of half-clothed white women.

On September 21, 1906, the Decatur Street dives were raided. It was reported with much sensation that pictures of nude white women were found on the premises. The story ran adjacent to the day's other provocative headline: "Half Clad Negro Tried to Break into the House"—a story of a *near* assault on Miss Orrie Bryan, a white. In case anyone had trouble getting from point A to point B, Hoke Smith's former *Atlanta Journal* published the story of the nude pictures of white women found in saloons under this provocative head: "Negro Dives and Clubs are the Cause of Frequent Assaults." The following day, the final catalyst for the Atlanta riots came—again in the daily papers, where it was reported that the "epidemic" of assaults on white women had hit a new high, with four attacks allegedly taking place over the preceding twenty-four hours.

This news hit the white saloons on Saturday afternoon and, by evening, a drunken mob took to the streets. En route to Decatur, the rabble beat a barbershop bootblack to death, then continued on, screaming, "Kill the Niggers" and "Save our Women." By nine o'clock, the riot hit Decatur which, fortunately, was nearly abandoned once its regulars heard about the oncoming mob. The rioters made do by demolishing the black-owned restaurants and saloons, then moved on to hunt down random individuals. Over three nights, between twenty-five and forty people were killed.

After the riot, it didn't take long for a concerted effort at closing Atlanta's black saloons to formulate. Many members of the black middle class had long wanted them closed, to address both the temptations of vice in their community and the image problem that went with it. (Drugs were a concern, too, of course, and, after Prohibition, cocaine and marijuana use by blacks would dominate the next wave of yellow journalism.) In *Voice of the Negro*, H. B. Watson wrote that the Decatur Street dives were "a veritable inferno where the souls of men and women are being gulped down at an appalling rate." This led to a massive increase in support for Prohibition among both blacks and whites, a movement to which many Southerners had, until then, been indifferent.[19]

Previously the South had not typically been much for abstinence of any sort. That was a Northern activity and associated with the same branch of evangelism that had agitated for abolition. Furthermore, drinking had been a major part of the culture in the southern United States since before the days of the Whiskey Rebellion. Still, between fear of black saloons threatening the chastity of the Southern belle and a mild eruption of evangelist faith amongst Southerners in the form of "holiness churches" in the early 1900s, temperance leaders and antisaloon organizers had finally gained a stronghold over Southern politics.

Where most reformers advocated the closing of all saloons (pointing out, accurately, that the violence had erupted from white establishments), many civic leaders briefly explored ways to close only the black ones. Smith, now the newly elected governor, suggested a prohibitively expensive licensing fee, accompanied by two-tiered tests for licensees. Naturally, these tests would mimic the ones for voting eligibility—a clear, straightforward one for whites; an incomprehensible test for black applicants. Smith's resistance to local prohibition was probably motivated, at least in part, by personal interests. He owned the Piedmont Hotel, the finest in Atlanta, whose bar was set to lose astounding amounts of money should all bars be closed. When all other alternatives for preventing black people from drinking were dismissed as unworkable, however, Georgia voted to go entirely dry. Smith signed the bill, despite the fact that it meant at least sixty thousand dollars (about one and a half million today) in personal losses over the first two years of state prohibition alone. While Smith didn't get to have it both ways by outlawing black saloons and keeping his own open, his consolation prize was that he got to push through many of the Jim Crow laws he had been championing since before the election, while simultaneously appearing as a reformer—of sorts.

The lessons from Atlanta were clear to many in the South and, indeed, across the country. In 1908, *Collier's* ran a series of articles by Will Irwin about "nigger gin" and the American saloon, which helped turn black saloons into a national concern. Samuel Mitchell, president of the University of South Carolina, remarked that "in any Southern community with a bar-room, a race war is a perilously possible occurrence." It didn't help that, just after Prohibition became state law in Georgia, the saloons in Springfield, Illinois, erupted in violence again. The story was familiar: alleged assaults or attempted assaults on white women, leading to drink-fortified white mobs agitating for a lynching—in this case, of two black men. This particular mob, roughly five thousand strong, descended on the Badlands and then to the Levee, where the black saloons were concentrated. Springfield was known as the center of vice for the region and considered second only to Chicago in terms of crime and unruliness. It also had the largest black population in Illinois and, in a neighborhood on Washington Street, a "block of crime" was associated with brothels, saloons, the buying of votes and the origin of almost every act of violence in the city.

In attempting to eradicate the Levee from Springfield, however, the mob met its match at one saloon. Armed blacks went to the roof of "Dandy" Jim Steele's Delmonico saloon and shot at the approaching rioters. Delmonico's was one of the few in the area that survived. Commentators were quick to point out the particular irony of the location and timing of the race riot: Springfield was Abraham Lincoln's birthplace and the city was just preparing to celebrate—on February 12, 1909—the centennial of his birth. The Lincoln centennial was repurposed and, instead of being a cause for celebration, it was used for a convention of reformers and activists to discuss "the negro question," from which came the institution of the National Association for the Advancement of Colored People (NAACP).[20]

This didn't mean the end of lynchings and race riots, of course. There were ten riots in cities across the United States when prize-fighter Jack Johnson beat Jim Jeffries on July 4, 1910. Roughly five thousand black Americans were killed as a result of mob violence between Reconstruction and the Civil Rights movement of the 1960s.

The sum total of these upheavals was almost all the help the prohibitionists needed. On top of anarchism, socialism, and labor movements, the threat of both machine politics and black political power was now firmly tied to the saloons. Before the race riots and the association of saloons with social ills, prohibition had been a tough sell in the South. After, the southern states were on board with the temperance leagues, the Prohibition Party and, of course, the Anti-Saloon League, which was about to show the antialcohol forces how to launch a successful political campaign.

11

CARRY
NATION
WIELDS
A HATCHET
IN A BAR

SUBWAY TAVERN ON BLEECKER STREET, 1905
*The Subway Tavern in New York was a bold
experiment—an attempt to create a respectable
saloon at 47 Bleecker Street. Image donated by
Corbis.*

Oberlin, Ohio might sound like a fairly inauspicious birthplace for the movement that was going to change America so profoundly in the twentieth century, but a meeting of the friends of temperance there on Sunday, June 4, 1893, was destined to do just that. This was where Reverend Howard H. Russell, Professor A. S. Root, Reverend John F. Brant, and General Giles Shurtleff decided to focus all further antialcohol activities on a single villain—the saloon.

Rev. Russell had already put some time into battling the saloon, spending much of the previous year trying to close Chicago's drinking establishments before the 1893 World's Fair—albeit unsuccessfully. He and his allies would advance the saloon as their primary target and, three months after the meeting, the Ohio Anti-Saloon League was formally launched. While the Oberlin group had high hopes, its members could not have fully grasped how important narrowing its agenda to the abolition of the saloon was going to be, in contrast with previous groups' wars on the large and amorphous target of the entire liquor, beer, and wine industry.

The Anti-Saloon League (ASL) would manage to succeed where the Women's Christian Temperance Union, the National Prohibition Party, and numerous other smaller, anti-alcohol societies did not. Much has been written on why it succeeded where others failed, but to sum up: It employed an aggressive yet nonpartisan approach; it identified the culprit as the saloon as opposed to alcohol; its organizational structure was corporate as opposed to democratic; and it had the single most ambitious publishing and public relations department of any organization to date, producing a barrage of incendiary literature pumped out in unprecedented volumes. The Anti-Saloon League is credited with having invented "pressure politics," a technique that involved a combination of aggressive fund-raising, back-room deals, and intimidation, and it wasn't above resorting to the occasional fraud and trickery.[1] Two hundred people worked full time at *American Issue* in Westerville, Ohio, the publishing organ of the Anti-Saloon League, cranking out an astonishing 250 million pages of material *per month* in the 1890s. The reams of propaganda took many forms—songs, plays, short stories, periodicals, flyers, books, and volumes of *The Standard Encyclopedia of the Alcohol Problem*. All of it had one thing in common: all saloons were evil. Never did the ASL concede that, somewhere, there might be a decently run saloon. It was instead asserted that the saloon was the "storm center of crime; the devil's headquarters on earth; the school-master of a broken

Decalogue; the defiler of youth; the enemy of the home; the foe of peace; the deceiver of nations; the beast of sensuality; the past master of intrigue; the vagabond of poverty; the social vulture; the rendezvous of demagogues; the enlisting office of sin; the serpent of Eden; a ponderous second edition of hell."[2]

Many, of course, drew out the relationships between the saloon and anarchy, the saloon and labor unions, the saloon and race riots, and the saloon and machine politics, which helped secure support for the Anti-Saloon League from wealthy industrialists, most notably John D. Rockefeller Sr., who began helping to finance the ASL in 1894. By the time the Rockefellers stopped supporting the League in 1926, the family had given it over a quarter of a million dollars (as much as six million today). Rockefeller was only one of many in a position of power who, despising the radical politics of the saloon and wishing for a more productive workforce, contributed to the League's efforts.

The rhetoric was extreme but, to be fair, there *were* some pretty bad saloons around the turn of the century. Stephen Crane described one in his 1893 novel, *Maggie: A Girl of the Streets*. "On a corner, a glass-fronted building shed a yellow glare upon the pavements. The open mouth of a saloon called seductively to passengers to enter and annihilate sorrow or create rage." To Crane and other contemporary writers, the saloon wasn't merely a setting, but a character in its own right, responsible, in part, for some of the damage inflicted upon the poorest populations of America.

Beer companies, such as Anheuser-Busch, Schlitz, Pabst, and Miller (and many of which are no longer household names, such as Blatz, Atlas, and Vienna Brewing) were only too happy to set up nearly anybody with a pulse with a saloon of their very own. In exchange, the new keeper would promise to sell their sponsor's beer exclusively—a "saloon mortgage" deal that was widely practiced. By 1916, for example, beer companies owned the furnishings—bar, back bar, shelves, and décor, essentially everything—of over four thousand of Chicago's seven thousand saloons.[3] At roughly the same time, in Los Angeles, *all* of the town's saloons were reportedly owned by a brewery. By 1918, 80 percent of America's drinking establishments were connected to a particular brewery. Obviously, this led to an explosion of saloons, enough to alarm reformers and even a fair number of nonreformers. But there was also an unintended consequence: The stiff competition meant that many saloonkeepers resorted to devious ways to attract customers and part them from their money.

Writing in 1950, nearly twenty years after Prohibition's end, Herbert Asbury chronicled many of the worst offenses. To read him, one might conclude (as he did) that there were no saloons with any redeeming qualities whatsoever. "Americans who lived . . . prior to prohibition, will recall the sidewalks slippery with slops and stale beer, the unpleasant odors, the drunks lurching through swinging doors, the loafers sitting on the curb, and the fighting and cursing inside the saloon." Asbury went on to call the saloon a "blight and a public stench," where "children, idiots and known drunkards" were served by bartenders who doubled as pimps and saloonkeepers who acted as the ward's "big boss."[4]

One of the more famous con men Asbury wrote about was Mickey Finn, who owned Chicago's Lone Star Saloon and Palm Garden, which gained notoriety for serving blacks alongside whites. Scandalous as this was, it would pale in comparison with his practice of selling the "Mickey Finn Special" to travelers and strangers—a knockout cocktail spiked with chloral hydrate. "Gold Tooth" Mary Thornton, one of Finn's saloon girls, would later testify that Finn had showed her a bottle of milky white liquid that he claimed to have bought from a voodoo doctor, throwing in an extra dollar to ensure its strength. He then told her, "We'll get the money with this." Gold Tooth Mary and other employees were then asked to use their charms to push this house "special." The poor fools who bought it would soon pass out, were taken into the back, and then robbed, beaten, and often stripped. The Lone Star Saloon and Palm Garden was closed in 1903, putting Finn out of business. Unlike many apocryphal or false etymologies related to the bar and booze industry, it's generally agreed that the term "Mickey Finn" does, indeed, derive from the Lone Star and its owner.[5]

While the Lone Star clearly represented an extreme, some saloon practices were arguably even more insidious than the Mickey Finn Special. All were striving to increase profit margins, which obviously involved enticing more Americans into drinking more alcohol. This included the Retail Liquor Dealers Association of Ohio, which, to counter the declining adult market, was quoted as endorsing the creation of an "appetite for liquor in the growing boys." The aforementioned saloon tokens and free lunches were one technique. In Upton Sinclair's *The Jungle*, the main character, Jurgis, describes the scene on "Whiskey Row," the not-so-fictional stretch of Chicago's Ashland Avenue near 47th, where twenty saloons per block catered to workers from the meat-packing plants and competed for their lunchtime business. Men, still clad in their blood-stained work clothes, would pour into the Whiskey Row saloons, many of which had apparently dubbed themselves "Union Headquarters." All held out a "welcome to workingmen" and a free lunch and, while penalties for helping oneself to the free lunch without drinking were swift and harsh, buying a beer seemed a fair exchange for the food. But, as Jurgis observes, "This did not always work out in practice, however, for there was pretty sure to be a friend who would treat you, and then you would have to treat him. Then some one else would come in—and, anyhow, a few drinks were good for a man who worked hard."

One can see why "treating" was a target for reformers. Occasionally, the practice was initiated by the bartender, who would roll dice to see whether he had to stand a round for the entire bar or simply his best customers. The hope was to start a wave of treating among the clientele. And once treating got rolling, it was almost unfathomable that a customer would fail to reciprocate—something Jack London learned when he was introduced to saloon culture and its code of masculinity as a young boy working the boats in Oakland. London described and analyzed the treating rituals in his 1913 *John Barleycorn*, quite possibly the strangest antialcohol piece ever written, given that it amounts to a love letter to the saloon. In his first foray, the young London is aghast at the money his colleagues spend in saloons. He also completely misunderstands the treating ritual and neglects to return the favor, his "duty," for several rounds in succession. When the truth finally dawns, he's embarrassed over his gaffe and sets about righting matters with a vengeance, buying rounds for any and all he meets. The ritual allowed London and friends to be "magnificently careless" and, in the choice between "money and men, between niggardliness and romance," London enthusiastically chose his comrades and romance. Buying rounds was empowering; in the name of generosity, "money no longer counted."

What London celebrated, however, others decried. Thorstein Veblen described treating as a form of working-class conspicuous consumption, while Sinclair saw it as a way of bankrupting the immigrant poor. Clearly, it amounted to a major concern to those who felt the practice only led to more drinking, which had been the case for eons—or at least as far back as to when it had been called "healthing." Several "antitreating" leagues and associations were formed and, in some instances, antitreating laws were put on the books. The treating debate was a hot topic outside America, too. Toronto enacted an antitreating law in 1913 and, in

London, similar legislation was passed two years later in the hope that it would cut the amount of liquor consumed by half. Antitreating associations were also popular in Ireland and, in "The Cyclops" chapter of James Joyce's *Ulysses*, when Leopold Bloom is at Barney Kiernan's pub, Bloom praises the antitreating league and champions it as a solution to the nation's drinking problem. This doesn't win him any friends at the bar, especially since several mistakenly believe that Bloom has won money on a horse race and is too cheap buy a round. Good luck was expected to be shared—another code of the bar.

Both abroad and in America, the war on the saloon made incremental gains, first by campaigning to get a number of states and municipalities to put local Prohibition to a vote. By 1913, there were nine dry states and more municipalities than can be counted that exercised the "local option" and voted its county or town dry. Between state and local laws, an estimated 50 percent of Americans lived in dry areas by the time of the Webb-Kenyon Act, the federal law passed that same year that prohibited the sale of alcohol between wet and dry states. Where campaigners failed to rouse citizens to vote dry, they often had luck winning the implementation of antitreating laws and/or blue laws that banned the sale of alcohol on Sundays. Sabbatarian closing laws, however, were no more popular at the turn of the century than they were when introduced by the Know-Nothings in the 1850s, and were widely ignored. In Bridgeport, Connecticut, in 1903, for instance, clergy pleaded with police to enforce the law, which saloonkeepers openly flouted, happily catering to the Sunday "rush" for "growlers"—take-away beer. The problem was that, if a police officer stepped up to his duty, he would only get grief from his largely corrupt department.

In other areas, things were done with slightly more discretion; patrons would enter through the back entrance on Sundays and saloonkeepers installed screens to shield the illicit activity. This, however, led to the passage of "screen laws" (or antiscreen laws), which prevented saloons from obstructing views of the interior from the street. In many places, screen laws provoked outright defiance on the part of saloonkeepers. The *Los Angeles Herald*, for instance, reported in 1905 "no disposition" to comply with such a law in San Diego. In Hoboken, New Jersey, in 1907, saloonists took a more subtle approach, claiming that the local antiscreen law didn't apply to them. As written, the law made an exemption for an "inn or tavern, or a hotel having at least ten rooms." The "joker" saloon men, as they were called by the *New York Times*, argued that the ten-room requirement only applied to hotels, not inns or taverns, as indicated by the position of the comma after "tavern."

One of the most famous blue laws was the previously mentioned Raines Law in New York, which led to "Raines Hotels"—flophouses that were used for prostitution, like the one that inspired Eugene O'Neill's 1939 play, *The Iceman Cometh*. But divvying up the public space into ten guest quarters provided only half the grounds for exemption. Hotels had to provide food, as well. As one might expect, the meals were often as makeshift as the "guest rooms." Frequently, altercations arose when a customer was naïve enough to attempt to eat the "meal." If an unwitting patron was lucky, he merely bit into something stale. Often it was far worse. Jacob Riis cited a common practice of serving "brick sandwiches, consisting of two pieces of bread with a brick between." Raines Hotels quickly became known as inhabiting the layer beneath the lowest scourge of bad saloons in New York State, a problem that eventually necessitated new legislation in the form of the 1907 Page-Prentice Bill, which gave state authorities the power to clean up the hotels.

Making a mockery of the law, whether by noncompliance, fake sandwichery, or the loophole of punctuation errors, became common practice among saloonists, many of whom refused to take the new Anti-Saloon League's encroachments any more seriously than they had taken temperance movements in the past. After all, many reasoned, temperance movements had been around since before the Civil War and none had been successful for long. And when they weren't sloughing off the law, saloon owners were often ridiculing the sentiment behind reform, occasionally giving reformers unintended assistance. Carrie Nation, for example, who cut a fairly ridiculous figure with her violent and hysterical "hachetations," might well have faded into the background were it not for the importance some saloonkeepers gave her. Nation wasn't actually "hacheting" licensed saloons but, rather, illegal saloons in already dry states, such as Kansas. Still, legal saloons gave her more airplay than she deserved by displaying signs like "All Nations Welcome but Carrie." Some made the papers by concocting Carrie Nation cocktails. (The recipe, it seems, was fairly similar to the contemporary "it" drink, the "Mamie Taylor"—consisting of scotch, lime and ginger beer. The difference was that the "Carrie" was made with more "antique" liquors and some rough "Kansas bitterness.") Journalist and playwright George Ade summed up the problem over the wets' nonchalant attitude toward the reformer: "The trouble with drink places is that they tried to think up cute ways of making a fool of the law instead of wisely endeavoring to keep up a semblance of decency and placate the non-customers."

Ade wasn't being entirely fair, however. Following in the footsteps of flashy Jerry Thomas was the next generation of barmen, some of whom were genuinely attempting to serve the public with creativity and integrity, and had been calling for a new push toward the professionalization of the industry. The United States Brewers Association, for one, tried to declare "war against the dives," an intention announced at its June, 1908 convention in Milwaukee. Also that year, the Knights of the Royal Arch, which was not a Masonic group but, rather, an association of cigar manufacturers and liquor distillers, was formed and lobbied for reform from within. "The most powerful argument the prohibitionist can present is the drunk man reeling from the doors of a saloon," read their mission statement. "Let us put ourselves right as a business before our fellow men. Let us cut off, root and branch, the minors, the drunkard, the tramp, the criminal, the dance hall, the vicious of every class and kind." On a more moderate note, the Modern Tavern League of Olympia, Washington, started an initiative to "stop sales to drunks."[6]

Harry Johnson, owner of a respectable Bowery saloon called Little Jumbo and author of another early bartending manual published in 1900, concurred when he wrote, "A good many people, I am sorry to say, are laboring under the impression that there is no such thing as a gentleman in the Liquor business. If those people, however, knew the inside of our business thoroughly or became acquainted with some good man employed therein, they soon would come to the conclusion that none but gentlemen could carry on the Liquor business in a strict and systematic way." Johnson continued: "The great trouble is, that most of those narrow-minded people don't know much about anything."[7]

While Johnson was an unlikely candidate for a Dale Carnegie award, he had clear ideas as to how bartenders were to behave in order to conform to the standards he and others had established. In his manual, he instructs bartenders to be cheerful and "strictly polite," to give "prompt answers to all questions as far as he has in his power" and to prepare drinks in a "neat, quick, and scientific way as to draw attention." Johnson conceded that some bartenders were guilty of a lack of professionalism: "They should not, like some bartenders do, have a toothpick in their mouth, or clean their fingernails, smoke or spit on the floor, or have other disgusting habits." He adds, "The swaggering air some bartenders have, and by which they think they impress the customers with their importance, should be studiously avoided."[8]

A good many followed Johnson's advice, too, if you take H. L. Mencken's word for it. In the Baltimore *Evening Sun*, the ombibulous Mencken wrote that the "average bartender, despite the slanders of professional moralists, is a man of self respect and self possession; a man who excels at a difficult art and is well aware of it; a man who shrinks from ruffianism as he does from uncleanliness." Mencken was not alone in his defense of the barman. In a letter to the editor published in *The North American Review* in October 1893, Thomas Mador Gilmore, one of the era's most outspoken wets, wrote that it required "an expert and an array of materials and conveniences to prepare a cocktail, a mint julep, a whiskey sour or any other of the many beverages so delightful to the average palate, and until something better and more convenient offers, the saloon will be retained to fulfill this office." He was apparently dismissing the possibility that people might concoct these delightful beverages at home. Later, in 1931, George Ade would argue, tongue only partly in cheek, that a good bartender "had to acquire almost a liberal education in order to know how to concoct all of the cocktails, rickeys, fizzes, cobblers, punches and other fearful and wonderful compounds. Only an artist of the first rank could properly build up a *pousse café* or permit the absinthe to drip so as to be properly opalescent and sufficiently potent."[9]

And although Herbert Asbury would claim that there were very few decent barrooms in the era, there were, in fact, a number of eminent bars. The best were distinguished by Ade from the average saloon as "gilt-edge and exceptional places." Ade listed the Sazerac and Ramos in New Orleans, the "splendiferous" Righeimer's in Chicago, the Planters' and Tony Faust's in St. Louis, the Antlers in San Antonio and the Palace in San Francisco. In addition, there were the "mint-julep headquarters in the old White at White Sulphur Spring [West Virginia], or the busy Waldorf in New York or the much frequented Touraine in Boston." While the saloon frequented by the working classes was under attack, the "gilt-edged" places were mythologized by the literary set and lifestyle writers of the day. Every city, Ade claimed, had at least one "expensively decorated 'buffet' where the socially elect could become pickled under polite auspices." None of this is to suggest that these were civilized hangouts in which a gentleman shared a cocktail after work and then rushed home to dinner. The Waldorf was crowded in the morning, right after its doors opened at eight, with people looking "for something to take away what was left of the jag of the night before."

One of the most eloquent, respected, and powerful voices in the wet camp urging professionalization was the aforementioned Colonel Gilmore, publisher of *Bonfort's Wine and Spirits Circular*. Gilmore consistently called for reforms in alcohol laws in lieu of Prohibition. He conceded that there were problems in the saloon, first and foremost that they were tangled up in politics, but argued that severing the saloon from politics would be achieved by doing away with "unjust taxation" and offering licenses to those who conducted business with decorum. Saloons, Gilmore argued, needed to be operated by a "better class of men," something that was unlikely to happen so long as saloonkeeping continued to be considered disreputable. Gilmore called for people to drink less—but also to drink better. He hoped that he would see a day when saloons would handle "pure and well-matured wines and liquors" but argued that high license fees and the fear of non-renewal led to a business philosophy which, by necessity, prioritized short-term profits and discouraged connoisseur drinking.

Gilmore's point was clear: Those who had spent the last few decades trying to degrade the profession had done a splendid job. However, he also noted that the legislation designed to hinder the saloonkeepers had managed to turn a number of honest and well-intentioned businessmen into disreputable grifters, just as T. S. Arthur had portrayed them in *Ten Nights in a Bar-Room*. Rather than punish them and risk making the situation worse, Gilmore was in favor of transforming saloons into clubs, offering "seats, tables, magazines and games" as well as "pure wine, beer, or spirits." There were actually some saloons in existence that already offered these amenities but these were mainly so-called continental style saloons, owned and frequented by European immigrants, primarily Italians and Germans.

A couple of attempts were made to run saloons along these lines, most notably New York's Subway Tavern, which opened at the corner of Bleecker and Mulberry in August, 1904. Designer Bishop Henry Codman Potter braved a bout of lumbago to attend the opening of his model saloon, which had been inspired by the Earl Grey pubs of England. The Earl, himself, had championed these as valuable weapons in the battle against the drink problem on a visit to America a couple of years earlier. Earl Grey pubs donated the majority of their profits to charity, stocked the finest wines, liquors and beers, and provided ample and edifying reading material for people who wished to stop by the club for a drink or two. The back room of the Subway Tavern was bipartisan, sporting pictures of both political candidates, offered a wholesome free lunch and even a path to sobriety—should a patron choose. This "path" involved a sign pointing to the front room (where women drank at the soda fountain and occasionally enjoyed a glass of beer) that read: "This way to the water wagon." There was little likelihood of women entering the back room given another sign which made it clear that their presence was strictly prohibited. Plus, the drinking chamber was well hidden behind swinging doors which, apparently, confounded the women on opening day when Potter gave a group a tour. But the Subway's firmest rule was its no treating policy. A year later, Des Moines, Iowa, would make history and take the Earl Grey model up a notch, when A. S. Kirkhart opened America's first explicitly Anti-Treating saloon.

Neither of these experiments lasted very long. The Subway was a spectacular failure, losing seventeen thousand dollars (some four hundred thousand today) in its first year of operation. It was soon sold to a new owner who had no intention of keeping any of the Subway's high-minded policies, nor the temperance slogans that adorned the mirrors ("Every inordinate cup is unblessed, and its ingredient is a devil"). "Benzine," the new guy reckoned, would do the trick.

Anti-treaters like Potter failed to understand just how important the ritual was to male bonding. Men gathered in the saloon, Jack London wrote, "as primitive men gathered about the fire at the mouth of the cave." Even the beer or whiskey ceased to matter after a while; what was important was "the spirit of comradeship of drinking together." The feeling that came with treating was one of acceptance, a sense of belonging to something larger. And, as London discovered, the feeling that came with being included in the club that was the saloon was thrilling, reassuring and, in addition, had an esoteric and unquantifiable attraction. "In the saloons life was different. Men talked with great voices, laughed great laughs, and there was an atmosphere of greatness. Here was something more than common every-day where nothing happened." The saloon was called the "poor man's club" for good reason. It catered to the many who would never come close to being admitted to a private club, and was an important part of their lives, just as it was for London: "They, too, must have found there that something different, that something beyond, which I sensed and groped after. What it was, I did not know; yet there it must be, for there men focused like buzzing flies about a honey pot."

The appeal of the saloon was hard to pin. Some of it stemmed from the camaraderie, the loose confederation whereby a patron could count on familiar faces but still be surprised by somebody new. Some of it was the whiskey. But it was the keeper who brought all of these elements together. For every one vilified by the Anti-Saloon League, there were several who were fulfilling the same role they had since the early colonial days—pillar of the community, arbiter of disputes, and tapper of strong waters. Add to this the fact that the saloon was still where working-class patrons were most likely to find and use a telephone, learn the score of a game (delivered by runners, kept track of on scorecards or even drawn out on blackboards at the bar), pick up their mail and, perhaps most controversially, cash a paycheck. (The Anti-Saloon League reported that one employer in Joliet, Illinois, discovered that all but one of the 3,600 paychecks it had issued during one pay-period had been cashed in a saloon. The sole exception had been cashed in a grocery store/saloon.) Not all keepers were in need of reform or professionalization, since they'd been diligently performing their duties all along. George Ade conceded that "not all proprietors were villains and it is a matter of history that nearly every bar-keep had to be guide, counselor, friend and sympathetic listener to any gentleman being buffeted by Fate, who wished to stay up until about midnight and have a good cry."

In a sentimental article for *The American Mercury* in 1925, B. J. Agnew wrote of his family's "grog-tainted" profession. His great-grandfather had kept a country tavern "during the frontier 'forties, the tindery fifties and the war-torn years of the next decade." The next two generations of Agnews followed suit. Agnew's grandfather wouldn't sell to "old soaks" even though he had sympathy for them, and owned and managed five saloons by the time he was fifty. His father carried on the tradition and Agnew recalled that, in the "days when mixing drinks was a profession and not a parlor sport," (referring to the home mixing of the Prohibition era in which he was writing), his father was a man of "infinite pride." He rejected the flashy attire made fashionable by Jerry Thomas and followers—"checked suitings . . . brilliant scarlet cravats and the blinding diamonds of the saloon-keeper of tradition"—and instead opted for the kind of attire that might suit a judge or clergyman. In addition, "the beer was always perfectly chilled, the more authoritative beverages unadulterated, the free lunch fresh and appetizing, and the bartenders sober, immaculate and courteous." To antisaloonists, Agnew Sr. must have seemed quite the anomaly. Instead of "plying men with liquor that they might buy more, he often promised bonuses to those he thought were drinking more than was good for them, provided they would go on the water-wagon for a certain period."

Agnew may have been the very model of a responsible saloonist but he was far from the only one. Saloon patrons had such affinity and loyalty to their owners because, in many cases, they did act responsibly, cared for their customers, and behaved as patriarchs of the community. Another saloon defender, journalist Travis Hoke, when recalling the corner saloon of his youth in a 1931 story for the unabashedly wet *American Mercury*, described the keeper as a "counsellor in all the ways of life, recipient of confidences, disburser of advice, arbiter of disputes, authority on every subject." Hoke argued that at his local, the saloonist never sold a drink to a drunken man, if you took into account the saloonkeeper's "distinctions between just feeling good, being a bit under the weather, having trouble at home, just needing a little straight rye to brace up" and, of course, as they'd say, "cut."

Even prohibitionist teetotaler Reverend Charles Stelzle defended the saloonkeeper in his 1926 memoir about growing up on the Bowery, where the saloon was the center of social life. There, he watched workingmen hold christenings, weddings, dances, singing society rehearsals and labor meetings; eat free lunches, bowl or play some billiards, pool and cards; even read newspapers. However, the "chief element of attraction," was the saloonkeeper himself, whom Stelzle described as a "social force in the community." Far from indicting the public face of the liquor industry, the reverend from the Bowery attacked the larger industry and defended its front man as generally cordial, neat and a devoted family and churchgoing soul who welcomed in the Salvation Army, "rarely permitted a man to become intoxicated" and generally didn't allow profanity on the premises. He secured work for his patrons and "loaned money," no questions asked, frequently hoping for "nothing in return."[10]

Stelzle identified the same problem Settlement House founder Jane Addams had when it came to winning the working classes over to Prohibition. Knowing the majority of saloonkeepers to be decent men, albeit with tight political affiliations, patrons would more often than not be put off by polarizing antisaloon hyperbole about how the bar was the devil's headquarters on earth.

The second problem Stelzle identified was that, were the saloon to be abolished, some reasonable substitute would have to come along to take its place. Also working on this problem was Raymond Calkins, author of the aforementioned *Substitutes for the Saloon*, a book commissioned by the Committee of Fifty for the Investigation of the Liquor Problem. Calkins's study revealed that the saloon did not simply quench "animal thirst" but also "social expression." As he wrote, "The saloon is the most democratic of institutions. It appeals at once to the common humanity of man . . . no questions are asked . . . the doors swing open before any man who chooses to enter."

When he was writing this in 1901, Calkins could not have imagined that the solution to the vexing problem of how to replace such a vital institution was already in existence, albeit in its infancy, in the form of Thomas Edison's Vitascope Theater, the first proto-movie theater. The earliest movies shown in America were in New York and New Orleans, the latter actually boasting the first permanent space in which films were viewed. It didn't take long for the phenomenon to become widespread. Starting in 1905, nickelodeon theaters became the rage in larger cities and, by 1908, evidence of "nickel madness" was to be found in almost every American mid- tolarge-sized town.

The early theaters weren't entirely uncontroversial. Some worried that they would become mere replacements for the concert saloons that had often been fronts for prostitution. Moving pictures had "been charged with strong criminal suggestiveness," said criminologist A. J. Todd in 1914 and the National Board of Censorship was soon working to police every film that came through American theaters. Films deemed tawdry or prurient either never made it to the cinema or were seized if shown without approval. In New York, an early piece of cinema verité was taken out of a theater and seized by police—because it revealed the inside of an opium den. Less controversial was *Cripple Creek Barroom* (1898), one of the earliest films of all time and generally thought to be the first movie in the Western genre. It gets pretty deep. In it, a woman saloonkeeper breaks up a fight, after which all her patrons return to happy drinking times.

The rapid proliferation of theaters that catered to children and sometimes hired vaudeville performers to provide sound created a new licensing problem for authorities and moral reformers. Those who believed that the best weapon against the saloon was the availability of alternate social spaces—positive substitutes—eventually embraced the movie house. It was generally free of alcohol and many people seemed to prefer the flickering lights of the silver screen to the yellow glare of the saloon. It also represented a welcome relief from nightly drinking. A Chicago police official summed it up: "Laboring men with their entire families trooped off to the pictures in the evening. The next morning the man finds his family happy, his own head clear, 35 to 50 (cents) in his pocket . . . and his conscience in good working order." Vachel Lindsay, an American poet, was one of the first to consider the new art form in a book-length work and, in his 1915 *Art of the Moving Picture*, he praised the cinemas, noting that, where a movie-house opened, the saloons on either side shuttered up. This was a good sign, according to Lindsay, who was encouraged by the transformation of the slums, where he saw "an astonishing assembly of cave-men crawling out of their shelters to exhibit for the first time in history a common interest on a tremendous scale in an art form." He continued, "Below the cliff caves were bar rooms in endless lines. There are almost as many bar rooms to-day. Yet this new thing breaks the lines as nothing else ever did. . . . Blood is drawn from the guts to the brain." Lindsay didn't let the fact that saloons were also used for the discussion of politics, opera, and Shakespeare get in the way of a good argument about the enlightening of cave-men through mass media. His is a telling statement and a clear marker of the ever-increasing sentiment regarding class and saloons.

In what was perhaps a preemptive move to appease censors and those with a more critical eye than Lindsay, a number of movies produced in the years leading up to Prohibition had a decidedly dry tone. In fact, a good number were simply film versions of the temperance weepies that had been so popular during the previous century. *Ten Nights in a Bar-Room*, in fact, was made several times over, twice by D. W. Griffiths who, apparently, was captivated by Simon Slade's villainy. The year 1915 was an intensely antialcoholic one on the screen. There was *Prohibition*, which featured speeches by William Jennings Bryan interspersed with a fictional tale of a man who gains revenge on his ex-girlfiend's fiancée by turning her upstanding sober young man into a drunk; *Distilled Spirits*, an early horror film in which an alcoholic hallucinates monsters; and, last but not least, *The Battle of the Ballots*, which was billed as a neutral and unbiased look at what local option votes were doing to people. In it, a saloonkeeper has a fight with his iceman after the latter votes to go dry. Later, the saloonkeeper dies of delirium tremens and a mob of tenderfoots tears the saloon down. It is later replaced by a movie house.[11]

Representatives from the liquor industry complained about the unfavorable light in which their product was consistently portrayed. According to antisaloonist Ernest Cherrington, writing in 1925, Wisconsin brewers charged producers with "a tendency to associate every dive scene, every human derelict, wayward son, or ruined home, with a beer sign or a mug of beer." Nonetheless, many praised the movie producers for their clear anti-alcohol message. In 1915, after the release of *Prohibition, Distilled Spirits* and *The Battle of the Ballots*, the mayor of Seattle called the film industry "directly responsible" for Washington State's decision to vote itself dry.[12]

The theater was also a far less threatening institution to the political status quo, despite the fact that occasionally lewd images appeared on screen. The interactivity of the saloon that had been responsible for so many riots, revolts, and rebellions was now being replaced by a one-sided exchange of information. Movie theaters led to a far more passive engagement with ideas than did bars or even live theater. The latter, traditionally characterized by spontaneity that was often triggered by interactivity with the audience, made the medium rife with revolutionary potential. Few, however, lamented the loss of the more engaging and stimulating forums. G. K. Chesterton, writing in his memoir *What I Saw in America* (1922), was a notable exception. "The cinema boasts of being a substitute for the tavern, but I think it a very bad substitute," Chesterton writes. "I think so quite apart from the question about fermented liquor. Nobody enjoys cinemas more than I, but to enjoy them a man has only to look and not even to listen, and in a tavern he has to talk. Occasionally, I admit, he has to fight; but he need never move at the movies."

The cinema was never going to be a substitute for the saloon in the realm of machine politics, which continued to grow more deeply entrenched in bars. Jack London wrote of a time when, out of cash, he went to a saloon around election time to wait for the doors to swing open and reveal "a bevy of well-dressed men." Before long, these men lined up at the bar to pour drinks down London's throat. By day's end, he was part of a parade of volunteer firemen, campaigning for his candidate through the town. He couldn't remember if the candidate was a Democrat or a Republican.

In 1912, the same year London was writing his alcoholic memoirs, Theodore Roosevelt was shot by John Schrank shortly before the former president was to give a speech in Milwaukee. Schrank was German-born and had been in his family's tavern business his entire life. With anti-German and antisaloon sentiments on the rise, though, Schrank's attempt, which wounded Roosevelt, was yet another nail used to seal up the saloon's coffin. The end seemed fore-ordained and the introduction of income tax in 1913 meant that the federal government could wean itself off the revenue it received from alcohol. Even fine-spirits booster Colonel Gilmore declared the saloon "doomed" in *Bonfort's Wine and Spirits Circular* and Jack London, to the shock of everyone, his wife included, declared he was going to vote for the dry candidate.

As if the ASL needed more help, there were a number of controversial labor disputes and work stoppages in the early twentieth century, many with discernible connections to saloons. The most notorious of the period, the Ludlow Massacre, was only tangentially connected to the saloon but nevertheless helped deliver one of the last blows. The incident occurred during the 1913–1914 Colorado coal miners' strike—an ugly fourteen-month dispute, largely between John D. Rockefeller's Colorado Fuel and Iron Company and Big Bill Haywood's old pals, the United Mine Workers. The set-up was familiar enough. The United States was in recession, so Rockefeller's firm had slashed wages. Worse even than the 1894 Pullman dispute, however, management then raised the prices in the company town, where, again, all employees had been forced to live, despite the fact that this practice had become illegal in the Pullman aftermath. One of the miners' key demands was that they be allowed to live wherever they chose. On April 20, 1914, after a particularly tense day of skirmishes, the Colorado National Guard looted some booze, got drunk and proceeded to take revenge on the tent city where the strikers lived. They killed twenty people, including four women and eleven children who'd been hiding in a tent when the Guard set it aflame.

The media and the public were shocked and horrified and, for once, the nation's newspapers were completely on labor's side. Rockefeller even agreed to a meeting with one of the coal miners' most hated leaders, "Mother" (Mary Harris) Jones, and, later made a visit to Ludlow. While he also requested there be an inquiry into the massacre, Rockefeller, it seemed, had already made up his mind as to the cause, since he immediately donated more money toward the forces working to vote Colorado dry. As an acknowledgment and thanks for the donation, Howard Russell, leader of the Colorado dry campaign, wrote that Prohibition would help maintain "the peace and order of the state against anarchy and red revolution." Colorado went dry in November and was soon joined by Arizona, Oregon, and Washington. (Ohio, by the way, remained "decidedly"—and likely maddeningly—wet, despite the best efforts of the Anti-Saloon League, for which home base was, somewhat ironically, still in Westerville, Ohio.)

As with other violent events, Ludlow gave Prohibitionists yet more ammunition. It was reasoned that closing the saloons would improve labor relations on two counts: Men wouldn't need higher wages if they didn't spend so much on drink; and employers would see higher productivity since hangovers and post-lunch inebriation would be a thing of the past.

Ludlow was closely followed by the East St. Louis race riots of 1917, where, at the trials, it was alleged that mobs had rallied in white saloons and that the perpetrators were "hangers-on," "saloon bums," "pimps," "machos," and employees and patrons of the bars. Crime boss and proprietor of the European Hotel, "Fat" Johnson, was said to have been a central player in rallying the rioters, who, again destroyed black-owned saloons such as Schreiber's and Fransen's on the grounds that they served as headquarters for black politicians. In total, over a hundred people were killed.

America's entry into World War I meant that anti-immigrant sentiment grew even stronger and that the German voice, which had remained anti-Prohibition, grew more irrelevant. Pabst, Schlitz, and Miller were officially declared enemies of the state. There were a few futile last-ditch attempts to push for professionalization and the depoliticization of saloons, including an article in a 1917 issue of *Mixer and Server*, published by the Hotel and Restaurant Employees' International Alliance and Bartenders' International League of America, which advised the bartender to pride himself on his cleanliness, to acquire an expert knowledge of drinks, and to always know his place: "He must not 'butt into' the conversation of his customer . . . (who) cares nothing for the opinions of the 'man behind' in politics or anything else."

Way too little and way too late. With an overwhelmingly dry Congress in power, a Congress that had been funded in part and supported by the Anti-Saloon League, the 18th Amendment to the Constitution (actually drafted by Wayne Wheeler, head of the ASL) was passed by both houses by the end of 1917. From that point, it needed ratification by three-quarters of the states (as all Constitutional amendments do). This was a relatively easy task, given the political and social climate resulting from years of antisaloon rhetoric and the ongoing war in Europe, which made sacrifice patriotic. In just over a year—on January 16, 1919—the amendment had mustered the required thirty-six of forty-eight states and was ratified. Ten more states came aboard within the next two months. In the end, Rhode Island and Connecticut were the only two to reject ratification.

Everybody got a year's grace period, though, and this saw American consumers going on the greatest survivalist spending binge ever known to the liquor industry. It was immediately understood that the Volstead Act was not going to make possession of alcohol a criminal activity. The party was simply going to move into the country's living rooms, where the well-heeled could drink as much as they wanted. J. P. Morgan, for example, purchased a thousand cases of French champagne, in the words of historian W. J. Rorabaugh, to "wait out the law."

By January 16, 1920, the night before Volstead took effect, newspapers reported that people actually seemed ready for Prohibition. They were still bloated and hung over from the long bender that was the previous year. There were also shortages of good liquor and, what *was* available, was exorbitantly expensive. Instead of wild last-night parties in the nation's saloons, the mood was gloomy. The *New York Times*, for example, reported few "wild orgies" but several "wet funerals" for John Barleycorn, including one at the Park Avenue Hotel where the room was painted black, with a coffin filled with black bottles for patrons to pay respects. Maxim's and Murray's Roman Gardens also staged "funerals" and, surely, every saloon worth its salt must have had some sort of ceremony to commemorate the passing of an era. One of the more lavish was a party at the Della Robbia Room at the Hotel Vanderbilt, where they were said to have drunk one hundred cases of champagne to the sound of the orchestra playing "Good-by, Forever."

Of course, as we know, America didn't say good-bye to the bar forever, merely see you later.

PART

III

12

A WOMAN WALKS INTO A SPEAKEASY

ACTRESS TEXAS GUINAN BEING ARRESTED, 1927

Speakeasy owner Texas Guinan about to step into paddy wagon. Image donated by Corbis.

As Will Rogers famously said, "Prohibition was better than no liquor at all." This sums up the lingering general perception that, during the period in which the Volstead Act was law, "dry" America was wetter than ever and that the moment the saloons closed up, opportunists immediately opened replacement speakeasies.

This version of history is heavily invested in the received wisdom that prohibitions don't work—an oversimplification. While a few speakeasies opened up in fairly short order, they were the exception rather than the rule. Were a parched soul looking for a drink in Manhattan in February 1920, for instance, his best bet might have been McSorley's "Wonderful" Saloon, where New York author Joseph Mitchell and others claimed they continued to get served a "near beer" that was remarkably *near* to the real thing. The establishment was, apparently, so profoundly respected by the police that they let it continue to operate unmolested. A number of artists who often camped out at McSorley's, including many from the Ashcan school (John Sloan did five paintings of the saloon between 1912 and 1930), were presumably grateful. Perhaps no one was more grateful than e. e. cummings, who, in 1923, wrote of the "glush of squirting taps" out of which flowed the "ale which never lets you grow old." Since the legendary watering hole had been left alone where others were shuttered, McSorley's Old Ale House, still on East 7th, can lay claim to the title of being New York's oldest continuously operating bar.

There were a few other brave—or desperate—restaurateurs who attempted to keep selling alcohol but, other than at these, a person's best shot at finding a drink was probably at a private party. Even then, the stockpiles weren't going to last forever, not even for the very wealthy. Although many believe people drank more during Prohibition, nearly everybody drank less. By the end of Prohibition, people drank about two-thirds of what they had prior to Volstead, according to economists Jeffrey Miron and Jeffrey Zweibel who, in 1991, published the results of their exhaustive study of the number of incidences of cirrhosis of the liver, alcoholism-caused deaths, or cases of psychosis and arrests for public drunkenness. If it were only measured in terms of reducing the per capita consumption of alcohol, Prohibition should actually be considered to have been a relatively successful experiment, especially in the first few years when it reduced the consumption of alcohol drastically, to about *one-third* of what it had been when it was still a legal commodity.[1]

A good bit of what *was* being consumed in America was going down in New Orleans, where many simply ignored the new law, and where liquor was imported from the Caribbean and Mexico with little interference. Daniel Okrent, Prohibition chronicler, writes of a found postcard from the Old Absinthe House in New Orleans mailed during the "dry" era. On the back was written: "From appearances, it is the only place where liquor is not sold here."[2] Thirsty travelers could go to New Orleans for an alco-holiday or, if they wanted fully legal alcohol in a saloon setting, take a sojourn to Quebec, where French-Canadians had reopened taverns the moment the war was over. Rows of roadhouses erupted in Quebec across the border from Maine, New Hampshire, and Vermont, and, as other provinces repealed dry laws, borderside bars were established from sea to shining sea.

It is often thought that Canada had no prohibition on alcohol but in fact it did, as part of its 1915 War Measures Act. When World War I ended, though, so did national prohibition and individual provinces were free to remain dry or opt to go wet. Quebec lost no time breaking out the wine and beer—an important part of its local culture and heritage. British Columbia went wet in 1920, while other provinces took their time. Ontario began allowing the sale of wine and beer in 1924, the same year Alberta and Saskatchewan repealed. Prince Edward Island—home to Anne of Green Gables—kept prohibition until 1948 and, by no small coincidence, that province also boasts, even today, a highly sophisticated moonshine culture.

With some provinces wet and others dry, Prohibition was effectively a farce in Canada. The country had no equivalent of the Webb-Kenyon Act, which had prohibited the shipment of alcohol from wet to dry states. Several distillers, most notably the Seagram Company, under the control of entrepreneurial Samuel Bronfman, took immediate advantage of this legal oversight and began building a mail-order alcohol empire within Canada. When America went dry, Canadian suppliers such as Bronfman saw the potential for sales south of the border and began ramping up production, ignoring ethical concerns. As Harry Hatch, president of Hiram Walker, another Canadian distillery, put it, "The Volstead Act does not prevent us from exporting at all. It prevents somebody over there from importing. There is a difference."

The establishment of the distribution network has been well-covered by the literature but, in a shot glass, much of the smuggling happened on the East Coast where fishermen pursued more lucrative endeavors, filling up on European imports from the French-owned islands of St. Pierre and Miquelon and delivering their cargo to "Rum Row"—an area three miles off the New Jersey coast where ships sat in international waters. (It's alleged that virtually the same routes are used for smuggling drugs today.) The rest of the hooch made its way across inland borders—particularly in Southern Ontario, where small crafts owned by companies like the Mexican Export Company regularly shipped whisky across the Detroit River to "Cuba" and "Mexico." The customs rosters indicate that a number of boats managed to make it to and from Cuba three times a day. When the Detroit-Windsor tunnel (soon to be known as the "funnel") opened in 1930, smugglers had one more avenue in a region that became rife with mob activity, which included a North American mafia first—a Godmother. A southern Ontario Calabrian crime family was nominally headed up by mobster Rocco Perri but actually under the control of his wife, Bessie Starkman.

Cuba and Mexico, of course, didn't need Canadian imports, since they had plenty of their own alcohol—enough to ship to American ports such as San Francisco, Miami, New Orleans, and Galveston, Texas. Antisaloonist Ernest Cherrington complained that most of the saloons in northern Mexico were owned by Americans and "operated for the benefit of American trade." Caribbean rum distillers were also happy to fill the void, not only by shipping to Florida, but also by playing host. The American bar was temporarily moved offshore during Prohibition—first to Bimini, to which the world's first booze cruises sailed, but most spectacularly to Havana, which became known as the "Paris of the Caribbean."

Aside from its architectural charms, Havana was a logical choice for the relocation of the party, being a relatively quick boat trip from Florida, from where shuttles operated out of Miami and Key West, the latter merely ninety miles from Cuba. Before long, even Northerners had the opportunity for speedy Caribbean alco-tourism. On November 1, 1920, war correspondent and *Good Housekeeping* editor Clara Savage flew (as a passenger) from New York to Havana (with a stop in the Keys) on a mail plane owned by the Aeromarine West Indies Airways Company and wrote about it for the *New York Times*. This sensational event struck a chord with thirsty Americans who might well have been enticed with a chance to see the "surprising maplike appearance of the earth below," but were also, no doubt, spurred toward an equally novel sight—a legal drink at a proper bar. "Don't be too sure, Mr. Stay-at-

Home, that you won't be flying hundreds of miles yourself, before very long!" taunted Savage. And, indeed, within a few years, Pan Am began shuttling former stay-at-homes from Key West to Havana—the world's first international passenger air service. By 1921—just eighteen years after Wilbur Wright became the first—an estimated 275,000 passengers were being flown around regularly in "flying machines," many owned by private individuals.

Antisaloonists were concerned at how easy smuggling was made by planes and, before long, ASL leader Cherrington was agitating for a solution to what had now become the "world liquor problem." Cherrington wanted the American government to pursue liquor treaties with foreign countries and even to employ the 1823 Monroe Doctrine to defend itself from the onslaught of foreign interests. The legacy of this line of thinking is still with us in the form of foreign interventions over drug policy. To justify an attack on Havana and its rum stores, Cherrington referred back to the Spanish-American War: "Were the reasons for interfering in Cuba any more important or demanding than those which now present themselves in connection with the international liquor problem, in the island of Cuba and especially in the city of Havana?"[3]

Evidence of Prohibition-era Havana still exists in the restored grand hotels—and their magnificent bars—such as the Nacional, the Sevilla, and the Telegrafo. In the latter, the bar was literally American, imported piece by piece from Newark, New Jersey, by an owner who refused to give up his profession just because of a little law known as Volstead.[4] There were also dozens of other establishments, such as the legendary El Floridita and Sloppy Joe's, in which countless American tourists and military servicemen stopped for their first drink. Sloppy's slogan was: "First port of call, out where the wet begins." Rowdy tourists, mafia opportunists, and unscrupulous developers attracted to Havana during Prohibition would eventually offend Cubans so profoundly that many wound up supporting Fidel Castro in his war to rid the country of foreign interests and influence. The American saloon continued to wreak political havoc, even when transplanted to other shores.

Relatively few could afford to travel to Cuba, the Bahamas, Mexico, or Canada simply to get a drink and, as a result, a slightly more affordable homegrown option began to emerge—new versions of the blind pig, blind tiger, and, finally, the 1920s innovation of the speakeasy. These options were not what anybody might call bargains—just slightly cheaper than traveling to another country for a drink. Drinking quickly became the province of the wealthy, what with contraband booze marked up to reflect both the disparity in demand and supply and also to account for the risk involved in smuggling and selling it. At no time in American drinking history had the class division become so clear. In *What I Saw in America*, Chesterton questioned whether anyone had ever even meant for the very wealthy to get on the water wagon. "It is to some extent enforced among the poor; at any rate it was intended to be enforced among the poor; though even among them I fancy it is much evaded. It is certainly not enforced among the rich; and I doubt whether it was intended to be."

Speakeasies, which often had first-rate entertainment and full dining options, proliferated, putting fine hotels and restaurants across the country out of business. In New York, unable to compete with places that sold alcohol, the Holland House, the Knickerbocker, the Manhattan, the Marlborough, the Buckingham, and, later, Delmonico's and the Waldorf-Astoria, fell victim to Prohibition. Bootlegger Sherman Billingsley's Stork Club was probably the most famous speakeasy, but closely rivaled by the 21 Club, Jack Kreindler's and Charlie Berns's iconic hotspot that had begun as a modest speakeasy in Greenwich Village called the Red Head, then worked its way up to 52nd Street via Washington Street, then to 49th, becoming a little more exclusive with each move. In the end, its owners were able to boast that the police precinct captain had a regular table.

Another club was the El Fey, which began as an upscale, Midtown venture and grew in popularity and fame on account of its wild hostess, Texas Guinan—a former screen and stage actress, who, during Prohibition, reinvented herself as the queen of the New York nightclubs. Guinan achieved near-royal status as a result of her charisma and reputation as a charming and outrageous straight-shooter who hailed from the frontier. She greeted customers with her trademark "Hello, suckers!" and candidly admitted that she'd be nothing without Prohibition. After the El Fey, Guinan opened her own speakeasy, the 300 Club. An egalitarian at heart, she was happy to take money from her "butter and egg men" but simultaneously looked out for her friends who couldn't afford to foot their bills. In her obituary, writer Heywood Broun recalled that he had once ordered champagne to impress a date at the club when Tex came to the table to discourage him: "You know we're charging $30 a quart for champagne and you know it isn't champagne. Tell your young lady to take gin and like it."[5]

At the El Fey, Rudolph Valentino, John Barrymore, Clara Bow, Gloria Swanson, Irving Berlin, and Peggy Hopkins Joyce mingled with wealthy and high society regulars—Vanderbilts, Morgans, and Chryslers. The wealthiest paid for the privilege of slumming with famous and often infamous characters, to the tune of nearly three-quarters of a million dollars (some $8 million today) in the El Fey's first seven months. Successful Prohibition-era nightclubs in urban areas were a mix of high society, artistic wits, and seedy mobsters. Guinan knew just how to achieve the right balance, courting high society types and writers while also tolerating the mafia, a necessary evil in the bar business during the period. She claimed to be old friends of semiregular patrons Lord Mountbatten and the Prince of Wales (the future King Edward VIII), the latter of which she had once protected during a raid by stashing him in the kitchen, disguising him as a short-order cook, and setting him about frying eggs. Her best stories were expertly publicized through her friend, gossip columnist Walter Winchell, whose career she helped launch.

If it seemed novel that women such as Texas Guinan should run and own nightclubs (Helen Morgan and Belle Livingston were two of her more famous competitors), it was also novel that young women should be going out and drinking in them, which they were. Texas's own Heywood Broun even commented, that in the old saloon, a man at least never had to try to compete with a crowd of schoolgirls for space at the bar.

There were actually plenty of women drinking in saloons before Prohibition—perhaps just not in Broun's circles. Many went to saloons to be social, slake a thirst, or take advantage of a free lunch. Dorothy Richardson, who, in 1905, published an account of her life as a New York wage-earner, describes a scene at a laundry where she and her female colleagues were being worked fairly mercilessly. When one fainted, an older co-worker suggested that the lady's weakness resulted from a lack of food. The following day, six women from the laundry ate at a saloon, ordering beers with "all the trimmings" and enjoyed a hearty hot lunch. Richardson, previously a teetotaler, grew to enjoy the beer that came with it.

Some women had been regular saloon patrons long before that, too, and a few—although fewer and fewer after the Civil War—were in the saloonkeeping business. In a number of jurisdictions, new legislation made it illegal for women to serve alcohol and saloons formerly run by married couples saw the woman relegated to the kitchen where she prepared the free lunch. Notable exceptions of the pre–Prohibition era, however, included "Big Tit Irene," who ran a saloon in Ashtabula, Ohio, and Chicago's "Peckerhead Kate." Chicago was also home to Dark Secret, an illegal joint in the "Bad Lands," run by neighborhood boss "Big Maud," who could offer "a drink, a woman, a bed for the night and nine times out of ten, a broken head." A brief look at Prohibition-era crime bosses of Chicago reveals that women were in the game almost as deeply as men. Herbert Asbury describes Maud as "another of the gigantic Negresses" of which he thought there was a surfeit in Chicago. She was preceded by the "Bengal Tigress," who specialized in procurement and was known for literally tearing down the shanties of her enemies. The Bengal Tigress competed with the 450-pound Black Susan Winslow, who, according to legend, couldn't be removed from her house upon arrest until the police removed the door frame and two feet of wall.[6]

Although few women were allowed to run saloons immediately prior to Prohibition, there were actually quite a few that allowed women to sit in the back rooms—accessed via a side "family entrance," so that the barroom remained the province of men. So long as they didn't have their foot on the brass rail, women were allowed to drink. In saloons where this was prohibited, women were encouraged to buy "growlers" of beer from saloon side doors and drink off-premises. Middle-class women favored "remedies"—bitters and blood tonics—which offered cures for nerves and various ailments, but were basically flavored alcohol. Among some women, including a number of temperance advocates, alcoholic tonics or laudanum (opium mixed with wine) were commonly consumed. Vin Mariani, a wine laced with coca was also extremely popular—especially after Pope Leo XIII and Thomas Edison both endorsed it. Queen Victoria, it seems, had a special fondness for the coked-up wine.

So women did drink, though there were rigid social guidelines governing where they drank and, until Prohibition, few middle- and upper-class women did so in public. This changed in the 1920s, however, and the young woman holding a cocktail in one hand and a "torch of freedom" (Lucky Strike cigarette) in the other, came to symbolize the changing role of women in the early twentieth century. Of course, Prohibition wasn't the only (or even the main) reason that women began taking on more assertive and powerful roles in the 1920s. They'd been empowered by suffrage (the Nineteenth Amendment was ratified in August, 1920) and emboldened by the final rejection of repressive

Victorian mores. A new openness about female sexuality was going to be developed in the speakeasies, where centuries of courtship tradition were discarded in a few short years. They provided illicit and exciting spaces where parental and legal authority no longer adhered, and youthful exuberance could be expressed honestly. In a way, speakeasies were where the American family would begin to be transformed.

One speakeasy story that captured the public's imagination symbolizes the changes in gender and class roles that shifted during Prohibition— the romantic affair between Irving Berlin and Ellin Mackay, which began in 1925. Berlin was a successful composer who enjoyed mingling with a wide swath of New York society in a range of Midtown and Downtown speakeasies—something that, ten years earlier, would have been nearly impossible for a Russian Jewish artist raised in the tenements. One evening, Berlin headed downtown rather than up, to Jimmy Kelly's at 181 Sullivan, where he met Mackay who, it turned out, had practically been stalking the lonely widower.

Mackay was not only stalking, she was also "slumming"—a practice established in the Victorian age, both in London and New York, in which the bourgeois actually took guided tours of poor inner-city neighborhoods, such as Whitechapel and the Bowery, for prurient interests. Mackay's father had made a sizeable fortune in telephone, telegraph and mining interests and the family was one of Long Island's most prominent. The family estate, Harbor Hill, boasted fifty bedrooms and sat on a six-hundred-acre piece of real estate overlooking Long Island Sound. In 1921, the young heiress had "been introduced" at one of New York's splashiest debutante balls; a thousand people had come to greet her, and other young things, at the Ritz-Carlton. Aside from many hopeful suitors, Mackay also had the pleasure of meeting the Prince of Wales, the very same man who had displayed such talent as a short-order cook, when he visited her family at Harbor Hill. Still, despite traveling in New York's very best social circles, Mackay preferred the speakeasies and, in 1925, took the bold move of declaring so in an article she penned for the then upstart magazine, *The New Yorker*. Editors were divided as to whether or not to publish her unsolicited piece. One iconoclast argued that they could not afford to turn it down, even had it been "written with her foot." The issue in which the article, *"Why We Go to Cabarets: A Post-Debutante Explains"* appeared, sold out and put the magazine on the map.

In it, Mackay explained the horrors of the "stag lines" of "extremely un-alluring specimens." These "objectionable men" frequenting the debutante balls would insist upon dancing poorly in crowded halls and the young women had no real choice but to accept their overtures. Courtship, with all its rigid rules and established codes, was precisely what was about to be discarded, replaced with the more casual "dating" that was being invented—or at least enabled—in the speakeasy. Dating was not only less formal; women had more power in initiating it. They were free, like Ellin Mackay, to meet a man in a nightclub and pursue a relationship that might or might not lead to marriage. None of this is to say that women like Mackay were typically spending time with members of *all* social classes in speakeasies, just the three strata Texas Guinan would have allowed in her club—high society, artists (struggling or established), and the mobsters who owned the clubs (or at least the booze sold therein). Ordinary people could not afford to drink regularly in even the low-end speakeasies, as prices were too steep for all but the rich. In 1926, according to Irving Fisher, contemporary economist and ardent prohibitionist, the average price of a quart of lager had risen eightfold since 1916 (from ten to eighty cents; about ten dollars today); a bottle of rye whiskey went from $1.70 to $7.00; a bottle of gin from ninety-five cents to nearly six dollars.

Jimmy Kelly's had become fashionable by the time Mackay and Berlin met, but it had been a long, tough climb up to semi-respectability. Kelly's original saloons—including the Mandarin Café, located on the "Bloody Angle" of Doyers in Chinatown and home to numerous gang incidents—were some of the most infamous in New York. Kelly (whose real name was James DiSalvio) was an ex-pugilist, fight matchmaker, and Tammany political organizer. He was also head of a gang that was engaged in several bitter rivalries, including one with the Jack Sirocco gang. One of the most infamous incidents in which Sirocco's and Kelly's soldiers clashed took place in 1913 at a Madison Square Gardens bicycle race. Because they had not been given the job of policing the Gardens, Kelly's men attacked it instead, firing on the Sirocco security men, seemingly oblivious to the crowds who were arriving to watch the race. The exchange lasted until both sides ran out of bullets. Police recovered six revolvers at the scene. Later that day, another gun battle broke out near Chick Tricker's saloon on the Bowery, one of Sirocco's main headquarters. In the end, Kelly would wrestle away control of Chinatown from his rivals. This all took place *before* the mob had control of alcohol distribution in America.

Twelve short years later, Berlin, Mackay, and Jimmy Kelly were all enjoying 181 Sullivan together and the "privacy" of the cabaret that

Mackay cherished. Henry Miller and his date (future wife, June) loved the place, too, and could be found there early in their relationship. In the previous decade, Kelly would never have been accepted into polite society, obviously, but neither would Berlin nor, for that matter, the German socialist Miller. Mackay wouldn't have been allowed to set foot outside of the Ritz-Carlton to meet any of those characters. The New York speakeasy brought them all together. In Mackay's follow-up article in *The New Yorker*, she announced that "modern girls [were] conscious of their identity and they marry who they choose, satisfied to satisfy themselves." The privacy wouldn't last, however, and public speculation that Berlin and Mackay would marry, despite her father's disapproval, was proved correct in 1926.

Many blamed Prohibition for the fact that women started drinking in semi-public, and saw it as a new low. Herbert Asbury claimed that women picked up drinking the moment it became illegal and conjectured that the reason lay "in the fact that women are naturally outlaws. . . . They'll do anything for love, and once in a while something for friendship," argued Asbury, "otherwise nobody can tell them what to do and get away with it."[7]

Asbury's explanation was written long after repeal, but it reflected the general concern over women and drinking during Prohibition, symbolized by Mackay and Berlin, who, in turn, represented a shift in public attitudes. Even stalwart teetotaling antisaloonists such as Rockefeller began to change his tune and soft-pedal his support for Prohibition when confronted with the speakeasy frequented by young middle- and upper-class thrillseekers of both genders. And if the speakeasies that debutantes frequented weren't dodgy enough, imagine the ones women weren't allowed into. Lucius Beebe wrote nostalgically about men's-only speak-easies, such as Jack Bleeck's Artists & Writers, which catered to the reporters at the nearby *New York Herald*, and Matt Winkle's on Park Avenue, which actually advertised in the Yale and Harvard student newspapers. Beebe was especially fond of Dan and Mort Moriarty's on 58th, in which "Prince" Michael Romanoff hid from immigration officers for three days, subsisting on sardines and scotch, and where author John Thomas almost died of liver complications. Thomas, a one-hit wonder who wrote a book called *Dry Martini* about life at the bar at the Paris Ritz, could have learned from Romanoff's sardine diet. His doctors had warned him that he would not survive if he did not have food with his drink and, from then on, Thomas carried a sandwich around with him and sat it on the bar.[8]

But women and Ivy Leaguers slumming with mobsters and alcoholic artists weren't the only reason for the downfall of Prohibition. Midway into the noble experiment, other problems, such as the inefficiencies and outright corruption of the enforcement agencies, began surfacing, and these marred the optics of the prohibitionists. Raids were frequent at Guinan's, as at every other speakeasy in America, but rarely resulted in closures. Among the few who actually managed to make arrests and accumulate enough evidence to convict, were famed cops Izzy and Moe, who disguised themselves to find illicit liquor on premises of New York speakeasies. Most club-owners accepted paying off police as part of the cost of doing business. Others regularly paid fines and considered those license fees, which really didn't cost much more than licenses had prior to Prohibition. Most considered the raids minor inconveniences. One place on the Lower East Side ran the length of an entire block and had two street entrances—one on Water, the other on Cherry; when one entrance was padlocked, they simply waited for the agents to leave and opened up for business on the other side. In San Francisco, The Eiffel Tower nightclub was raided on New Year's Eve and reopened a half-hour later. Texas Guinan herself, was never seriously charged with anything until her 300 Club was padlocked in February 1927. She claimed that she was only an employee, however, and managed to avoid jail.

The poor and working classes, by contrast, faced more serious consequences far more frequently. Unable to afford a club like the 300, many were only occasionally able to afford a more downscale version of the speakeasy—a blind pig or blind tiger or, worse, the outright rip-off clip joints that had spread across America and sold liquids of varying degrees of quality. "Smoke"—often made with industrial alcohol—was available in most urban areas for ten cents a glass. "Yack Yack" bourbon was popular in Chicago, while, in Philadelphia, they preferred "Soda Pop Moon."[9] People from all over drank Goat Whiskey, Squirrel Whiskey, Panther Whiskey, Coroner's Cocktails, Jackass bourbon, and White Mule (because of its kick). Some of these fine hand-crafted spirits were made from diverted industrial alcohol, some of it from moonshine.

One of the more terrifying products sold during Prohibition was "jake," which was said to be Jamaican ginger extract. An epidemic of paralysis cases broke out in Kansas and was eventually traced back to jake, or more specifically, to the denatured alcohol (made for industrial use, but poisoned to thwart human consumption) that gave jake its potency. It left its victims permanently paralyzed with—"jake-leg" or "jake-foot." And they were among the lucky ones. Wood alcohol (methanol, often used to denature industrial alcohol) left thousands blind and killed roughly ten thousand a year.

All this underscored the concerns of moderates, who worried from the onset that Prohibition would lead to more dangerous drinking. It also undermined the efforts of the Anti-Saloon League. Though it had succeeded in shuttering the saloon in 1919, the League was still working hard and, as we've seen, had no sooner won the war at home than set its sites on worldwide prohibition. It continued to publish reams of anti-saloon material, aiming not just at adults but at the younger generation, lest it forget the evils of the saloon. In one tract called *The Outcast*, presumably meant to be a parable and read to youth, a group of children are described as playing "city" and begin by building a fictional town. When one of the kids, Ray, wants to build a saloon, the other children throw him out of the game and ostracize him. His friend chides him: "You not only act like a wet man, but you talk like one. Wet men are always talking about their rights." The friend concludes with the assertion that God is on his side and, with that, Ray reforms and gives up his dreams of saloon-ownership.

Things were nonetheless starting to fall apart for the ASL, and one of its biggest public relations problems was its relationship with the Ku Klux Klan. In the early years, this alliance had been crucial for getting Prohibition accepted in the Southern states; but it was a dubious long-term strategy. By the mid-1920s, the association between the two had been made very clear in the media. As Clarence Darrow said to a reporter for the *Baltimore Evening Sun* in 1924: "The father and mother of the Ku Klux is the Anti-Saloon League. I would not say every Anti-Saloon Leaguer is a Ku Kluxer, but every Ku Kluxer is an Anti-Saloon Leaguer." In his 1922 book, *What Prohibition Has Done to America*, economist Fabian Franklin noted that the whole course of the Prohibition movement had been "profoundly" affected by the desire to keep blacks from drinking alcohol. He went on to lament that the New Yorkers were being deprived of "their right to the harmless enjoyment of wine and beer in order that the negroes of Alabama and Texas may not get beastly drunk on rotgut whiskey."

At the same time, there were several high-profile battles involving the KKK's sometimes violent enforcement of Prohibition. In Williamson County, Indiana, where the KKK and the ASL had been collapsed into the "Williamson County Law Enforcement League," a vicious and bloody drug war was being waged between the Klan and Catholic bootleggers. Long before Al Capone became a household name, the public and media considered "Bloody Williamson" to be an early instance of increased criminal activity directly attributable to Prohibition.

While some critiques of the enforcement of Prohibition stemmed from the violence, others involved civil liberties. Many were concerned about the number of officers who were hired to root out "sauce" (over three thousand federal agents alone) and feared the formation of a police state, replete with unwarranted invasions of private property. To some, Prohibition represented a well-meaning attempt to redress social issues and public health—two concerns that became paramount in the early twentieth century thanks to the efforts of muckrakers such as Jacob Riis and Upton Sinclair. But as Michael Lerner points out in *Dry Manhattan*, his book on Prohibition in New York, the Eighteenth Amendment was the only one that *restricted* personal liberties. But, then again, the wets are always talking about their rights.

There were also the mishaps and embarrassments. When the San Jose Bar in San Francisco's Chinatown was raided, a police officer's service revolver was found, one of several pieces of evidence that pointed to police involvement in the actual running of the resort. On the other coast was the Bridge Whist Club at 14 East 44th, a speakeasy that was opened up by federal authorities in order to penetrate the network of big-time smugglers who supplied New York. The Bridge Whist Club was not unique in this regard; there were other "bait" speakeasies around the country, including one well-known club in Norfolk, Virginia. According to *Collier's*, the Bridge Whist trap never snared any bootleggers, but did manage to do "a roaring business at all hours of the day and night." People were also grateful for the state-run speakeasy, since it was renowned for offering an outstanding free lunch. One sting attempt at the Bridge Whist led to a bootlegger (who apparently knew he was being overheard) outlining the drinking habits of all the ASL leaders and government officials he had come to know over the years.[10] *Collier's* also took aim at Prohibition in 1929 by publishing a "Bartender's Guide to Washington," exposing the many speakeasies frequented by those in office. However, perhaps no one did more damage to the ASL than William H. Anderson, general state superintendent of the League's New York chapter. In 1917, Anderson had managed the seemingly impossible by getting a local option law passed in the city. In 1924, however, Anderson, the League's golden boy and greatest hope, was charged with cooking the ASL's books, possibly to free up some money to bribe Tammany politicians to stay dry. Despite the fact that Anderson's actions were almost certainly approved by the top ranks, his colleagues abandoned him.

This was also the year Rockefeller stopped contributing money to the ASL. By the late 1920s, some industrialists were going so far as to denounce the law. One of the most stunning about-faces of the era involved Pierre S. du Pont, who, before Prohibition, had a reputation for being as intolerant of alcohol as Henry Ford. Indeed, du Pont had enforced strict no-drinking policies for his employees, even eradicating all saloons from Penns Grove, New Jersey, home to one of his largest factories. Workers had to cross the river and drink in Delaware. Eventually, however, du Pont began to register his concern for "my sons and daughters," who saw "thoroughly respectable and successful men and women drinking, talking about their bootleggers, the good 'stuff' they get, expressing their contempt for the Volstead law." He even went so far as to denounce the hypocrisy of businessmen who drank while condemning the working man for doing the same.

Henry Ford, by contrast, never did moderate his position that America was better without alcohol and opposed the repeal of Prohibition. "If the law were changed," Ford said, "we'd have to shut down our plants. Everything in the United States is keyed up to a new pace which started with Prohibition. The speed at which we run our motor cars, operate our intricate machinery, and generally live, would be impossible with liquor."

While Ford remained unmoved by the argument that Prohibition had led to hypocrisy and a dangerous contempt for the law, others were becoming convinced by it. Hollywood producers took up the notion enthusiastically, despite the fact that Prohibition was at least partly responsible for their continually growing audiences—those who couldn't afford the price of speakeasies. The flickers weren't the only forms of entertainment benefiting from Prohibition. The radio industry credited the abolition of the saloon with the rapid growth of home radio sales. Those without the cash to go out slumming stayed home with the radio and maybe some bootleg liquor. Those who couldn't afford bootleg went to the movies instead, where they could sublimate their desire by watching people drink on the silver screen. Reacting to this new demand for "alcohol porn," films evolved from a dry medium into a wet one, as the public enthusiastically lined up to watch Bert Wheeler and Robert

Woolsey getting *Caught Plastered*; Stan Laurel and Oliver Hardy getting blottoed in *Blotto*; and pretty well anything with W. C. Fields in it. But it wasn't all just hijinks with "snake medicine." Alcohol researcher Robin Room points out that, by 1928, films like *Our Dancing Daughters* were openly critical of the hypocrisy that many felt tainted Prohibition. In this film, the girl who claims to be a teetotaler is really an immoral drunk and the girl who admits to having a drink once in a while is the healthy, upstanding heroine. This message not only reflected the changing public opinion but helped form it. An MGM director in 1935 credited his medium with helping shift both opinion and policy by showing that "liquor was an immense factor in human life."

The enormous and far-reaching consequences of Prohibition apparently shocked men such as William Randolph Hearst, another original stalwart of Prohibition who switched sides not long after Pierre du Pont. Scores of other influential people followed, citing the same reasons: that Prohibition sparked contempt for the law and increased criminality, set back the cause of temperance, and encouraged young, middle-class men and women to drink in public. Often this drinking would go on in inappropriate places like Jimmy Kelly's or, worse, Harlem, prompting a mixing of social classes and ethnicities that not long before would have been unthinkable. The numerous articles in contemporary newspapers purporting to teach people the new Volstead lingo are testament to the anxiety over the new mixing of the races and possible miscegenation. From the *New York Sunday News*, November 3, 1929: "Blue means a very dark colored person; Freakish is used to describe an effeminate man or a mannish woman; Sweet man is a lover; Chitterlings is a tripe-like food, made from the lining of a pig's stomach; Snouts are pickled pig's snouts, a popular delicacy; Hunching is a dance."

There's no doubt that the image of Ellin Mackay types hanging out in mixed-race black and tans or in Greenwich Village with Italian mobsters, Russian-Jewish musicians, and Socialist writers was disturbing to many social and political leaders of the time—particularly at a moment when the pseudoscience of eugenics was capturing the imagination of many. In 1929, the Committee of Fourteen (a New York panel appointed to study the effects of Prohibition) reported that New York had sunk to new depths thanks to speakeasies that attracted young men and women who would otherwise "never have visited the old-time Raines-law hotel." It also cautioned that the speakeasy's cloak of "respectability" might throw its young patrons "off their guard." Further terrifying those concerned about their sons and daughters was the spate of violent incidents in these clubs, such as the sensational shooting of the Hotsy Totsy Club owners, and the open and widespread mob involvement. Men such as Jack Diamond (whose underlings had gunned down the owners in the Hotsy Totsy), Arnold Rothstein, Dutch Schultz, Charley Luciano, Lepke Buchalter, Bugsy Siegel, Jake Gurrah Shapiro, and Meyer Lansky all had shares in places such as the Cotton Club, Silver Slipper, Rendezvous, Les Ambassadeurs, Embassy Club, and the Club La Vie.

These concerns alone, however, weren't enough to summon the political will required to repeal a constitutional amendment—an incredibly daunting task. What finally tipped the scales in favor of repeal was the economy and, to be more precise, the dip in income tax caused by the Great Depression. The government, whose implementation of income tax in 1913 made Prohibition possible to consider, now needed a new revenue stream and would have to turn back to an alcohol tax to dig its way out. Franklin Roosevelt began with the Wine and Beer Revenue Act, which he signed March 22, 1933. Patrons jammed restaurants, including Luchow's in New York City, until it ran out of beer. Later that year, on December 5, Prohibition was fully repealed.

All this was not meant to encourage the rebirth of the saloon. In fact, Proclamation 2065 (the Repeal of the Eighteenth Amendment) contained this specific mandate from Roosevelt: "I ask especially that no state shall by law or otherwise authorize the return of the saloon either in its old form or in some modern guise." It was a nice thought. But, as Roosevelt must have known, the saloon hadn't really gone away, even during Prohibition. It had merely evolved, as it would continue to after repeal.

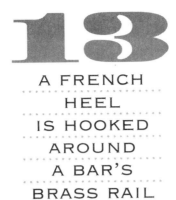

13

A FRENCH
HEEL
IS HOOKED
AROUND
A BAR'S
BRASS RAIL

STORMING THE SAZERAC, 1949

*These ladies are "Storming the Sazerac"—a bar at
the Roosevelt Hotel in New Orleans that was men's
only until Friday, September 25, 1949, when it
finally opened its doors to women. Image courtesy
of The Sazerac Company.*

"The lid is off!" announced the enthusiastic voice on a 1933 newsreel. Presumably it was playing to mostly empty theaters, since, according to the narrator, just about everyone was off celebrating the news in wetter venues. Some folks, as the voiceover pointed out, hadn't even waited for the official return of legal and licensed premises and were already out at hotels and nightclubs, renewing "old acquaintances" and reveling with "old time hilarity." Everyone, it was reported, was in a "real pre-War spirit."

That bit about the pre-War spirit, though, was perhaps a little exaggerated, given that some had never really changed their drinking habits, Prohibition or not. If anything, at least at the outset, the time right around repeal might even have been a little dryer than the tail end of Prohibition, because some speakeasies shuttered themselves up to avoid fines for serving without a license. There were a few brave soldiers and, on December 5, 1933, H. L. Mencken found one in the Rennert Hotel in Baltimore, where he celebrated "liberty restored" a few hours after news that the vote from Utah had carried the Twenty-First Amendment—the one that brought repeal. In preparation, the people of New Orleans had somehow managed to have fifty thousand gallons of imported liquor at the ready, much of it drunk in the streets to the sound of cannon fire. In Chicago, people crammed into Berghoff's and the Drake Hotel's Coq d'Or to raise a glass—the town's first establishments to secure licenses postrepeal. In Pittsburgh, the Pittsburgh Athletic Association was one of the first places up and serving. And then there was New York's Waldorf Astoria, which had a special punch made up as the pre-dinner cocktail when Pierre du Pont and other members of the Association Against the Prohibition Amendment met to toast victory. Mission accomplished, the members celebrated and made plans to disband the association the very next morning.

No women were invited to the Waldorf that night, but there were plenty out drinking. In a footnote to its story on repeal celebrations, *Time* magazine reported that, "many a woman, taught to drink by Prohibition, last week hooked a French heel over a brass rail."

Texas Guinan, who was so instrumental in that education, was not one of them. She died a month before repeal and would never have a chance to find out if she really was "nothing without Prohibition." Others who had profited off Volstead, however, simply went legit. Canadian suppliers, for example, were still associated with the highest-quality whiskey and had stores of properly aged product and a good distribution network in place to supply the thirsty market. American distillers didn't take long to get in the game, though, and the associated industries—grain growers, keg and barrel makers, and bottle manufacturers—rejoiced. An estimated half-million jobs would be created by repeal. Those who weren't looking for jobs in manufacturing plants were thinking entrepreneurially. There was a crush of people applying for licenses to sell beer the moment it became legal (on April 7, 1933) and another rush on liquor licenses when full repeal followed eight months later. In addition to struggling to keep up with the demand, licensing agencies were confronted with a new challenge: How could they issue licenses without also bringing back the saloon?

In some places, the solution was as simple as calling it by a different name. Herbert Asbury would later write that the word "saloon" had been transformed into "one of the most horrid words in the English language; it was officially eliminated from the nation's vocabulary by the Eighteenth Amendment and the Volstead Act, and remained under a ban after the Amendment had been repealed"—a reference to Roosevelt's plea that the saloon not be resurrected. "Even today," Asbury continued, writing in 1950, "it is nowhere permitted to call a retail liquor establishment a saloon." While the actual word might have been eliminated, a saloon by any other name would still be a saloon. Legislators therefore had to make sure that strict licensing regulations accompanied the return of legal public drinking, in order to ensure those old saloon evils—machine politics, miscegenation, gambling, narcotics, and prostitution—weren't also revived. How best to control the bar was left up to individual states.

Not every state had to deal with the problem immediately. Maine, for example, postponed legal drinking for a year and, state by state, different types of beverages were allowed in different proportions. Every state, save Alabama and Kansas, allowed light beer. In Connecticut, Indiana, Colorado, and California, legislators banned hard liquor from bars, which were only licensed to sell wine, beer, and cider. This failed spectacularly in California, where so many licensed establishments were openly defying this law that, by 1935, the state had to scrap it altogether. Arkansas, Texas, and South Carolina also tried on-premises liquor prohibitions, which had greater longevity. In Texas, right up to 1970, customers were obliged to bring their own liquor into bars and then charged for "set-ups" (ice, mixes, swizzle sticks, etc.). Kansas went wet in 1948 but really only legalized full liquor service in bars in the 1980s. And, in

South Carolina, hard liquor could only be served from airplane-style miniature bottles until 2005. Aside from environmental implications, such restrictions preemptively destroyed any chance of the development of a cocktail culture in bars. Then again, that may have been the point. Of the fifteen states that initially opted to stay dry, before long, many trickled into the wet column. By 1936, only seven remained dry. Mississippi, last of the latecomers, was entirely dry until 1966.

Many today still lament the legacy of these laws, claiming that they led to an overall degradation of the quality of drinks and bar service (begun with Prohibition, of course, but carried on with tight post-Prohibition regulations) that dogged American bars for most of the twentieth century. Instead of encouraging bartenders to reclaim the tradition of acquiring a "liberal education" in mixing spirits and cordials (of which George Ade and Thomas Mador Gilmore spoke of with such reverence), new regulations attempted to take the fun, flair, and glamour out of bartending and increasingly reduced barmen's roles from craftsmen to mere servers. As curious as these controls might sound now, at the time, most people didn't fret. Some states— New Hampshire, for example—implemented monopoly liquor stores, while others enacted legislation regulating the sale of beer and hard liquor in retail outlets. For the most part, the idea was to encourage home drinking, discourage public drinking, and to keep off-sales segregated from on-premises drinking. While beer was allowed in any bar, wine and liquor were often confined to "bona fide" hotels and restaurants. In addition, the old screen laws were brought back, on the grounds that "vice" and "debauchery" flourished in the relative privacy afforded by screens and curtains in bar windows.

Another attempt at discouraging the return of the saloon involved the actual physical bar. The long counter and brass rail, fixtures in so many saloons, had become so associated with drunken behavior that some states only allowed patrons to drink at tables. Similarly, a few Canadian provinces had launched repeal with "tap rooms," which were licensed to sell beer—and beer only—to patrons seated at tables. This arrangement was reminiscent of the German beer gardens and European-style bars (essentially cafes) that some argued led to a less violent and debaucherous sort of drinking. One major difference between some American tap rooms and German beer gardens was a prohibition on music. A number of states barred live music in any establishment selling liquor; those states that did allow it tightly regulated the musicians through cabaret licensing. Limits were put on the number of musicians who could play at one time in a single venue, severely restricting the performance of jazz, which was still considered racy and even dangerous.

Again, no matter which system was implemented, public interest in the details, rationale, or repercussions was limited. As suggested by the authors of *After Repeal*, a 1936 study of postrepeal alcohol licensing and use commissioned by John D. Rockefeller Jr., this might have been because of the public's general fatigue with alcohol-related issues that had occupied the minds and conversations of so many Americans for so many years. The authors describe a public apathy and a willingness to let the subject "drop." Yes, there were still a few dry stalwarts who howled against repeal, but most were simply and wordlessly happy to have drinking made cheaper and more convenient.

The federal government was especially mute on the matter. The only regulations it pushed for were those that discouraged tied-houses—the system by which a particular brewery subsidized (if not outright funded) saloonkeepers' startup and operating costs with the understanding that the saloon would carry its product exclusively. To discourage the resumption of a practice that had seemed responsible for so much irresponsibility prior to Prohibition, it was made illegal for a producer to own or invest in a tavern, even to provide signs or supplies, or to offer a quota system or credit. Such measures, however, were hard, if not impossible, to enforce. Bar owners couldn't be forced to carry a variety of beers and, if one chose to favor Pabst over Schlitz, liquor inspectors needed to prove that this was a result of financial incentives. Before long, unofficial versions of the tied-house system were common in most wet states.

New York Times writer H. I. Brock argued that, in New York's nightclubs, "control was the word, no longer abandon." Nonetheless, many state laws were ineffective. In California, as mentioned, a majority of establishments simply disregarded the liquor prohibition. In places where restaurants and hotels were the only outlets licensed to sell alcohol, modern versions of Raines law hotels would eventually surface. Even many once-decent restaurants and legitimate hotels slowly degenerated to mere liquor retailers. Liquor sales were extremely lucrative and it became tempting for many to let other aspects of the business slide in pursuit of the highest profits. Legislation in various municipalities that required a fifty-fifty ratio between food and drink sales was circumvented through creative bookkeeping; soda, coffee, and even cigarettes became defined as "food." Before long, the stale cheese sandwich was back on the table, especially on Sundays in states with "new blue." Old-timers in any state with blue laws will recall how you could always tell an out-of-towner because he would actually try to eat the sandwich. (In Ontario, they say that about Americans; in Michigan, they say it about Canadians.) Also widely disregarded was the outlawing of the physical bar. Within a couple of years of repeal, owners were insisting that their bar-like structure over which they served drinks was not a bar at all but, rather, a "counter," upon which it was convenient to serve food. In New York State, legislators had to give up on this prohibition within two years, modifying the law to require simply that the bar not be the "predominant feature" of the tavern. It nearly always was, of course.

As bad as the sale of liquor was to some, most opponents of repeal despised taverns that sold beer exclusively. These were described as places that sold to anyone, be they minors or already intoxicated, and catered to "loiterers and law violators."[1] Before long, antirepeal militants charged that "dive" bars and beer taverns had picked up where the worst saloons had left off and that, in many urban areas, youth drinking (under twenty-one—the legal drinking age in almost every jurisdiction in the 1930s) and prostitution was as bad as it had been before the noble experiment. In February 1935, a report on the new drinking establishments in Chicago by the Juvenile Protective Association declared the "Return of the Saloon" and claimed that vice in the city's "saloon-taverns" was rampant. "Some saloons are simply houses of prostitution, having adjacent rooms used for vice; hostesses solicited at the bars and tables, thence repairing to connecting quarters with the patrons." The more legitimate bars also still had to deal with prostitution where "streetwalkers" came "to solicit," often in plain view of the minors who were being served illegally. The report charged that "Children in liquor resorts watched prostitutes openly offer themselves to men, and witnessed appalling scenes of intoxication and debauchery."

We see concern over the return of the old saloon articulated in William Saroyan's Pulitzer Prize–winning play, *The Time of Your Life*, which takes place in Nick's Pacific Street Saloon, Restaurant and Entertainment Palace, a San Francisco dive. Although the play is ultimately redemptive, the characters who loiter in the bar include a drunkard, an out-of-work philosopher, a vice-squad bully, and a prostitute named Kitty Duval. New public drinking was beginning to look a lot like the old public drinking. Of all the anxieties expressed over the new legal "saloons", the presence of women in bars (whether of Kitty Duval's profession or not) was one of the most profound. Working-class women could afford to drink again in the new, legitimate, and relatively afford-able bars. And, although the middle and upper classes were being encouraged to buy packaged liquor for home consumption, the genie had been let out of the bottle during Prohibition.

A few, such as actor/singer Carl Brisson, championed the new era of female sipping with the song "Cocktails for Two" in the 1934 film, *Murder at the Vanities*: "Oh what delight to be given the right; To be carefree and gay once again; No longer slinking, respectfully drinking; Like civilized ladies and men."

A large number of men, however, lamented the loss of a male-only public sphere. None more than Don Marquis, newspaper columnist, playwright, and creator of Archy and Mehitabel as well as the "the Old Soak," a voice introduced in 1914 to complain about prohibition-ists. In 1935, Marquis privately published a small book devoted en-tirely to the problem of the presence of women in the "New Barroom," a state of affairs with which he and the "Old Soak" were "profoundly disappointed."

"What we had wanted, what we had hoped and prayed for, what we had fought, bled, died and lied for, was the return of the Old Barroom," he writes. "The vision of its return, just as it used to be, cheered us and sustained us through all these desert years of drought (mitigated by speakeasy cases) known as the 'prohibition' era."

Instead of the Old Barroom, Marquis and the Old Soak walked into a place that was "abominably and inescapably" open—a complaint about the screen laws. "Your wife, your sister, your maiden aunt, your little golden-haired daughter, your mother-in-law, the pastor of your church, the boss at your office, the wife of your boss and the wife of your pastor, the man you are trying to get a contract out of, your creditors, may look right through the window and count every drop of liquid damnation you dribble down your gullet." As if all that weren't bad enough, women could come "right through the front door" and even sit at the bar. "They put a foot on the brass railing. They order; they are served; they bend the elbow; they hoist; they toss down the feminine esophagus the brew that was really meant for men—stout and wicked men." Marquis knew that this change was likely to be permanent. Once a woman's foot "sets itself anywhere it never retreats."

Women's presence in the barroom would remain contentious for the next forty years. Some of the better bars and hotels instituted men-only policies and, before long, men came to dominate the high-end service industry, too. Working-class women had broken into the ranks of serving the public in restaurants and hotels in the 1920s, after Prohibition had come into effect right at the same moment their wealthier counterparts were getting into speakeasies. Prior to Prohibition, food and beverage service was almost exclusively the province of men, largely European immigrants. After Prohibition, as women such as Texas Guinan took over the running of nightclubs, the less glamorous jobs of working coffee shops and lunch counters began falling to women, who would work for less money than men. In addition, the 1924 Immigration Law, influenced by, among other things, Madison Grant's 1916 eugenist treatise, *The Passing of the Great Race*, limited the number of Europeans who could come to America each year (and prohibited Asian immigration entirely); this meant fewer European immigrants competing for jobs. Not only were women cheaper labor, the fact that alcohol wasn't served at luncheonettes and cafes helped them break into an industry from which they were largely barred, thanks to the feeling that women serving alcohol was a recipe for immorality. Now the girls of the concert saloon and other waitresses of the early twentieth century, described by sociologist Frances Donovan as "genuine Bohemians" living lives of "semi-prostitution," were being replaced by "girls" serving coffee, who were preferred by management and patrons over European waiters for their friendly demeanor.[2]

Male waiters felt threatened by the swarms of women moving from rural areas to take over urban food service and hospitality jobs, but managed to keep control of the more lucrative fine-dining jobs. Women were free to run the lunch counter, creating a pink ghetto. When alcohol came back into the picture, male waiters' unions petitioned politicians for clauses in all new legislation prohibiting women from handling liquor. This wasn't entirely without precedent. Ordinances banning women from working in saloons had been part of many state legislations and local option laws in pre-Prohibition days. In 1892, there was a crackdown on St. Louis proprietors employing "females in dramshops" and, around the turn of the century, a woman mixing a sling in Missouri was charged with a *felony*. You wouldn't have seen this every day, of course, since, according to an 1895 census, there were only 147 female bartenders in all of America compared to 55,660 men.

Still, just about every restaurant in the wet states was planning to offer alcohol as soon as it legally could, so prohibiting women from working these jobs would have been grossly unfair to those already working the lunch counter. Waitress' locals organized against local ordinances preventing them from night-shift work and the prospect of being legally shut out of all the lucrative jobs that involved liquor sales and service. Then again, even the most radical among them weren't entirely comfortable with women working in beer taverns and establishments that dealt exclusively in liquor. Few would have applied for such jobs and fewer still would actually have got them, so the prohibition on women bartenders was largely self-enforcing.

With the arrival of World War II, however, this was all about to change. Remarkably, there was little serious talk of revisiting Prohibition when America entered the war. Not none, simply very little. There had been a small groundswell of anti-alcohol sentiment in the early 1940s that resulted in a few local option ordinances; but perhaps because people on both sides were still suffering from Prohibition-fatigue syndrome, these generated little steam. If anything, prohibitionist groups were met with ridicule and derision. One particularly dismissive critique came from Theodore Geisel (Dr. Seuss), who lampooned the wartime prohibition movement with a 1942 cartoon of a crazy, axe-wielding woman riding a camel. The caption read, "Your Nutty Aunt Carry is Loose Again." (Nation used both "Carry" and "Carrie.") Seuss's biographer Philip Nel speculates that Seuss, in keeping with his lifelong grudge against the women who put his father, president of the Springfield Brewery of Massachusetts, out of work in 1920, also resurrects Nation in his 1954 *Horton Hears a Who!* in the character of misguided reformer Arabella Godiva.[3]

Rather than try to put taverns out of business, people were instead using them as places to unwind and reduce wartime stress. Even before the war, people turned to bars, which were simultaneously places to escape from dark news from Europe and places to discuss the severity of the situation. In the poem "September 1, 1939," W.H. Auden immortalized one of his locals, the Dizzy Club on 52nd Street in New York, a bar he frequented apparently for the purpose of forgetting the impending war. Its fifth stanza reads:

Faces along the bar
Cling to their average day:
The lights must never go out,

The music must always play,
All the conventions conspire
To make this fort assume
The furniture of home;
Lest we should see where we are,
Lost in a haunted wood,
Children afraid of the night
Who have never been happy or good.

In an admittedly limited fashion, the bar again reprised its role as a community and communications center, a place where people dropped in to exchange news and listen to the radio. While many had radios at home, they often still opted to listen in groups. Unfortunately, just when they were most needed, there was a shortage of bartenders, since so many were off fighting. Women, as we might expect, filled in. We hear a lot about Rosie the Riveter but not nearly so much about the lesser-known "Bessie the Bartender," as cocktail writer Eric Felten calls her. (One day, perhaps, she, too, will have a lunch box.) "Yes, we can," said the women who comprised Brooklyn's Bar Maids Local 101. Some critics still worried that the combination of alcohol and women would lead to debauchery and, as a compromise, Local 101 agreed that members were not to work past midnight or give out their last names. Women tended bars and even acted as sommeliers in restaurants all across the country. Even male food service unions and organizations had to admit that the desperate situation called for extreme measures.

But just as women machinists had to relinquish their jobs when the veterans returned from the war, so was Bessie the Bartender expected to give her shift back to male counterparts. When some refused, the scene grew ugly. Bartenders picketed establishments that kept female employees and pushed for state intervention. In Brooklyn, Bartenders Local 70 was out picketing in full force against The Mechlan and the Little Old New York Café, since they had been "locked out" of their work and replaced by "lady bartenders." *The Brooklyn Eagle* covered both sides of the equation. Barmaid Loretta (still careful not to divulge her last name) countered: "A woman has to make a living, and what's wrong with bartending? During the war it was patriotic for us to work."

Although the move was sparked by employment issues, it was helped by those who, like Don Marquis, still longed for the return of the saloon as a retreat from women. Opponents of women behind bars argued that they couldn't handle the potential violence of a barroom nor the complicated recipes for cocktails and, of course, that the pressure to earn a good tip might lead them astray. To others, it was plain unseemly. Newspapers such as the respected *Troy Record* concurred: "Who wants the hand that rocks the cradle mixing whisky sours?" Barmaid activists pointed out that it was no coincidence that those expressing the most concern for womens' moral well-being were almost universally their male competition.

As a result of similar protests and union pressure, which preyed on people's concerns for the family unit and female virtue, and fears over the evils of saloon prostitution, Michigan instituted a law prohibiting women bartenders in 1945—unless they were either the wife or daughter of a male proprietor. A female bar-owner not only could not employ her own daughter but couldn't tend bar herself. And pioneering entrepreneur Valentine Goesaert wanted to do just that. She had bought a bar in Dearborn and wanted to run it with her daughter and two female employees. The women challenged the law on the grounds that it discriminated against female bar-owners and took the case to the Supreme Court. In 1948, the law was upheld, although Supreme Court Justice Felix Frankfurter first paid lip service to the important role played by female servers: "We are, to be sure, dealing with a historic calling. We meet the alewife, sprightly and ribald, in Shakespeare, but, centuries before him, she played a role in the social life of England." Still, claimed Frankfurter, the regulation of liquor traffic was so important that it remained perfectly fine for Michigan to forbid all women from working behind the bar.

With Frankfurter's decision, prospective female bartenders in the sixteen other states that barred women from handling liquor lost hope. The ruling seemed to encourage the institution of new and similar laws across America. Bessie the Bartender was out of work in more than half of American states by the early 1960s and it would take another unrelated Supreme Court challenge in the mid-1970s for laws prohibiting women behind bars to be finally declared a violation of the Fourteenth Amendment. The 1976 *Craig v. Boren* ruling determined that discrimination on the basis of gender was only justified when it was "substantially related to the achievement of important governmental objectives." At stake in *Craig v. Boren* was a young man's right to buy 3.2 percent alcohol in Oklahoma. There, the law stated that women over eighteen could buy near-beer but men had to wait until they were twenty-one. By this point, however, many states had already dismantled laws prohibiting women behind the bar, with Michigan actually doing so quite early, in 1955. In "progressive" California, it took a 1971 Supreme Court Challenge—*Sail'er Inn v Kirby*—to rectify the discrimination. Here, topless waitresses wanted the right to become topless bartenders—and won. Another blow to the patriarchy.

Somewhere in between the two spheres of women—drinking in bars and those working in them—were the B-Girls of the 1940s and 1950s. Although often framed as a new offshoot of vice, Bar-Girls were, in fact, yet another version of concert saloon waitresses and "percentage girls," who were employed by establishments to entice men into drinking more and buying drinks, a percentage of which was given back to the working woman. It was an old game and, for the large part, the minor fraud didn't register very highly on most people's list of national emergencies. In the 1940s, most major cities had a section of town known as "B-Girl Row," which was periodically raided, then left to go back to business as usual. A *Los Angeles Times* reporter joked that there was so much B-Girl activity on "skid row" that there was a plan to organize a union. And, indeed, many did try to join the waitresses' union, so that they might have greater legal protection should the bar be raided.

In no way did these women appear to be waitresses within the bar, however. They were often modestly dressed and claimed to be typists or nurses en route home from work. After they hooked a willing pigeon, they would ask him to buy drinks all night, most of which were iced tea or soft drinks doctored to look like fancy cocktails. B-Girls would typically flirt with the man, leading him to believe he had found a date for the night. After a phenomenal number of fancy, overpriced drinks, the girl would suddenly excuse herself, leaving her poor fella with a huge bar tab. Marilyn Monroe famously played a B-Girl named Cherie in the 1956 film *Bus Stop* (also called *The Wrong Kind of Girl*) and, in it, complains about sometimes having to drink fifteen faux cocktails a night. Interestingly, the concern here was not so much for the women who had to resort to this work, nor the fact that it must have exposed them to some dangerous situations. Rather, the concern was for the male victims. In a 1952 *Life* magazine article, Chicago police captain Johnny Warren cautioned visiting political conventioneers to avoid "low taverns . . . strange girls and strange perfume." Anticipating a feeding frenzy, he predicted that the cocktail lounges, taverns, and hotel lobbies would be full of B-Girls. "Men are funny people at conventions. They're away from home plate. They're on first base and they think they're going to score. That's where they're wrong. They're only going to get clipped."

In California in the early 1950s, there was a full-on moral panic over the "boobytrap sisterhood" being played out in the sensational journalism of some West Coast newspapers. The *Los Angeles Times* ran an exposé of B-Girl Row at Main and East 5th Streets, where five taverns faced having their licenses revoked in May 1956. Later that summer, the paper ran a follow-up story on "Sin Street!" accompanied by a true confessional: "The shocking inside story of a B-Girl." San Francisco papers frequently ran similar front-page stories, tantalizing suburban readers and reconfirming their ideas that the city was a den of immorality. Amanda Littauer, who researches the history of sexuality in postwar America, associates the extreme and almost unfathomable moral panic over B-Girls as the earliest whiffs of McCarthyism and the Red Scare. B-Girls frequently targeted servicemen, many of whom might have believed they had fortuitously run into a "Victory Girl," women who reputedly "rewarded" soldiers for their bravery by having sex with them. The B-Girls represented an attack on the American family and way of life.

The B-Girl threat was used to justify barring women from the barroom, a hot political issue in the 1960s. It may seem fairly frivolous in the context of the arguably bigger issues second-wave feminists were dealing with (such as the wage gap), but some forward-thinking women such as Karen DeCrow and Betty Friedan recognized that keeping women out of bars not only denied them lucrative work but also kept them out of a powerful "public" sphere. In addition to the prohibition on tending bar, women were also denied admittance to "stag" bars and restaurants that had "stag lunches." For example, the Oak Room in New York's Plaza Hotel—where Cary Grant was duped and kidnapped in 1959's *North by Northwest*—didn't admit women before three in the afternoon. While the official rationale for these policies was that banning women in bars discouraged prostitution and the slightly lesser saloon evil, B-Girls, in 1967, some Syracuse University students recognized it as segregation. This wide-scale discrimination had been almost universally and unquestioningly accepted until the day some women had what philosophers call an "ontological shock"—the moment in which a commonly accepted practice is suddenly thrown into question.

It started one evening in late December when Joan Kennedy, a student at the Newhouse journalism school, and her mother, parched from a long day's Christmas shopping, decided to take a breather in the Rainbow Lounge of the Hotel Syracuse, only to be turned away on the grounds that they had no escorts. Kennedy immediately went to law student Karen DeCrow, who was active in Syracuse's brand new chapter of the National Organization for Women (NOW). Initially, there had been a lot of disagreement within the chapter over whether or not to push the issue. "A lot of people said we should back off, since people will think all we want to do is drink in bars," said DeCrow, still active, still living in Syracuse.

Many did not want NOW, as a new organization, to appear frivolous; but Kennedy's case caught DeCrow's imagination as a "symbol of being a free person." It was segregation, argued DeCrow, who had experience working against Jim Crow laws and who later went on to fight for women's rights to gain admission to private clubs and golf courses. It was also a barrier to her goal "to get women out into the marketplace" and prove that they weren't "sweet flowers who couldn't leave the home." She pointed out the absurdity that a woman could pick up a guy in the street and go to the hotel bar, but would be considered indecent if she went in with her mother. Further, DeCrow argued, in these men's only spaces, a lot more than recreation was happening. "Most business decisions don't happen because somebody calls a meeting at ten in the morning, at which all issues are to be decided," says DeCrow. "They happen informally over drinks after work."

DeCrow's arguments prevailed and a modest-sized crowd of people came from around the country to support the sit-in she organized at the Rainbow Lounge. DeCrow recalls that the hotel had taken pre-emptive measures against the sit-in (which had been announced to the press) and had removed all the seats from the bar stools. "They also changed the numbers on the sign from the fire department that determines the number of people allowed in the room from one hundred and ten—to six," says DeCrow. "You'd have to be an idiot to fall for that."

DeCrow then organized a sit-in at a bar in Syracuse called McCarthy's, "a male-only place catering to a less-than-carriage trade." When the media arrived for a quote, DeCrow recalls that they interviewed "a man dressed in a torn sweat shirt, unshaven and with a few teeth . . . (who) told television cameras that 'he didn't come here to pick up girls.'" Next came the lawsuit against the Hotel Syracuse. When DeCrow brought news of her chapter's activities to the NOW convention in New York in May 1968, the issue seemed ready to explode. That convention was held at the Biltmore Hotel, which just happened to have a men's-only bar, at which powerful men, such as Governor Al Smith—the 1928 Democratic Party candidate for president—historically had congregated.

The following February, DeCrow and others orchestrated the national "Public Accommodations Week," for which NOW members organized "drink-ins" at men's-only bars across America. Among the splashier drink-ins was Judith Meuli's group's descent on the Polo Lounge in Los Angeles' Beverly Hills Hotel; the invasion of The Retreat, Washington, DC's male enclave; and Betty Friedan's party of three, which demanded but was refused service at the Plaza Hotel's Oak Room. Also noteworthy were the seven NOW members who descended on Berghoff's in Chicago, a male-only institution distinguished, as we've seen, for having received the city's very first postrepeal liquor license, and for having complied with the law throughout Prohibition by serving only near-beer, just as McSorley's Old Ale House had.

McSorley's had one other thing in common with Berghoff's. Other than the occasional ale served to Mother Fresh-Roasted, a widowed panhandler whose husband had apparently died from the bite of a poisoned lizard in Cuba during the Spanish-American War, McSorley's had never, in its alleged 115 years of business, served a woman. It even had a sign posted at the front door that read: "No Back Room in Here for Ladies." Having thrived for over a century on "good ale, raw onions and no women," McSorley's wasn't about to cave just because Karen DeCrow and colleague Faith Seidenberg bellied up to the bar in protest. In a *New Yorker* article, DeCrow recalled it seeming like a very large bar, a distortion she attributes to her fear. "We went in," said DeCrow, "and guys were hooting at us." Her request for a glass of ale was ignored. "So a man sitting at the bar bought us drinks. The crowd didn't turn on us, but they threw him out the door bodily. His face was covered with blood."

In 1969, Seidenberg launched a lawsuit against McSorley's, but it never got to court since a New York City law would go into effect the following year that eliminated discriminatory practices in all public spaces. Barbara Schaum, who owned a nearby leather goods store, was reportedly the first female patron to be served in the bar (other than Mother Fresh-Roasted, of course).

While McSorley's had to be forced to open its doors to women, most bars willingly changed policy. Berghoff's, for example, even invited Gloria Steinem (and media) to have a drink. There were other bars, however, that offered a thoroughly intimidating atmosphere for their unwelcome new guests. In Judith Rossner's 1975 novel *Looking for Mr. Goodbar*, this anxiety is expressed when the main character refers to the chasm between the media attention and legal gains made by women such as Karen DeCrow, and the reality of walking into a bar alone. "However much she might have read in recent years about women in bars, they were still in her mind very much a male preserve, an almost magical kind of place where men went to get away from women."

Don Marquis had been proved right: A woman's foot was now set firmly on the brass rail, even in bars in which she clearly wasn't welcome. And if Marquis was right about women inhibiting men's ability to enjoy themselves, whether or not these women were trying to, they were precisely the civilizing force needed to prolong the life of the tavern. America's anxiety had shifted away from its brief period of vilifying all saloons back to the time-honored tradition of denigrating only the bad ones—the ones with brawls and excessive drinking, as well as another type of men-only bar—the gay bar.

14

JOE MCCARTHY STORMS INTO A BAR

José Sarria performing Faust in San Francisco's Black Cat Café, circa 1961. Photo courtesy of The José Sarria Collection.

Christmas Eve. A depressed George Bailey walks into Martini's bar and starts demanding service. When George gets uncharacteristically drunk, Nick the bartender and the proprietor, Mr. Martini, grow concerned about the well-being of their friend and banker. A couple of scenes later in *It's a Wonderful Life*, George—having now been given the gift of never having been born—returns to the bar with the angel Clarence, who asks for a mulled wine, "heavy on the cinnamon and light on the cloves." Bartender Nick doesn't have any mulled wine in this alternate reality but, instead, the order elicits this response: "Hey, look, mister, we serve hard drinks in here for men who want to get drunk fast. And we don't need any characters around to give the joint atmosphere. Is that clear? Do I have to slip you my left for a convincer?"

There is, of course, a dark side to Frank Capra's Christmas classic— the one in which George Bailey has not been born. Even before the transformation, George, as a result of his drinking, gets into a bar fight and rams a tree with his car; but the truly dark side is the one Nick articulates—post transformation—when he makes a clear division between the dives that cater to serious drinkers and the ones with "atmosphere." The division wasn't merely a part of the vernacular of the day; it was a bona fide academic subject. In 1945, Yale published twenty-nine lectures from a summer session in Alcohol Studies—one of which, John Dollard's "*Drinking Mores of the Social Classes*", was a splendid example of the attitudes that continued to shape alcohol policy in America. Dollard's lecture is not a study in hidden class assumptions. Rather, they are overt: "In the Upper classes, drinking is not a moral issue. People at the top of our social structure drink a good deal; both sexes drink. Men and women drink in the same groups, in party style. There are, however, certain stiff controls here which do not exist in some of the lower classes."

Even Dollard's divisions are telling. He divides American society into a taxonomy of six classes, starting with the Upper-Uppers, descending into the "Upper-Lower" ("poor but honest folk; the working element") and, at the bottom, the "Lower-Lower," whom he describes as the "no 'count poor," "the ignorant," and the "shiftless." Members of the lower classes were characterized as "openly aggressive" when drinking, thanks to a lack of training. They were missing something called the "drink like a gentleman taboo." Obviously, this behavior extended to the bars in which they drank. There was, therefore, no need to police establishments catering to the Upper-Uppers or even Upper-Middle men. Upper-Middle women weren't a problem since they didn't drink at all.

Nick's statement in *It's a Wonderful Life* seems to allude to something else, too. Clarence's drink choice is obviously too effeminate for a bar where "men" drink "hard drinks." His choice labels him as a "character" who threatens to give the joint "atmosphere"—something Nick threatens to shut down with his fist. He has these two "pixies"—Clarence and George—thrown out. It doesn't require much of a stretch of the imagination to situate this in the context of the most feared bar patron in America at the time—the gay male, worse even than the threat of a B-Girl or a feminist with her foot on the brass rail.

For gay clientele, there was something even more fundamental at stake than there was for pioneering women, who had been denied access to better-paying jobs and the unofficial business boardroom. For gay men in America, the restrictions against gay bars and the constant harassment of the few bars that operated outside of the laws also represented a denial of their basic right to associate. And the whole point of freedom in the context of American democracy is this freedom of association.

People tend to think of gay bars as a relatively recent phenomenon. But they've always been there, usually covert, and typically falling into one of two categories—those that were circumspect and the ones that regularly got raided. Laying claim to the title of "America's Oldest Gay Bar" is New Orleans' Café Lafitte in Exile, which was founded by Tom Caplinger in 1953, when he and other gay patrons (including Tennessee Williams) were made to feel unwelcome at Lafitte's Blacksmith Bar, a few blocks down along Bourbon Street. (The Blacksmith, by the way, lays claim to being the oldest structure in America [1772, at least] currently housing a bar.)

Lafitte in Exile's claim is disputed. Other contenders are Twin Peaks in San Francisco's Castro district (early 1970s) and the 1957 trio of Nob Hill in Washington, DC, Leon's in Baltimore, and Radio City Lounge in Salt Lake City, Utah. Additionally, there are the Double Header in Seattle's Pioneer Square and the White Horse Tavern in Oakland, California. The Double Header has a good case for being America's oldest gay bar, since it was established in 1933 and started attracting a gay clientele (at least to its basement area) right from the outset. After World War II, the main floor became a gay bar, too. Today it's primarily a straight bar. And, if that disqualifies the Double Header, there remains the White Horse, which can and does boast continuous operation with a gay clientele since 1936.

Not that this makes it the first. We certainly know, for example, that Pfaff's beer cellar, which notable New York bohemians frequented in the

1860s and 1870s, catered to a gay clientele that Whitman described as "beautiful young men" with "bright eyes" who "flit along." Foreshadowing the phenomenon of slumming, Whitman described well-heeled New Yorkers who enjoyed mixing with "bohemians and bummers."[1] Since so many gay bars were covert, it's difficult to delineate a clear early history; but, starting in the 1870s, there are numerous reports of "resorts" catering to a gay clientele—largely men, of course—in the red light districts of many urban areas. In Herbert Asbury's 1936 "informal" history of the French Quarter in New Orleans, he describes the aforementioned multiracial, gay bar/bordello, run by Big Nellie at Lafayette near Baronne. Asbury claims it had "permanent roomers" by the names of "Lady Richard, Lady Beulah Toto, Lady Fresh and Chicago Belle," and was home to many balls at "which both white and Negro men were invited." This sort of bar/bordello was probably not entirely uncommon in New Orleans, which had had a "great influx" of gay men around 1890; but there were also queer red-light districts in urban areas across America.[2] Of these, perhaps none was as infamous as the Bowery, which, again in the 1890s, was a major attraction on slumming tours. According to historian George Chauncey, one of the tour's principal attractions were the "degenerates" and "inverts" who frequented resorts such as Columbia Hall, better known as Paresis Hall (a reference to the insanity one was likely to pick up if he had contact with its patrons). Paresis, Manilla Hall, the Black Rabbit, and Slide were some of the better-known resorts at the turn of the century that were relatively open about their patronage. But they always faced the risk of harassment from reformers like Anthony Comstock, who made a career out of fighting vice.[3]

During Prohibition and for the decade or so after repeal, many newly opened gay bars and speakeasies were actually left alone, despite the fact that "indecent" and "immoral" behavior was grounds for revocation of a license. The word "gay," in fact, was initially part of a code used mainly to describe bars (for instance, a speakeasy said to be in the "Gay 20s") to cue potential clientele. Others advertised by means of slightly more obscure references, like Bonnie's Stone Wall tea room in New York's West Village, which was very likely named after a 1930 lesbian autobiography, *The Stone Wall*.

It was only postwar, in the late 1940s and early 1950s, that gay bars became a target for the first time since the Comstock era at the turn of the century. Once again, gay bars began to be pathologized as places for dangerous, out-of-control binge-drinking, recruitment, "infection," and, of course, indecent and immoral activities, which were seemingly a result of the disinhibition caused by excessive drinking. The reason for this surge in harassment and intolerance is easily traced to McCarthyism and its accompanying values, constructed in opposition to notions of "bohemianism" and the supposed anti-family values of the left, as well as to labor and women's movements. While we associate Senator Joseph McCarthy primarily with anticommunism and the blacklist, another significant contribution he made was to the culture of homophobia. McCarthy began purging the government and military of homosexuals on the grounds that they could more easily be blackmailed and turned into communist spies. Obviously, the potential for blackmail was much greater for those who now worked in an even less tolerant workplace, making McCarthy's fears a self-fulfilling prophecy, if not outright circular reasoning.

Homophobia soon informed government policy at all levels and inspired police raids. For the most part, the raids were confined to men's bars; but there was certainly plenty of harassment on the street, in parks, and at some lesbian bars, too. John D'Emilio, author of 1983's seminal *Sexual Politics, Sexual Communities*, describes an orchestrated raid in New Orleans on both gay and lesbian bars in 1953 that resulted in sixty-three women taken into custody. A few years later, the Alamo Club of San Francisco was raided, resulting in the arrest of thirty-six women, one of whom recalled being in a state of "paralyzing fear" and running for cover—"again." Raids on lesbian bars were actually common and, as D'Emilio explains, the numbers seem even more skewed since there weren't nearly as many lesbian bars as there were those that catered to gay men.[4] One post-war estimate places the total number of lesbian bars in America at about thirty. At the time, there were roughly thirty gay bars in San Francisco, alone, and an estimated forty in New York City.

One of those San Francisco bars was the Black Cat Café on Montgomery Street, which, according to Allen Ginsberg, was the greatest gay bar in the world. Ginsberg wasn't the only literary character to hang out at the Black Cat; William Saroyan and John Steinbeck were regulars, too. The place was immortalized by Jack Kerouac as the setting for much of the action in *On the Road*. The Black Cat was a thorn in the side of vice squads and policemen before, during and after Prohibition. It had once been a vaudeville theatre, which was often suspected of being a front for prostitution, and, after the war, reopened as a bar with a honky-tonk piano where Ginsberg recalled "gay screaming queens" mingled with poets, longshoremen and "heterosexual gray flannel suit types." The bohemian scene was closely observed by Alfred C. Kinsey, who apparently spent a month observing the Black Cat's star attraction José Sarria, a waiter-turned-drag-performer who specialized in torch songs and "satirical operas," and who will credit himself for introducing opera to San Francisco's gay community. The Black Cat's license was constantly under threat from the California Alcohol and Beverage Control Board (ABC), which suspended it periodically, since the owner, Sol Stoumen, refused to pay the bribes necessary for the maintenance of a gay bar in that era. Although many have claimed that the mafia ownership of gay bars didn't really begin until the 1960s and was primarily an east coast phenomenon, owners had to be prepared to deal with a certain level of local corruption; there were frequent shakedowns, especially in states where there were laws on the books specifically designed to thwart the assembly of gay men in licensed establishments. In some states, gay bars were explicitly illegal; but, in reality, even in states where they weren't prohibited, all gay bars actually bordered on the illegal, given how easy it was for authorities to declare them "disorderly." In that owners often needed help facilitating payoffs to police, bars that operated on the outskirts of the law needed outlaws to run them.

Stoumen's license was revoked in 1948 on the grounds that he was keeping a "disorderly house." He took the ruling to the California Supreme Court and, in 1951, since there was no specific law in the state prohibiting gay bars, had his license restored. This would hardly be the end of his legal troubles, though. The Black Cat would be repeatedly raided, with patrons arrested for cross-dressing and other "lewd" and indecent behavior. Sarria counseled the clientele to attach signs to their clothes reading, "I'm a Boy," so that they couldn't be charged with female impersonation "with intent to deceive." All of the Black Cat's trials and tribulations were made even more challenging by the addition, in 1955, of a statute that specifically made gay bars illegal in the state of California. In his book, D'Emilio connects the dots between bar patronage in the gay community, sexual identity, and the politics of resistance. His project was spurred on by the assumption that members of the queer community lived in isolation and had no real communal association prior to the Stonewall Inn riots of 1969 in New York, universally regarded as the catalyst for the gay pride movement. For all its significance, Stonewall, in itself, was a clear indication that a tight-knit and well-organized community existed prior to 1969, one that was sufficiently politicized to launch a major revolution overnight. D'Emilio's work demonstrates that gay pride evolved from well-established networks that had developed throughout the 1950s and 1960s—almost entirely in gay bars.

The gay bars in which these networks were established, proliferated—much to McCarthy's chagrin—in the post-war period as gay military personnel, previously closeted in small towns, moved to larger urban areas and "came out." (What did you think The Village People's "In the Navy" was about?) In Seattle, San Francisco, Los Angeles and New York, bars offered what D'Emilio describes as "an all-gay environment where patrons dropped the pretension of heterosexuality, socializing with friends as well as searching for a sexual partner."[5] In the conservative climate of the 1950s, however, police forces consistently raided any place that came to be known as even tolerant of a gay clientele.

Ironically, the campaigns of police harassment and vigilante violence that were meant to break up the gay communities wound up uniting them. As D'Emilio puts it, "When trouble struck, as it often did in the form of a police raid, the crowd suffered as a group," making the bars "seedbeds for a collective consciousness that might one day flower politically."[6] Whether the rationale for harassing and shuttering gay bars stemmed from an understanding that they were venues for political organization or, more likely, a fear of "recruitment" and an ensuing epidemic of immorality, crackdowns were frequent. In New York in 1960, police managed a near-complete eradication of all the gay bars in the city; only the Cherry Lane Theater was left operating. In protest, hundreds of men, maybe even thousands, took to the streets and cruised Greenwich Avenue and Third Avenue between 50th and 60th Streets until the police, officials, and the general public had time to rethink their stance on gay bars. One by one, the bars were quietly reopened.

In 1961, back in San Francisco, Stoumen was again in trouble with the ABC—along with half of the city's forty-nine gay bars, all of which had been closed down sporadically for most of 1960 and 1961. This had been in retribution for the assertiveness of several Polk Gulch bar owners who, the previous year, had the audacity to charge eight San Francisco police officers with soliciting bribes in what would become known as the "Gayola" scandal. After the officers were acquitted, the payoffs subsided but closures increased.[7] It had become increasingly clear to some that it was time to take the persecution into the political arena. And who better to represent not only Stoumen but the entire community than Jose Sarria, the

Black Cat waiter whose Sunday afternoon "satirical operas" had become a neighborhood mainstay Sarria's camp performances, which the dowager queen always closed with: "All right, you nellie queens, on your feet! United we stand, divided they'll catch us one by one," had become a rallying call. Sarria ran for City Supervisor that year, in 1961—a full twelve years before Harvey Milk's first try at public office—and while the odds were stacked against him, he came close to winning one of the six spots on the Board. Sarria says he never wanted to win but, rather, to prove that gay people had the right to run for public office. He was the first openly gay candidate for public office anywhere in America—not that he was the first gay politician, Sarria is quick to point out. He explains that he was also the first to say: "There's no crime in being gay, the crime lies in getting caught."

Sarria's run for office helped the gay community grasp that the personal was political and that political organization would be necessary to protect it. The League for Civil Education was born in San Francisco's gay bars, where it also distributed its newsletters—just as early Revolutionary pamphleteering had taken place primarily in the taverns of Boston, Philadelphia and New York. Bar-owners, themselves, organized and formed the Tavern Guild, which began fighting the ABC and asserting members' rights to own and operate bars catering to a gay clientele.

This would all come too late for the Black Cat, however. Stoumen simply couldn't afford to keep the good fight going and would lose his license yet again—the night before Halloween 1963. The following year, he closed up shop for good, a victim of both legislation and its enforcement. Two new organizations, however—the Lesbian Daughters of Bilitis and the Society for Individual Rights—would continue to defend other bar owners and the newfound understanding that the struggle against discrimination *was* political and that a fundamental right—the right to associate—was being denied to the community.

The crackdown on the gay community in San Francisco seems to have encouraged some to venture up the coast, seeking greener pastures in Oregon and Washington State, where major cities already had large gay communities and seemingly more lax regulations surrounding their association and public drinking. Even the response to this influx of gay residents was decidedly humane, at least compared with the reactions in Los Angeles, San Francisco, and New York. Still, there was some opposition. Portland Mayor Terry Schrunk, for example, declared in 1964 that he wasn't about to let his city become a "small San Francisco."

Accordingly, Schrunk launched the first campaign to revoke licenses from the city's gay bars since an early 1950s purge led by Mayor Dorothy McCullough Lee; but his attempts were thwarted by legal action and an uncooperative state licensing board. As a result, argues historian Peter Boag, the gay population of Portland was decidedly apolitical. Having freedom of association meant there was less need to form a Tavern Guild and make political stands.[8] The other main area San Francisco refugees fled to was Seattle. Before long, there was a small backlash there, too. The Seattle City Council, however, decided it preferred a few explicitly gay bars than to have gays "scattered" in bars across the city, and negotiated for legal licenses to be maintained by owners who would exercise tight control over patrons' behavior. This would lead to Seattle becoming one of the first major American cities where the bars weren't run by the mafia. No shakedowns, no mob.

In the summer of 1964, *Life* magazine tackled the gay bar in a special report on "Homosexuality in America." Aside from trying to answer the questions "Why does it happen?" and "How can it be prevented?," writer Paul Welch profiled the culture in San Francisco, which he claimed was the "Gay Capital" of America. There, Welch found a "sad and often sordid world" of increasingly bold men who even had "their own drinking places." Of course, for every bold and "obvious homosexual," there were "probably nine" who were "nearly impossible to detect." They were pretty easy to detect over at the Tool Box, a leather bar that was photographed (but never named) for the first couple of pages of the article. Proprietor Paul Ruquy was famously quoted as saying that his bar represented the "anti-feminine side of homosexuality." Welch portrayed the Tool Box as the most pathological of San Francisco's bars and represented the "far-out fringe" of the community. He contrasted it with the Jumpin' Frog, a cruising bar where men drank "inexpensive beer," and the slightly more respectable gay bars, such as the Black Cat, which Welch noted had recently closed down. He determined that the average lifespan of a gay bar in San Francisco was about eighteen months.

But where one Black Cat was shuttered, a new one opened up. In this case, in terms of the name, literally. In 1966, two years after the San Francisco Black Cat closed, a Black Cat Tavern in the Silver Lake district of Los Angeles opened at the corner of Sunset and Sanborn. Thanks in part to magazines that were declaring San Francisco the gay capital and the dramatic events that would soon follow in New York City, Los Angeles may not immediately come to mind when thinking about the struggle for gay rights. However, as a port city, Los Angeles rivaled San Francisco, Miami, Chicago, New Orleans, and New York for the size of the gay community that settled there after the war. In the early 1950s, at least a half dozen of America's lesbian bars—the If Club and the Lakeshore (established in the 1940s), along with the Pink Glove, the Cork Room, the Star Room, and the Open Door—were located in Los Angeles.[9]

Back at the Black Cat, as 1966 turned into 1967, the patrons sang "Auld Lang Syne" and kissed—as people often do on New Year's Eve. At that moment, police officers, who had been in the bar the entire night posing as customers, came out of the woodwork and randomly arrested and beat patrons. This was justified on the grounds that the gay and lesbian kissing had lasted more than a "reasonable" number of seconds and couples, therefore, had crossed the line into the realm of the lewd. The tactic was not an uncommon one in policing gay bars.[10] In fact, Los Angeles police inspector James Fisk, in that same Paul Welch article in *Life*, described the undercover sting used to root out homosexuality. It involved sending police "dressed to look like homosexuals—tight pants, sneakers, sweaters or jackets" to "prowl the streets and bars." In the community, these undercover cops were known as "Betty Badge" or "Lily Law." Despite the efforts of the Los Angeles Police Department (LAPD) in their "unrelenting crackdown"—over three thousand arrests for homosexual offenses in 1963 alone—Fisk lamented that they were "barely touching the surface of the problem. The pervert is no longer as secretive as he once was. He's aggressive and his aggressiveness is getting worse because of more homosexual activity."

Despite fears of police brutality in Los Angeles, within six weeks of the raid on the Black Cat, a protest was organized for the corner of Sunset and Sanborn. Two hundred people registered their disapproval of the "arbitrary" arrests and held placards reading: "No More Abuse of Our Rights and Dignity." The protest received scant coverage and support in the mainstream media and, though the Los Angeles Tavern Guild raised money to cover the legal costs of those arrested, the kissers were eventually convicted of lewd acts. Perhaps because of the clear systemic dismissal of this injustice and subsequent political action, critical studies scholar Belinda Baldwin points out that several associations grew more militant and vocal. Two community members, Richard Mitch and Bill Rau, decided to start their own gay publication—*The Advocate*.

While the Black Cats, the Tool Box, and numerous other gay bars in major cities were being harassed to the point of extinction, there were actually a few that were never once raided or persecuted—those that simply paid off police regularly. Some suspect the White Horse in Oakland managed to stay open for a record-setting seventy-plus years precisely because of prompt payment of bribes. Other bars—the swank ones *Life* magazine described as "just off the lobbies" of the country's grand hotels—didn't need to bribe police at all; they and their wealthy and respectable clientele were generally left alone. In the article, customers are classified as one of three sorts: "Local businessmen and out-of-town visitors—plus occasional innocent heterosexual travelers."

Welch neglected to identify any of these gay cocktail bars but, in Los Angeles, the bar at the Biltmore Hotel was notorious, as was the Marine Room at the Olympic Hotel in Seattle, the bar at Portland's Multnomah, The Monteleone's Carousel bar in New Orleans, and the Viking Room in Minneapolis's Radisson Hotel. The local businessmen who cruised the Viking were referred to as "piss elegant" by memoirist Ricardo J. Brown, while the "ribbon clerks" (a term used in poker to denote players who bet too little) preferred a working-class bar across the river in St. Paul.[11] In New York, the Oak Room in the Plaza Hotel was a famous cruising bar in the 1950s and 1960s. This may add a layer of meaning (or perhaps irony) to Betty Friedan's feminist gesture there in February 1969. Even the men's only bar in New York's Biltmore—the hotel where feminists organized to gain admittance into male bars—had been an important cruising spot. None of New York's swank cruise bars, however, was quite as famous as the men's bar at the Astor Hotel, which had been, more or less, happily serving a gay clientele since pre-Prohibition times. After repeal, the Astor resumed its traditions and allowed gay men to drink at the bar, provided they didn't become so "obvious" that they scared off any of the "innocent heterosexual travelers."

Why wouldn't the Astor's management serve openly gay men? There was no law against serving homosexuals. Or was there? This was a question that plagued the gay community of New York for some time. And a 1966 protest was designed to determine exactly that. This was the Sip-In, at which four members of Mattachine (the most prominent gay rights group prior to 1965) intended to demand drinks at bars where they were unwelcome. Unlike Stonewall, the Sip-In was not a spontaneous uprising. It was a staged event, explicitly intended to gain publicity for the gay community, but also to force the State Liquor Authority (SLA) and the police to define the legality of gay bars in New York. Contrary to most people's understanding, the New York SLA had never had any explicit rule against gay bars—only a rule against "disorderly" bars. Then again, the mere presence of a single homosexual could turn a bar from a perfectly respectable place into one rife with disorderliness.[12]

There had been one previous court challenge to this SLA policy, in the 1950s, when police raided the Fifth Avenue Bar (oddly enough, located on Broadway) that was part of a well-respected and long-established cafeteria complex on the Upper West Side. Despite the Fifth Avenue's reputation for generally responsible management, police dropped in late one night and found fifteen men believed to be homosexuals, one of whom was arrested for soliciting an undercover officer. This was enough evidence for the SLA to revoke the bar's license; but the owners fought the ruling in court, where it was determined the SLA did not have enough evidence to prove that the bar had knowingly courted a gay clientele. Any bar-owner could have unwittingly done so (after all, nine out of ten were virtually "impossible to detect") and the court ruled that a bar could only lose its license if it could be shown that it had catered to the "disorderly" on purpose.

While the ruling would appear to represent some progress (in that, at least bar owners couldn't simply have licenses revoked at the sight of a gay patron), historian George Chauncey argues that neither the SLA nor the police paid much attention to the court ruling and continued to raid and revoke licenses pretty much as they had before.

What this did, however, was encourage management to be more rigorous in policing their own bars. Many bars had signs indicating their policy against serving homosexuals. In that 1964 *Life* story, the editors included what might be the most shockingly incendiary part of the article, a photo of a bartender with a sign behind him reading: "Fagots—Stay Out." Perhaps the most appalling aspect of the photo's inclusion in the article is that it seems completely gratuitous. The article is about gay bars and the policing of them, not straight bars with a no-homosexual policy. Perhaps to justify its inclusion, the caption included a micro-interview with Barney Anthony, spelling bee champion and owner of the Santa Monica Boulevard bar with the aforementioned sign. "I don't like 'em," he says. "There's no excuse. They'll approach any nice-looking guy. Anybody does any recruiting, I say shoot him. Who cares?"

There were hundreds of similar signs across America in straight bars in or near gay neighborhoods. One, at the Ukrainian-American Village Restaurant on New York's Lower East Side read, "If You Are Gay, Please Go Away," and was destined to become at least a small footnote in New

York bar history. Led by Dick Leitsch, a New York Mattachine activist, four men planned to enter the restaurant on April 21, 1966, declare themselves "orderly homosexuals" and demand service. Leitsch, though, had tipped off the press about his plans and the reporters, in turn, had tipped off the restaurant. When Leitsch arrived, the place had closed for the day, unwilling to be a part of the event.

Things got even more anticlimactic after that. Leitsch and company then went to several neighborhood bars and, despite their open admission that they were homosexuals, got served everywhere they went, until they hit the Julius on West 10th Street in Greenwich Village. Famous for having been patronized by both Truman Capote and Tennessee Williams, the Julius may well have been the oldest continuously operating gay bar in New York. Since the Julius regularly served a gay clientele, the foursome had to convince the manager that, with his license already facing suspension, he simply couldn't afford to serve self-declared homosexuals. When this logic prevailed, the four were refused service and Leitsch, finally, could stage his "Sip-In" and hand the media a story. In exchange for the Julius' cooperation, Leitsch promised to use Mattachine funds to help it deal with its troubles with the SLA.

Sensing entrapment, the SLA denied that it had played any role in the large number of bars in New York that refused service to the gay community or in the regular closings of those that did. Again, it claimed to only be suspending licenses in places where there were established cases of disorderly conduct. Leitsch's campaign, then, was not destined to be the watershed moment he had planned—one that would help free the gay bar community from the exploitative yoke of oppression by the mafia, which charged outrageous prices to run what were, despite SLA denials, essentially illegal bars. In a sense, while the rest of the country celebrated repeal in 1933 and the return of safe and legal public drinking, Prohibition lingered on in the gay community for nearly forty more years.

Just one short block south of the Julius was the epitome of unsafe and illegal drinking in New York brought about by this unofficial prohibition. Almost a year after the slightly underwhelming Sip-In, the Genovese crime family opened the Stonewall Inn. Even before it became indelibly associated with the riots that would kick-start the world-wide revolution, the Stonewall was famous. Or, at least, infamous.

Located at 53 Christopher Street, Stonewall was slapped together by "Fat" Tony Lauria and a couple of associates for $3,500, despite Fat's father's protestations that it was beneath the family's position in the mob hierarchy to run a gay bar. The investment was destined to pay off in spades. The Genovese family, one of the largest in New York City's "five families," immediately became involved in the venture—an inevitability since Genovese family Capo, Matty "the Horse" Ianniello, had a stake in almost every gay bar in New York at the time. This underground empire was so incredibly lucrative because the New York police were so repressive. While one might expect New York to have been a relatively safe place to be gay in the 1960s, many contemporaries remarked on how dangerous a place it was to be an "obvious" homosexual. In smaller towns, where gay communities were less visible, many enjoyed relative freedom; but, in New York and its burgeoning gay community, police reacted with systematic violence.

The mafia did more than simply run interference against the police, however; it also took advantage of the situation to justify charging exorbitant prices in what were essentially dismal and unsafe drinking spaces. Moreover, just because the police were paid off didn't guarantee that fairly regular raids—with patrons hauled off to the station—wouldn't occur. The payoffs really only guaranteed that the illegal bar could reopen immediately after a raid. In the worst places, mob-run prostitution was part of the package, and many were part of blackmail rings, in which money was extorted from closeted gay patrons.

Stonewall was the poster child for all of these negative attributes. Despite paying an alleged twelve hundred dollars per month in bribes—generally thought to be the most exorbitant monthly gayola rate charged to any bar—it was subject to frequent raids. Cover—three dollars to get in—was expensive and didn't get you much—two watered-down drinks served in glasses that were "cleaned" with a dip into a bucket of soapy water that was rarely changed throughout the evening. The plumbing in the bathrooms was constantly backed up and the floors were covered in raw sewage most nights. As a result, unsurprisingly, the place was said to reek. There were also allegations that there was an upstairs space where underage boys were procured—and perhaps even murdered—by bouncer Ed "the Skull," who was also almost certainly involved in the blackmail schemes. In a Mattachine society publication, *Gay Scene Guide*, potential patrons were warned to maintain privacy at Stonewall: "We caution our readers NEVER to use your real name when cruising, NEVER to give your address." They were also advised to be on guard against the trick or hustler who may be "working for the management."[13] And there was no fire exit. As writer James Waller would put it, the bar was only "infinitesimally safer than descending into a West Virginia coal mine."[14]

As unpleasant as the whole experience sounds, the Stonewall Inn became the "it" place of the West Village because it was one of the few gay bars that permitted dancing and also had an extremely liberal policy when it came to serving the more "obvious" homosexuals. Transvestites, bull dykes, and flame queens were among the regulars and, partly as a result, it also became a popular place for ostensibly straight wealthy people to go slumming, just like the Bowery had been decades prior.

But there were no wealthy tourists at Stonewall on June 28, 1969, the night that Inspector Seymour Pine showed up. Actually, Pine had been there more than just that one night. A few nights earlier, on June 24, there had been a raid on Stonewall and three other village bars, victims of a stepped-up campaign of harassment in the area for the entire summer. Indeed, the Stonewall riots were the result of built-up frustrations within the community over a series of raids, not simply a reaction to the one that took place in the early hours of that Saturday morning. David Carter, author of *Stonewall: The Riots That Sparked the Gay Revolution*, argues that the prevailing mood three days before Stonewall was one of agitation that could be summed up with one line: "This shit has got to stop."

When Pine returned to Stonewall to raid the place for the second time in a week, the crowd didn't disperse as it had on previous occasions. Instead, it jeered as police shunted people from the bar to police wagons. The crowd, as we know, grew and grew as police continued to either release patrons or arrest them. In a tremendous reversal of sentiment, the crowd, soon swelled by sympathetic bystanders, actually cheered on the ruthlessly exploitative mob owners and management as they were carted off by police. The violence seems to have begun when a transvestite hit a policeman over the head with a purse and was further fueled by a fight between a bull dyke and a cop that had started inside the bar and continued as she was being escorted into a wagon. Within minutes, the crowd was threatening to overturn the wagon; rioters had scared police back into the Stonewall Inn, where they bolted the door shut for forty-five minutes, waiting for backup. Rioters rammed the door and windows and, with police inside, tried to light the place on fire. Reinforcements arrived, managed to break up the crowd, and rescued the "prisoners." This was only the beginning of the rioting and ensuing political action. Three days of violence and unrest would lead to massive media coverage, the formation of the Gay Liberation Front, and, one year later, the inception of New York's Gay Pride Parade with ten thousand participants.

Stonewall was the catalyst. Nonetheless, the groundwork for the revolution that sprang from it had been laid out in illegal bars in San Francisco, Los Angeles, and other port cities, and in places such as the Tool Box and Black Cat. There, as well as at the Stonewall Inn, the gay community had fought for, and eventually won, the freedom to associate.

15

CHANGE
STROLLS
INTO
THE BAR

FOUR-YEAR-OLD BARTENDER, SLOPPY JOE, JR., 1931
Image donated by Corbis.

Remarkable as it might seem, the word "saloon" only became legal again in New York in 1973. That didn't matter much, though, since almost everyone was happy to call it a bar—a term that became fairly ubiquitous over the last half of the twentieth century. The word "bar," of course, is a synecdoche—a word in which a part refers to the whole—and in this case serves to illustrate just how important that one feature became, despite repeated attempts to rid the country of those long wooden fixtures over which drinks were served, raised, and dispatched. Nonetheless, no legislation that barred drinking while standing ever survived terribly long and, as a result, "beer taverns" and "tap rooms" faded into old-timers's memories.

In the 1970s and 1980s, a few bars ventured to call themselves "saloons," but none in homage to the watering holes that had been frequented by urban radicals and immigrants. Rather, the new "saloons" attempted to evoke the romance of the Wild West. Replete with swinging doors, sawdust, and player pianos, these faux-saloons sometimes cropped up in urban areas in attempts to capitalize on the popularity of Hollywood Westerns and television shows from the 1950s and 1960s. Westerns, both in the silent era and the mid-century revival that featured *High Noon, Shane* and *The Gunfighter*, depicted the saloon as a standard fixture, often the center of action—a historically accurate portrayal of the frontier institution. Even in an imagined final frontier, the Mos Eisley Cantina is where a hero like Luke Skywalker hooks up with smuggler Han Solo to form a rebel alliance, this time for the purpose of blowing up the Death Star.

On TV shows such as *Bonanza* and *Gunsmoke*, saloons were featured as regular settings for the week's drama. The latter show's Long Branch Saloon was named after Chalk Beeson's Dodge City saloon, where Wyatt Earp dealt cards to friends Bat Masterson and Doc Holliday. In a bizarre turn of life imitating art imitating reality, there are now many "Long Branch Saloons" in towns and cities throughout America, including a facsimile in Dodge City, Kansas—not a facsimile of the original but of the *Gunsmoke* version. Many of these places featured bucking mechanical bulls, such as Gilley's in Pasadena, Texas, used in John Travolta's 1980 film *Urban Cowboy*. Gilley's was actually more of a honky-tonk than a saloon, as was its contemporary cousin, the Boar's Nest in Hazzard County, Georgia, where the Dukes unwound with a beer at the end of most episodes.

Somewhere between the honky-tonk and the saloon lay the roadhouse. Made notorious in films such as the *The Wild One* and *Easy Rider*, biker hangouts managed to scare middle-class Americans driving station wagons into worrying over which roadhouses to stop in, for fear of running into hostile locals or motorcycle gangs. This fear was featured in any number of films and satirized in Tim Burton's *Pee-Wee's Big Adventure*, wherein our hero escapes biker wrath by dancing table-top to "Tequila"—in platform shoes. Post-Prohibition roadhouses were typically set up on the wet side of a county line, catering to patrons who lived under local option but, before long, the aesthetic behind them thrived and eventually became sanitized, as we can see in corporate bars of the 1980s. Although Patrick Swayze and franchisees did their best to soften the roadhouse's image, its sordid past as a quasi-speakeasy came back to haunt it in popular culture as a place where, in movies such as *Thelma and Louise* and *The Accused*, women found themselves vulnerable. If you're a woman and can recall going to a suburban "O'Toole's" in that era, there was often something a little creepy about these masculine environments, even if the idea of a biker gang hanging out in the back, waiting to prey on unsuspecting middle-class families was a little extreme.

On the subject of bad bars, it would be impossible not to mention the poet Charles Bukowski and his muse, the dive bar, which Bukowski used as both his escape and inspiration when he couldn't afford Hollywood's Musso and Frank Grill. These days, "dive bar"—like the roadhouse—is actually an aesthetic which some owners try to mimic for patrons wishing to bask in the irony of "faux dive," in the hopes of escaping bourgeoisdom. The ersatz dive, however, is infinitely preferable to the most dominant form of bar in America today, the TV-littered sports bar, which was the first theme bar to properly cross over from the working-class domain into the mainstream. The sports bar evolved from beer taverns such as the one 1970s sitcom icon Archie Bunker frequented (and eventually owned). Its ancestor is surely the pre-Prohibition saloon where runners relayed race results or sports scores to patrons. Even the bars with rat/terrier fights can be considered early predecessors. Many people are of the opinion that any bar with a television is really a sports bar, since it invariably gets turned over to the game of the night and eventually sucks up all the attention in the room.

Of course, so do live performances in bars. Music was eventually allowed back into bars as states that had stipulations on live music loosened legislation, thereby restoring an important tradition for creative expression in public spaces in America. Jazz, for example, was essentially invented in bars and "juke-joints," the early unlicensed rural saloons that catered to the black populations during slavery and after Emancipation. While jazz and ragtime were widespread over the Southern states, Herbert Asbury has traced the birth of the actual word "jazz" to one of two competing "spasm" bands that played in New Orleans' brothel ballrooms and bars. The first was a seven-man spasm band (members of which, astonishingly, were all between the ages of twelve and fifteen), advertised as the Razzy Dazzy Spasm Band. The second, apparently hoping to take things up a notch and borrow on its rival's success, christened itself the Razzy Dazzy Jazz Band, possibly coining the term "jazz."

After Prohibition, jazz and other forms of live music found their way back into the bar, although not without a struggle, since live music was prohibited in many licensed establishments, according to local or state licensing laws. In seemingly liberal New York, with its legendary music scene, the cabaret law actually limited the number of band members who could take the stage at a single time to three. New York's cabaret licensing was instituted in 1926 in an attempt to control what the Board of Alderman's Committee on Local Laws called "wild strangers" and "foolish natives" at speakeasies and rent parties.[1] Three may seem an arbitrary number but, in fact, it was a fairly precise way of ensuring that no razzy-dazzy-heavy-on-the-horn-and-saxophone bands could per- form in New York, since jazz was associated with drugs, loose sexual mores, and miscegenation. After Prohibition, some bars could apply for a cabaret license but this was nearly impossible to obtain in residential areas, which, then as now, covered much of Manhattan. Bars that allowed a visiting musician to join in and jam with the house band risked fines and/or the loss of a license until as recently as 1988, when lawyer Paul Chevigny fought for the right of the visiting saxophonist. The Cab- aret Law was no dead letter law, either. The *New York Times* reported that police descended upon Mikell's on Columbus near 97th Street on February 10, 1987, padlocking the joint for having had more than three musicians on stage the preceding weekend. Saxophones, a patently racy instrument, were heavily discouraged in many places by state licensing boards. The antisax discrimination also carried across borders to places such as Toronto, where a legendary music venue named Albert's Hall had its requests for saxophonists continually denied. Meanwhile, in the lounge bars of that city's preeminent hotels, saxophonists were free to blow away. Back in the United States, exceptions were made, but many state control boards tried to discourage any jazz other than the mellow keyboard and string duos and trios. Eventually, however, music resumed its role as an integral aspect of any bar experience, even if it wasn't always live.

Singles bars took off in the 1960s and 1970s, representing some of the earliest spots in which women were truly welcomed and not simply tolerated. At roughly the same time, there was an advent of "fern bars," beginning with the grand opening of Henry Africa's in San Francisco in 1970, which distinguished itself from its competition with better lighting and explicitly catering to a clientele of both women and men. So named for its abundant plants, these places also featured more comfortable seating, like booths and upholstered barstools and "feminine" touches like tiffany glassware and spawned chains such as T.G.I. Friday's and Bennigan's. Sam Malone's bar on the TV show *Cheers* and the Regal Beagle on *Three's Company* were both loosely modeled on the fern bar, where young professionals, men and women, could feel comfortable unwinding with working-class bartenders, wait staff, and the occasional postal worker. Expanding the client base proved extremely lucrative to bar owners since, while women still don't spend as much in bars as men do, they tend to attract male customers—and their wallets. In the last couple of decades of the twentieth century, then, almost as much effort was put into attracting women to bars as had once been spent keeping them out. Some efforts have been more subtle than others. There are crass "ladies' nights" in a few places, especially those located in spring break zones; but, for the large part, attempts to diversify the patronage are manifest in making the venue safe, appealing, and, often, offering something a little more refined. Ersatz British pubs of the 1970s and 1980s paved the way for a beer renaissance, that would result in a massive movement toward better beer—first imports, then local microbrews, and, now, cask-conditioned ale. Wine bars have had a slightly spottier success record than beer places but, where there were once none, almost every major city now typically houses many. The other form of connoisseur drinking that also helped grow a client base of women was the cocktail. There was no shortage of bad cocktail bars in the 1990s and, indeed, cocktail lounges have never been hard to find in states where they've been legal since repeal. However, the "drinkways" that allowed bartenders to pass on their craft from one generation to the next had been cut off by Prohibition. Gone, therefore, were the alcoholic minglings of George Ade's day and, in its place, sprouted a fairly alcoholic culture in the 1950s, with the result that cocktails tended to grow larger and more potent. There are many who love Tiki, being fond of both finely crafted rum drinks and over-the-top kitsch, but they would be the first to admit that these drinks are not for the weak-livered and that they have been part of the trend toward oversyrupification of potent, over-sized drinks. This trend only got worse when vodka marketers and candy manufacturers joined forces to produce a line of pink drinks and alco-pops. The number of ounces listed on the drink menu became its primary virtue, and the blood-sugar testing industry wound up the only real winner.

Angel's Share changed all that. In 1994, a handful of Japanese cocktail enthusiasts opened a little cocktail den at the back of a restaurant in the East Village. It took the name Angel's Share for that portion of alcohol that mysteriously disappears in the barrel-aging process. The bartenders imported Japanese cocktail-making techniques which, it turned out, had actually been imported from America—from the days when Jerry Thomas and Harry Johnson ruled the world and America's bars were cultural attaches. In Japan, where there had been no Prohibition, cocktail makers had preserved American pre-Prohibition traditions—nearly intact. This sparked a few notable imitators, who recognized that drinks really were a lot better circa 1890 and set about resurrecting that past. Sasha Petraske, whose first bar was Milk and Honey, is one of the best-known early pioneers and is credited with having reinvented the New York cocktail scene. Petraske is always quick to remind people that much of the credit belongs to Angel's Share. There are now bars special-izing in pre-Prohibition cocktails in nearly every major American city. Women feel quite comfortable frequenting them, in part, because of the rarefied and civilized atmosphere that Petraske and other similar bar-owners have created.

Along with a more diverse clientele, however, have come several new problems. As the bar has increasingly been defined as a public space, there has been a corresponding crush of regulation detailing how that space should be used. Restrictions covering nomenclature, furniture, and entertainment have been relaxed; others have correspondingly tightened. The most obvious regulation is the one against smoking, for which some form of legislation exists in the majority of American urban areas. When tobacco became the great pariah in the 1980s, few expected anti-smoking legislation to make its way into the last piece of real estate smokers had managed to hold onto—bars. Nevertheless, it has, and, in each jurisdiction, its opponents have braced themselves for bar closings and layoffs, only to find that very little of the sort has happened. While non-smoking bars could not have survived in competition with smoking bars, in places where the playing field was fairly even, non-smoking bars have thrived. There are few jurisdictions where it is still legal to smoke in bars and, of major cities, Las Vegas, Pittsburgh, and San Antonio, at this time of writing, are some of the more notable holdouts. By contrast, many cities offer some form of exemption for cigar bars, hookah bars, and owner-operated bars and there's a certain level of alleged non-compliance in the higher-end bars and clubs. Still, the movement for smoke-free bars must be considered overwhelmingly successful, especially given the widespread skepticism initially held by almost all bar-owners and regular customers that smokers would ever be able to adjust to the idea of taking a drink without an accompanying cigarette.

There were a few problems at the outset. Bartenders complained that people went out for a smoke and never came back to settle their bills and, as a result, it's generally harder to run a tab these days in a place where you don't know the bartender. In dense urban areas, the problems have not resolved themselves so neatly, however, since many people who live in mixed residential and commercial neighborhoods complain about the noise stemming from the sidewalks as barflies and clubgoers gather for a smoke break. Martha's Vineyard even temporarily repealed its smoking by-law in 2002 in response to complaints about the throngs of smokers on the sidewalks. Patios—many of which still allow smoking—have become an increasingly popular and noisy option, much to the chagrin of an aging, wealthy population of urban homeowners who know what NIMBY stands for and how to manipulate city councils and neighborhood politics.

The clean air *inside* bars also led to an unintended consequence: It cleared the way for a whole new crop of patrons—babies. As soon as it became clear that bars in most urban areas were going to act in compliance with the law, in came the parents who, presumably, bored to tears with baby were looking for a little adult companionship.

Although this controversial practice seemed to explode in the first decade of the twentieth century, children in bars is not a new phenomenon. In many other cultures, children are almost *welcomed* into some bars. When George Orwell envisioned his ideal bar in his 1946 essay *The Moon Under Water*, he imagined a garden at the back, so that "whole families" could go there "instead of Mum having to stay at home and mind the baby while Dad goes out alone." Orwell continues, "And although, strictly speaking, they are only allowed in the garden, the children tend to seep into the pub and even to fetch drinks for their parents. This, I believe, is against the law, but it is a law that deserves to be broken, for it is the puritanical nonsense of excluding children—and therefore, to some extent, women—from pubs that has turned these places into mere boozing-shops instead of the family gathering-places that they ought to be." Children are allowed into many pubs in Ireland and England, although not all. J. D. Wetherspoon's, an English pub chain (that has a pub called, ironically, The Moon under Water in its portfolio) recently limited the number of drinks that could be served to parents visiting with children to two per visit.

In many parts of continental Europe, it is not at all uncommon to see children running around a pedestrian square surrounded by cafés or asleep in strollers as parents socialize past midnight. Even more fun than watching the little urchins is watching North American tourists' eyes pop when they see children in an adult sphere after bed-time. In Quebec, where the social code is a little tighter than in the rest of North America, the sight of relatively well-behaved children joining their parents in adult spaces is routine. Proponents of integrating children into adult social life point out that, in places where this is common practice (and where the drinking age is lower), problem-drinking—like binge-drinking, drunken violence, and drinking and driving—is less of a problem than it is in North America. There are a few mitigating factors, however. Binge-drinking is said to be on the rise in Italy, Spain and France, for example, and fewer people drive throughout Europe, period. Nonetheless, on an intuitive level, it makes sense that children who have watched adults socialize as they grew up would fare better than those who were sent to bed as the guests arrived or, were left home with a babysitter while parents went out to have adult time in adult spaces. And, if spring break (in, say, Daytona Beach or Fort Lauderdale) provides any evidence of how these sheltered children turn out, all parents should consider taking their toddler out for a pint or two as part of a daily regimen, perhaps between Lachlan's soccer and Oona's banjo practice.

In fact, plenty of neighborhood bars have tolerated children in the late afternoons and early evenings for many years, even in staid North America. Children have traditionally been accepted in a number of venues, including bars that cater to families on vacation and those that are clearly family-friendly hybrids of bars and restaurants. In urban areas, neighborhood bars and pubs have always accommodated families at dinner hour and even into the early evening. For special events, such as the Olympics, the World Cup, or the World Series, adolescents are often allowed to sit and watch a game in a bar as a treat. And, as anyone who ever sat at the top of the stairs and listened to the sounds of the party can attest, there is something magical about adult parties from a child's perspective. In *A Drinking Life*, Pete Hamill describes the thrill of finally getting to spend a bit of an afternoon at his father's bar as an eight-year-old in 1943 Park Slope, Brooklyn. Jack London recalls the saloons of his boyhood as the highlight of his days helping his father with deliveries. San Francisco saloons were London's favorites, since the barkeeper would usually treat him to some "delicious dainties" of sardines and sausage, along with a syrup and soda temperance drink. "And he became my ideal of a good, kind man. I dreamed day-dreams of him for years." More recently, J. R. Moehringer's *The Tender Bar*—a memoir *cum* love letter to his own local, Dickens—credits the Manhasset, Long Island bar for having restored his faith when he was a boy and "tending" him as a teenager in the 1970s. At the age of eight, Moehringer found a "committee" of surrogate fathers who took the place of his absent dad.

The feelings aren't so tender these days. At least not in several rapidly gentrifying urban neighborhoods across America, where the presence of mothers who have organized "Mommy and Me" cocktail hours in bars have raised hackles. The most famous example of this has been in Park Slope—not far from where a young Pete Hamill first felt a tavern's warmth—where, in 2005, Andy Heidel, a bartender at the Patio Lounge posted the "Stroller Manifesto" that barred children. Heidel taped his theses to the door after enduring one miserable shift too many tripping over young children and their trappings. "What is it with people bringing their kids into bars?" Heidel asked. "A bar is a place for adults to kick back and relax. How can you do that with a toddler running around or crying, getting changed on the table next to you, or being breast-fed?" Heidel continued his rant: "Listen, if you're a parent now, your child doesn't have to be the center of everyone else's universe, too. Get a babysitter if you want to go out to a bar, or buy a bottle of wine and invite your friends over, just stop imposing your lifestyle on the rest of us in our sanctuary of choice . . . If you can't find a sitter and have to go out with your child, for the love of god, go to a family restaurant like Two

Boots or the Tea Lounge, for I declare today and all future Sundays, Stroller Free."

The point of view is understandable. Children are noisy, messy, eat and drink small amounts, and are notoriously lousy tippers. Servers generally make no more money for every child they serve and often deal with at least twice the aggravation. And blocking a busy pathway with a SUV-sized stroller is obviously an unacceptable hazard to workers and other patrons. Heidel also claimed to be speaking for more than simply his fellow waiters and bartenders, noting that the rest of the community was tired of negotiating around children and strollers in bars. It turned out that he was correct. He *did* speak for many members of the public, who registered their agreement through on-line chat boards, in interviews with the media, and in bar banter. Members of the Park Slope bar community complained about sling-wearing dads drunkenly dribbling beer on babies' heads and tipsy women crashing their strollers into bar furniture. Regulars have been shocked when asked to stop swearing, smoking in outdoor spaces, drinking, and even to leave if overly refreshed, on the grounds that they were setting a bad example. Won't somebody please think about the children?

Park Slope patrons claim that bars are the last space in the whole neighborhood where they aren't consistently reminded that they should be thinking about the children. The neighborhood has been almost cartoonishly overwhelmed by Park Slope mothers and fathers who, some claim, practice an aggressively indulgent and child-centered parenting style with their "spawn." It seems to some as if the new mothers are practicing a secular "cult of domesticity," mimicking women from the mid-nineteenth century, and then again from the 1950s, who strove to be perfect mothers. Except in place of milk, casseroles, and good manners, we now have soy, organics, and an aggressive and paranoid political correctness. In 2006, much was made over the seemingly innocent posting, "Found: boy's hat" on a Park Slope Parents email forum. Gallons of digital ink were spilled over the poster's assumption that it was a *boy's* hat: "It's innocent little comments like this that I find the most hurtful . . ."

One might keep the extreme nature of Park Slope parenting in mind if tempted to jump to conclusions about universal and growing anti-child sentiment. Non-parent residents in Park Slope are articulating a frustration with gentrification in general and their feelings that the neighborhood has been flooded with "entitled" parents who seemingly want it both ways—refusing to give up their fleeting youth and simultaneously wanting their children around them at all times. Despite charges that these parents neurotically over-parent, they've also been observed under-parenting in the bar and have been seen sipping away obliviously while other customers and staff dealt with unruly children who occasionally put themselves into harm's way. And, if a bartender or customer dared to steer a child away from danger or simply said "no," the Park Slope parent would suddenly be roused from drink and conversation to scold the "offenders," asking that they refrain from disciplining other people's children. So much for anyone's dream of a village raising a child.

It's a striking contrast to the warmth associated with Jack London's, Pete Hamill's, and J. R. Moehringer's early bar stories. Then again, those boys had been brought in as part of an initiation into a male ritual by their fathers (or surrogates in Moehringer's case) and were almost certainly expected to conform to the space, not the other way around. In our contemporary case, it seems clear that the Slope mothers and fathers do expect the bar to be further sanitized in order to accommodate their needs. Were it not for that mitigating factor, it would be hard not to think of gender bias at work here, since the wrath of Park Slopers is aimed primarily at the stroller *moms*. Despite the fact that the barrier for women drinking in bars has been crossed, a lingering tendency to define women who drink as slightly unseemly remains—especially if they're married and have kids. Children witnessing maternal drinking represents another loaded issue, one that borders, to some, on child abuse. Nor is the Park Slope manifesto the first time a publican's decision to enforce his own notions about drinking while parenting has been controversial. In 1991, a waiter was fired after he tried to refuse a pregnant woman a strawberry daiquiri in a Seattle restaurant. Our attitudes toward pre-natal and child safety have become increasingly vigilant over the past few years—some say bordering on hysterical—especially where alcohol or tobacco is concerned.

Most parents who bring their children to bars point out that they don't take their kids out and proceed to get sloshed. For the large part, they are having a couple of drinks in the late afternoon or, perhaps over dinner, and enjoying a brief respite from the grinding isolation of stay-at-home parenthood. (As an aside, there may well be room for another larger critique—whether or not full-time, stay-at-home mothering is a realistic plan for many women who, shortly after the honeymoon period that follows not working wears off, crave companionship and stimulation. In the case of Park Slope, however, the socioeconomic status of these stay-at-home mothers—they are still overwhelmingly women—almost works against them. One of the most common critiques of these bibulous parents is that they should hire a sitter; there's little doubt that most can afford it. Were it a more marginal coterie of mothers, it would be a lot easier to frame the issue as an isolated group denied the right to try to establish social connections and enjoy a few hours in their local "third place," where community members catch up with casual acquaintances and mix with people they might not have met in other work or home arenas. But between their apparent plethora of options and the poor parenting and sense of entitlement the Park Slope mothers are accused of, rolling a stroller into a licensed establishment represents the most recent battle to define the public space that is the American bar.

The issue came front and center again in January, 2008, when Brooklyn bar Union Hall, instituted a no-stroller policy and moved its "No Admittance under 21" sign to a more conspicuous location. The interweb chat board lit up again but, this time, with an equally strong and vocal group of parents who objected to having one of their regular activities denied. They asserted their right to frequent the semi-public space and complained the action was discriminatory. In addition, the group claimed that it was insulting to have parenting choices dictated and critiqued by the local bar manager. The parents could have been said to have won the first round since Union Hall owners apologized for their lack of tact and agreed to allow mothers back in for a few afternoons. As a result, the "nonbreeding" Park Slope residents seemingly have little choice but to retreat into upstairs spaces that can't be accessed or, to move to Greenpoint or Williamsburg and suffer all the hipsters. They could also visit faux-dives, notably stroller-free.

Perhaps the most interesting aspect of the rhetoric being used against the stroller moms is the consistency with which one meme comes up, namely, "This is a bar." Sometimes that phrase is punctuated with an exclamation point. At other times, the word "bar" is italicized, as if it referred to a clearly defined entity, as it did in the day when the word was pronounced "saloon." With all the vitriol associated with the word, you might expect to find a Roman orgy, or rat and terrier fights. Or, perhaps, people sucking booze out of a barrel through a straw. Or drunken concert saloon girls getting taken advantage of by sleazy owners and patrons. Or Gold Tooth Mary stripping and robbing unconscious patrons after they have unsuspectingly ordered the house special.

And yet, in bars in Park Slope and across America, people mostly just sit, sip drinks, and talk to the person next to them. In some places, patrons talk about sports; in others, about vintages; in others, members of the community get together to unwind and talk about their lives and how quickly their neighborhood is changing. We wonder what the Park Slope regulars think they're doing in the bar that children so desperately need to be protected from. There's a sense, perhaps, that the presence of children in the bar forecloses the fantasy that life there is really as debauched as some of its participants like to imagine.

This episode can also be viewed as a confirmation that, even as drink has become domesticated and mundane since pre-Prohibition, and chain restaurants offer two-ounce dessert cocktails to suburban moms in Middle America, we are still a little hung up on bars. They remain, to some small degree, Satan's headquarters on earth.

It's hard to imagine that anyone would ever visualize the goings-on in a pub in Oxford, or the local beer garden in Hamburg, or the Spanish café in a square in La Rioja, as being so scandalous that children needed to be shielded from them. Then again, for at least the past two hundred years, we've had a far more troubled relationship with our public drinking spaces than in the United Kingdom and continental Europe, where cafes and pubs are cherished—even revered. Whether it is blamed on evangelism, the puritan work ethic, or its past as a space for radicals, immigrants, and the disenfranchised, even the most sanitized corporate ersatz roadhouse, replete with piped-in elevator music and bartenders adorned with eighteen pieces of "flair," the American bar retains a tiny bit of grime that simply cannot be washed off. And that stubborn residue is the hangover from three centuries—going on four— of vilification, adoration, rabble-rousing, escapism, and revolutionary idealism at work.

The story of the American bar is a love–hate story. There's a heavy dose of narcissism in it, too, since the story of the bar is, really, the story of America itself. As we grapple with the gritty truth that so many of our greats—the revolution, republican egalitarianism, checks against federalist tyranny, labor unions, and gay rights—were born out of a union between half-drunk radicals and punch, it becomes hard not to simultaneously feel smirking pride and self-reproach.

The bar began by being all things to all people and, within its confines, the nation's personality was formed. In the tavern, it was decided that the government should try to be fair to all people—except, of course, those not wanted on the voyage. And when those people excluded from the great American dream demanded to be a part of it all, the places in which they rallied for inclusion were the taverns, saloons, speakeasies, and grog shops, striving to make the bar—and the country—truly all things to all people.

A book about the American bar can never be exhaustive, of course. We have got to this point, for instance, and only now mention Hemingway (a Guinness world record for consecutive Hemingway-free pages in a drinking-related book), Rick's American Café, or even Tom Cruise. There are so many great bars (nobody can know all their names) and too many great stories. Perhaps this is why Walt Whitman left his great elegy, his toast and treat, to the American bar—and to Pfaff's in particular—unfinished:

> The vault at Pfaffs where the drinkers and laughers meet to eat and
> drink and carouse
> While on the walk immediately overhead pass the myriad feet of
> Broadway
> As the dead in their graves are underfoot hidden
> And the living pass over them, recking not of them,
> Laugh on laughers!
> Drink on drinkers!

SIGNS BEHIND THE BAR, IN BIRNEY, MONTANA, 1941

Photo taken by Marion Wolcott. Image courtesy of the Library of Congress.

NOTES

CHAPTER I

1. Curtis, *And a Bottle of Rum*, 28.

2. Thompson, *Rum Punch and Revolution*, 3.

3. Salinger, *Taverns and Drinking in Early America*, 115.

4. Field. *The Colonial Tavern*, 4.

5. Conroy, *In Public Houses*, 14.

6. Popham, "The Social History of the Tavern," in *Research Advances in Alcohol and Drug Problems*, 243.

7. Foot, *Monastic Life in Anglo-Saxon England c. 600–900*, 237.

8. Gately, *Drink: A Cultural History of Alcohol*, 86.

9. Standage, *A History of the World in Six Glasses*, 21.

10. Albertson, "Puritan Liquor in the Planting of New England," 479.

11. Josselyn, *New England's Rarities Discovered*, 90.

12. Kobler, *Ardent Sprits*, 26.

13. Barr, *Drink: A Social History of America*, 32.

14. Frethorne, Richard, Letter to his Father and Mother, March 20, April 2, and April 3, 1623, in Susan M. Kingsbury, ed., *The Records of the Virginia Company of London, IV* (Washington, D.C., 1935), pp. 58–62. Originally found reference to its existence in Barr's *Drink*.

15. Yenne, *The American Brewery*, 8.

16. Lender and Martin. *Drinking in America*, 14.

17. Lossing, *The American Historical Record*, 53.

18. Brown, *Early American Beverages*, 10–15.

19. Ibid., 19.

20. Walton, Out of It: A Cultural History of Intoxication, 76–77.

21. Eggleston, 342.

22. Bliss, *Side-Glimpses of a Colonial Meeting-House*, 32.

23. Field, 30.

24. Yoder, "Tavern Regulation in Virginia: Rationale and Reality," in *The Virginia Magazine of History and Biography*, 262.

25. Conroy, 214.

26. Ibid., 214.

27. Sandoval-Strausz, *Hotel: An American History*, 17.

28. Knight, in *Colonial American Travel Narratives*, ed. Martin, 54.

29. Browne, *Archives of Maryland*, vol. 2, 346.

30. Rorabaugh, *The Alcoholic Republic*, 20.

31. Conroy, 39.

32. Yoder, *Virgina*, 261.

33. Thomann, *Colonial Liquor Laws*, 47.

34. Saltonstall letter December 1696—found in Field, 33–36.

35. Earle, 8.

36. Ibid.

37. Thomann, 4.

38. Winsor, *History of the Town of Duxbury, Massachusetts*, 296.

39. Ibid, 8.

40. Ibid, 13.

41. Shurtleff and Pulsifer, *Records of the Colony of New Plymouth*, 113.

42. Field, 33.

43. Salinger, 24.

44. Bushman, From Puritan to Yankee, 5.

45. Crawford, *Little Pilgrimages among Old New England Inns*, 136.

46. Mancall, *Deadly Medicine*, 68.

47. Ibid.

48. Lender and Martin make this assertion.

49. Burns, *The Spirits of America*, 47.

50. Thomann, 55.

51. Thomann, 59.

52. Thomann, 81.

53. Conroy, "In the Public Sphere" in Holt, ed., *Alcohol*, 41–59.

54. Baldwin, *Colonial Liquor Legislation*, 22.

55. Thomann, 21.

56. Conroy, *In Public Houses*, 29.

57. Ed Cray estimates that this song was very old by the early 1700s, when it was first found in print. Located in Cray's *The Erotic Muse*.

58. Lender and Martin, for example.

CHAPTER 2

1. Perley, *History of Salem*, 266.

2. Earle, 5.

3. There is, incidentally, a pub in Boston's North End called Goody Glover's, replete with a plaque commemorating poor Ann Glover.

4. Boyer, *Salem Possessed*, 60–110. This entire section is informed heavily by Boyer and Nissenbaum's research into the social and political context of the Salem hysteria.

5. Thompson, 28.

6. Harris, *In the Shadow of Slavery*, 20–28.

7. Launitz-Schurer Jr., "Slave Resistance in Colonial New York: An Interpretation of Daniel Horsmanden's New York Conspiracy," 140.

8. These quotes and larger story are assembled from multiple sources: Horsmanden's *The New York Conspiracy*, Foote's *Black and White Manhattan*, and Burrows's *Gotham*, primarily.

9. Horsmanden, *The New York Conspiracy*, 37.

10. Horsmanden, 37.

11. Horsmanden, 113.

12. Carp, *Rebels Rising*, 177.

13. Salinger, 73.

14. Cohen, "The Philadelphia Election Riot of 1742," 312

CHAPTER 3

1. Thompson, 82, and Bayles, *Old Taverns of New York*, 147.

2. Thompson, 79, and Carl Bridenbaugh, *Cities in Revolt*, 213.

3. De Tocqueville, *Democracy in America*, 114.

4. Hamilton, in *Colonial American Travel Narratives* (ed. Martin), 207–310.

5. Livingston, "Of Elections, and Election Jobbers," in *The Independent Reflector*, 279.

6. Burns, 23, and Conroy, 224.

7. Adams, 85 and 187.

8. Habermas, *The Structural Transformation of the Public Sphere.*, 14–43.

9. Thompson, 79.

10. Hamilton, in Martin, 191.

11. James, *The Varieties of Religious Experience*, 282.

12. Crevecoeur, From Moore, ed., *More Letters From an American Farmer*. Originally found in Carp *Rebels Rising*.

13. Cooper, *Campaign of '84*, 258.

14. Warden, "The Caucus and Democracy in Colonial Boston," 27.

15. Nash, *Urban Crucible*, 52.

16. Nash, 51.

17. Carp, 80–81.

18. Miller, *Pioneer in Propaganda*, 40.

19. Alexander, *Samuel Adams: America's Revolutionary Politician*, 13.

20. Alexander.

21. Burrows, 199.

22. Carp, 87.

CHAPTER 4

1. Carp, 68.

2. Thompson, 102.

3. Manigault, "The Letterbook of Peter Manigault, 1763–1773" (ed. Crouse), 87.

4. Moore, *Diary of the American Revolution*, 9–10.

CHAPTER 5

1. Szatmary, *Shays' Rebellion*, 63.

2. Szatmary, 64.

3. Batterberry, *Out on the Town in New York*, 24.

4. Batterberry, 21.

5. Smith, *The City of New York in the Year of Washington's Inauguration, 1789*, 73.

6. Travers, *Celebrating the Fourth*, 92.

7. Garvin, *On the Road North of Boston*, 144.

8. Link, *Democratic-Republican Societies 1790–1800*, 253.

9. Garvin, 144.

10. Bernstein, *Wedding of the Waters*, 241.

11. Binkley, *American Political Parties*, 51.

12. Baldwin, Whiskey Rebels, 27.

13. Baldwin, 25.

14. Rorabaugh, 52.

15. Baldwin, 63.

16. Pittsburgh Historical Society.

17. Slaughter, *The Whiskey Rebellion*, 272.

18. Notably Slaughter.

19. Baldwin, *Pittsburgh: The Story of a City, 1750–1865*, 119.

20. Baldwin, 175.

21. Wondrich, *Imbibe! From Absinthe Cocktail to Whiskey Smash, a Salute in Stories and Drinks to "Professor" Jerry Thomas, Pioneer of the American Bar*, 175.

CHAPTER 6

1. Alexander, *Transatlantic Sketches*, 103. (Originally found in Hooker, *Food and Drink in America*.)

2. Hooker, 145–149.

3. Sandoval-Strausz, *Hotel: An American History*, 14.

4. Hooker, 149.

5. Sandoval-Strausz, 23–24.

6. Weiser, *The Great American Bars and Saloons*, 6.

7. Selcer, *Legendary Watering Holes*, 10; Erdoes, *Saloons of the Old West*, 16–20.

8. Rea is the author of the forthcoming B.A.S.T.A.R.D.S. and www.thebarkeeper.com. Confirmed via interview.

9. Selcer, *Legendary Watering Holes*, 15.

10. Sante, *Low Life*, 104–105.

11. Sante, 105.

12. Sante, 106.

13. Asbury, *The French Quarter*, 319.

14. Ade, *The Old-Time Saloon.*

15. Bayles, 373.

16. Atkinson, *Atkinson's Casket, Volume 10*, 624.

17. Murray, *Travels in North America during the Years 1834, 1835 & 1836*, vol. 1, 68.

18. Buel, "Columbian Exposition: Preliminary Glimpses of the Past," *The Century*, 45 (1893), 622.

19. Thoreau, *Excursions*, 97–108.

20. Hawthorne, *American Notebooks*, 119.

21. Marryat, *A Diary in America*, 47.

22. Kobler, 59–62.

23. The phrase "temperance weepies" was coined by Jessica Warner in *All or Nothing: A Short History of Abstinence in America*. At least that's the only reference to it I've ever found.

CHAPTER 7

1. Garvin, 144.

2. Austin, *Tale of a Dedham Tavern*, 88.

3. Hildreth, The Boston Opposition to the new law for the suppression of rum shops, 3.

4. Hildreth, *An American Utilitarian*, 179.

5. Bacon, A discourse on the traffic in spirituous liquors, 41.

6. Dannenbaum, *Drink and Disorder*. Original quote from *Crusader*, a temperance publication.

7. Warner, *All or Nothing: A Short History of Abstinence in America*, 43–47.

8. Laband, *Blue Laws*, 16.

9. Asbury, *Gem of the Prairie*, 45. It's unclear how accurate this quote is, given Asbury's unreliability. But it seems to come from Flinn's *History of Chicago*, 1887.

10. *Chicago Times*. August 5, 1877.

CHAPTER 8

1. Smith, *Notable Black American Women*, 141.

2. Asbury, *Gem of the Prairie*, 64–65.

3. Graham, *Two Decades*, 23.

4. Ibid., 24.

5. Asbury, *The Great Illusion*, 83.

6. Powers, *Faces Along the Bar*, 104.

CHAPTER 9

1. Chance, H. M., "An Analysis of the Fire Damp Explosions in the 1881 Anthracite Coal Mines from 1870 to 1880." Read Before the American Philosophical Society, May 6, 1881.

2. Kumin, *The World of the Tavern*.

3. "The Sunday School Chronicle," April 12, 1878,

4. Adelman, *Haymarket Revisited*, 90–95.

5. Goldman. *Living My Life*, 9–10.

6. Powers, 55.

7. Hapgood in 1913. Quote found in Powers, 176.

8. Barker, *The Saloon Problem and Social Reform*, 63.

9. Pickard, Douglas. "The 1892 Homestead Strike: A Story of Social Conflict in Industrial America." 2007 thesis, Harvard University. Quote from July 7, 1892.

10. Goyens, *Beer and Revolution*, 38.

11. Schaack, *Anarchy and Anarchists*, 216.

12. Hills, Timothy. Unpublished research.

CHAPTER 10

1. Pringle, *Theodore Roosevelt*, 61.

2. Dorchester, *The Problem of Religious Progress*, 24.

3. Powers, 69; Warner, *Prohibition: An Adventure in Freedom*, 20; Steffens, *The Shame of the Cities*, 34.

4. Asbury, *Gem of the Prairie*, 142–154.

5. Calkins, *Substitutes for the Saloon*, 10.

6. Woods, *The City Wilderness*, 129.

7. Lerner, *Dry Manhattan*, 23.

8. Roosevelt, *New York*, 266.

9. Addams, "The Subtle Problems of Charity," in *The Atlantic Monthly*, February 1899.

10. Riis, *How the Other Half Lives*, 97.

11. Stivers, *A Hair of the Dog*, 159.

12. Noel, *The City and the Saloon*, 27.

13. Selcer, 92.

14. Selcer, 230.

15. Cha-Jua, *America's First Black Town*, 165.

16. Crowe, "Racial Violence and Social Reform-Origins of the Atlanta Riot of 1906," 236.

17. Hammel "The Negro Problem and the Liquor Problem." Quoted in Warner, *All or Nothing*, 116.

18. Crowe describes all of this in greater detail—all unattributed quotes from newspapers were originally found in his excellent article.

19. Burns, *Rage in the Gate City*, 83.

20. Crouthamel, "The Springfield Race Riot," 181.

CHAPTER 11

1. Notably in Odegaard's *Pressure Politics*.

2. "American Issue"—Kentucky Edition, April 1912.

3. Duis, *The Saloon*, 25.

4. Asbury, *The Great Illusion*, 114.

5. Asbury, *Gem of the Prairie*, 172–176.

6. Clark, *The Dry Years*, 61.

7. Johnson, *Harry's Johnson's Bartenders' Manual*, 40.

8. Ibid., 21–26.

9. Sparks, *The North American Review*, vol. 157, 1893.

10. Stelzle, *A Son of the Bowery*, 46–51.

11. Room, "The Movies and the Wettening of America," 12–13.

12. Cherrington, *Standard Encyclopedia of the Alcohol Problem*, in Room, The Movies and the Wettening of America," 12.

CHAPTER 12

1. Miron and Zweibel, "Alcohol Consumption During Prohibition," 245.

2. Okrent, *Last Call*, 259.

3. Cherrington, *America and the World Liquor Problem*, 104.

4. Curtis, 165.

5. Berliner, *Texas Guinan, Queen of the Night Clubs*, 115.

6. Asbury, *Gem of the Prairie*, 106.

7. Asbury, *The Great Illusion*.

8. Beebe, "Moriarty's Wonderful Saloon."

9. Burns, 220.

10. Lerner, 235.

CHAPTER 13

1. Harrison, *After Repeal*, 66.

2. Donovan, *The Woman Who Waits*, 140.

3. Nel, *Doctor Seuss*, 106.

CHAPTER 14

1. Gilfoyle, *City of Eros*, 122.

2. Asbury, *The French Quarter*, 393.

3. Chauncey, *Gay New York*, 33.

4. D'Emilio, *Sexual Politics, Sexual Communities*, 50.

5. D'Emilio, 33.

6. D'Emilio, 33.

7. Agee, "Gayola: Police Professionalization and the Politics of San Francisco's Gay Bars, 1950–1968," 478–480.

8. Boag, "Does Portland Need a Homophile Society?"

9. Faderman, *Gay L.A.*, 285.

10. Faderman, 154–156.

11. Brown, *The Evening Crowd at Kirmser's*, 8.

12. Carter, *Stonewall*, 50–54.

13. Carter, 97.

14. Waller, "It's a Wonderful Strife," *Out Week*, June 26, 1989.

CHAPTER 15

1. Chevigny, *Gigs*, 97.

BIBLIOGRAPHY

Adams, John, and Charles Francis Adams. *The Works [of] John Adams, Second President of the United States.* 1 AMS ed. New York: AMS Press, 1971; 1856.

Ade, George. *The Old-Time Saloon: Not Wet-Not Dry, Just History.* New York: R. Long & R.R. Smith, 1931.

Adelman, William J., and Press Collection. *Haymarket Revisited: A Tour Guide of Labor History Sites and Ethnic Neighborhoods Connected with the Haymarket Affair.* Chicago: Illinois Labor History Society, 1976.

Agee, Christopher. "Gayola: Police Professionalization and the Politics of San Francisco's Gay Bars, 1950–1968." *Journal of the History of Sexuality* 15.3 (2006): 462–489.

Albertson, Dean. "Puritan Liquor in the Planting of New England." *The New England Quarterly* 23.4 (1950): 477–490.

Alexander, James Edward. *Transatlantic Sketches, Comprising Visits to the most Interesting Scenes in North and South America, and the West Indies. With Notes on Negro Slavery and Canadian Emigration.* London: R. Bentley, 1833.

Alexander, John K. *Samuel Adams: America's Revolutionary Politician.* Lanham, Md.: Rowman & Littlefield, 2002.

Asbury, Herbert. The French Quarter; An Informal History of the New Orleans Underworld. *New York*, London: A.A. Knopf, 1936.

———. *Gem of the Prairie: An Informal History of the Chicago Underworld.* DeKalb, Ill.: Northern Illinois University Press, 1986; 1940.

———. *The Great Illusion: An Informal History of Prohibition.* New York: Greenwood Press, 1968; 1950.

Atkinson, Samuel Coate. "Atkinson's Casket." Philadelphia: Samuel C. Atkinson, (1839).

Austin, Walter. *Tale of a Dedham Tavern; History of the Norfolk Hotel, Dedham. Massachusetts.* Cambridge: Private printing at the Riverside Press, 1912.

Bacon, Leonard. *A Discourse on the Traffic in Spirituous Liquors.* New Haven: B.L. Hamlen, 1838.

Baldwin, Leland Dewitt, Western Pennsylvania Historical Survey, and Buhl Foundation. *Pittsburgh: The Story of a City, 1750–1865.* Vol. 56. Pittsburgh: University of Pittsburgh Press, 1970; 1937.

Baldwin, Leland Dewitt, and Western Pennsylvania Historical Survey. *Whiskey Rebels: The Story of a Frontier Uprising.* Pittsburgh: University of Pittsburgh Press, 1939.

Barker, Charles R. "Colonial Taverns of Lower Merion." *The Pennsylvania Magazine of History and Biography* 52.3 (1928): 205–228.

Barker, John Marshall. *The Saloon Problem and Social Reform*. New York: Arno Press, 1970.

Barr, Andrew. *Drink: A Social History of America*. New York: Carroll & Graf, 1999.

Batterberry, Michael, and Ariane Ruskin Batterberry. *On the Town in New York, from 1776 to the Present*. New York: Scribner, 1973.

Bayles, William Harrison. *Old Taverns of New York*. New York: Frank Allaben genealogical company, 1915.

Bendroth, Margaret. "Rum, Romanism, and Evangelism: Protestants and Catholics in Late-Nineteenth-Century Boston." *Church History* 68.3 (1999): 627–647.

Berliner, Louise. *Texas Guinan, Queen of the Night Clubs*. 1st ed. Austin: University of Texas Press, 1993.

Bernstein, Peter L. *Wedding of the Waters: The Erie Canal and the Making of a Great Nation*. 1st ed. New York: W.W. Norton, 2005.

Binkley, Wilfred E. *American Political Parties, their Natural History*. New York: A.A. Knopf, 1943.

Bliss, William Root. *Side Glimpses from the Colonial Meeting-House*. Boston, New York: Houghton, Mifflin and Company, 1894.

Boyer, Paul S., and Stephen Nissenbaum. *Salem Possessed; the Social Origins of Witchcraft*. Cambridge, Mass.: Harvard University Press, 1974.

Bridenbaugh, Carl. *Cities in Revolt: Urban Life in America, 1743–1776*. Capricorn Books ed. New York: Capricorn Books, 1964.

Brown, Ricardo J. *The Evening Crowd at Kirmser's: A Gay Life in the 1940s*. Minneapolis: University of Minnesota Press, 2001.

Burke, W.M. "The Anti-Saloon League as a Political Force." *Annals of the American Academy of Political and Social Science* 32, Regulation of the Liquor Traffic (1908): 27–37.

Burns, Eric. *The Spirits of America: A Social History of Alcohol*. Philadelphia, PA: Temple University Press, 2004.

Burns, Rebecca. *Rage in the Gate City: The Story of the 1906 Atlanta Race Riot*. Rev ed. Athens: University of Georgia Press, 2009.

Burrows, Edwin G., and Mike Wallace. *Gotham: A History of New York City to 1898*. New York: Oxford University Press, 1999.

Bushman, Richard L. *From Puritan to Yankee; Character and the Social Order in Connecticut, 1690–1765*. Cambridge, Mass.: Harvard University Press, 1967.

Calkins, Raymond, and Committee of Fifty for the Investigation of the Liquor Problem. *Substitutes for the Saloon*. Boston: Houghton, Mifflin and Co, 1901.

Carp, Benjamin L. *Rebels Rising: Cities and the American Revolution*. Oxford; New York: Oxford University Press, 2007.

Carter, David. *Stonewall: The Riots that Sparked the Gay Revolution*. 1st ed. New York: St. Martin's Press, 2004.

Cavan, Sherri. *Liquor License: An Ethnography of Bar Behavior*. Chicago: Aldine, 1966.

Cha-Jua, Sundiata Keita. *America's First Black Town: Brooklyn, Illinois, 1830–1915*. Urbana: University of Illinois Press, 2000.

Chauncey, George. *Gay New York: Gender, Urban Culture, and the Makings of the Gay Male World, 1890–1940*. New York: Basic Books, 1994.

Cherrington, Ernest Hurst. *The Anti-Saloon League Year Book; an Encyclopedia of Facts and Figures Dealing with the Liquor Traffic and the Temperance Reform*. Columbus and Chicago: The Anti-Saloon League of America, 1908.

Cherrington, Ernest Hurst. *America and the World Liquor Problem*. Westerville, Ohio: American Issue Press, 1922.

Chevigny, Paul. *Gigs: Jazz and the Cabaret Laws in New York City*. 2nd ed. Vol. 2. London; New York: Routledge, 2005.

Clark, Norman H. *The Dry Years; Prohibition and Social Change in Washington*. Seattle: University of Washington Press, 1965.

Cohen, Norman S. "The Philadelphia Election Riot of 1742." *The Pennsylvania Magazine of History and Biography* 92.3 (1968): 306–319.

Conroy, David W., and Institute of Early American History and Culture. In *Public Houses: Drink & the Revolution of Authority in Colonial Massachusetts*. Chapel Hill, N.C.: Published for the Institute of Early American History and Culture, Williamsburg, Virginia, by the University of North Carolina Press, 1995.

Cooper, Thomas V., and Hector Fenton. *Campaign of '84. Biographies of James G. Blaine, the Republican Candidate for President, and John A. Logan, the Republican Candidate for Vice-President. With a Description of the Leading Issues and the Proceedings of the National Convention. Together with a History of the Political Parties of the United States: Comparisons of Platforms on all Important Questions, and Political Tables for Ready Reference*. Chicago, New York: Baird & Dillon, 1884.

Crawford, Mary Caroline. *Little Pilgrimages among Old New England Inns: Being an Account of Little Journeys to various Quaint Inns and Hostelries of Colonial New England*. Bowie, Md.: Heritage Books, 1998; 1907.

Cray. *The Erotic Muse: American Bawdy Songs*. 2nd ed. Urbana: University of Illinois Press, 1992.

Crowe, Charles. "Racial Violence and Social Reform-Origins of the Atlanta Riot of 1906." *The Journal of Negro History* 53.3 (1968): 234–256.

Curtis, Wayne. *And a Bottle of Rum: A History of the New World in Ten Cocktails*. New York, Crown Publishers, 2006.

Czitrom, Daniel. "The Politics of Performance: From Theater Licensing to Movie Censorship in Turn-of-the-Century New York." *American Quarterly* 44.4, Special Issue: Hollywood, Censorship, and American Culture (1992): 525–553.

Dannenbaum, Jed. *Drink and Disorder: Temperance Reform in Cincinnati from the Washingtonian Revival to the WCTU*. Urbana: University of Illinois Press, 1984.

Davis, Thomas J. "The New York Slave Conspiracy of 1741 as Black Protest." *The Journal of Negro History* 56.1 (1971): 17–30.

D'Emilio, John. *Sexual Politics, Sexual Communities: The Making of a Homosexual Minority in the United States, 1940–1970*. Chicago: University of Chicago Press, 1983.

Doane, William Croswell. "The Excise Law and the Saloon." *The North American Review* 155.431 (1892): 395–400.

Donovan, Frances R. *The Woman Who Waits*. New York: Arno Press, 1974.

Dorchester, Daniel. *The Problem of Religious Progress*. New York: Phillips & Hunt, 1900.

Duis, Perry. *The Saloon: Public Drinking in Chicago and Boston, 1880–1920*. Illini Books ed. Urbana: University of Illinois Press, 1999.

Earle, Alice Morse. *Stage-Coach and Tavern Days*. New York: B. Blom, 1969.

Eggert, Gerald G. ""Seeing Sam": The Know Nothing Episode in Harrisburg." *The Pennsylvania Magazine of History and Biography* 111.3 (1987): 305–340.

Eggleston, Edward. *The Beginners of a Nation; a History of the Source and Rise of the Earliest English Settlements in America, with Special Reference to the Life and Character of the People*. New York: D. Appleton, 1896.

Erdoes, Richard. *Saloons of the Old West*. 1st ed. New York: Knopf, 1979.

Erenberg, Lewis A. "From New York to Middletown: Repeal and the Legitimization of Nightlife in the Great Depression." *American Quarterly* 38.5 (1986): 761–778.

Faderman, Lillian, and Stuart Timmons. *Gay L.A.: A History of Sexual Outlaws, Power Politics, and Lipstick Lesbians*. Berkeley: University of California Press, 2006.

Ferdinand C. Iglehart. "The Saloon and the Sabbath." *The North American Review* 161.467 (1895): 467–475.

Field, Edward. *The Colonial Tavern*. Providence, R.I.: Preston and Rounds, 1897.

Foot, Sarah. *Monastic Life in Anglo-Saxon England, c. 600–900*. Cambridge, U.K., and New York: Cambridge University Press, 2006.

Foote, Thelma Wills. *Black and White Manhattan: The History of Racial Formation in Colonial New York City*. New York: Oxford University Press, 2004.

Fowler, William M., and Oscar Handlin. *Samuel Adams: Radical Puritan*. New York: Longman, 1997.

Fox, Hugh F. "The Saloon Problem." *Annals of the American Academy of Political and Social Science 32.*, Regulation of the Liquor Traffic (1908): 61–68.

Funderburg, Anne Cooper. *Sundae Best: A History of Soda Fountains*. Bowling Green, Ohio: Bowling Green State University Popular Press, 2002.

Furbay, Harvey Graeme. "The Anti-Saloon League." *The North American Review* 177.562 (1903): 434–439.

Garvin, Donna-Belle, James L. Garvin, and New Hampshire Historical Society. *On the Road North of Boston: New Hampshire Taverns and Turnpikes, 1700–1900*. Concord, N.H.: New Hampshire Historical Society, 1988.

Gately, Iain. *Drink: A Cultural History of Alcohol*. 1st ed. New York: Gotham, 2008.

Gilfoyle, Timothy J. *City of Eros: New York City, Prostitution, and the Commercialization of Sex, 1790–1920*. 1st ed. New York: W.W. Norton, 1992.

Gilmore, Thomas Mador. "The Saloon as a Club." *The North American Review* 157.443 (1893): 511–512.

Glenn, Thomas Allen. "The Blue Anchor Tavern." *The Pennsylvania Magazine of History and Biography* 20.4 (1896): 427–434.

Goldman, Emma. *Living My Life*. New York: Da Capo Press, 1970.

Gottlieb, David. "The Neighborhood Tavern and the Cocktail Lounge a Study of Class Differences." *The American Journal of Sociology* 62.6 (1957): 559–562.

Goyens, Tom. *Beer and Revolution: The German Anarchist Movement in New York City, 1880–1914*. Urbana: University of Illinois Press, 2007.

Graham, Frances W., and Georgeanna M. Gardenier. *Two Decades: A History of the First Twenty Years' Work of the Woman's Christian Temperance Union of the State of New York*. Oswego, N.Y.: Press of R.J. Oliphant, 1894.

Habermas, Jürgen. *The Structural Transformation of the Public Sphere: An Inquiry into a Category of Bourgeois Society*. Cambridge, Mass.: MIT Press, 1989.

Hamilton, Alexander, Carl Bridenbaugh, and Institute of Early American History and Culture (Williamsburg, Va.). *Gentleman's Progress: The Itinerarium of Dr. Alexander Hamilton, 1744*. Chapel Hill: Pub. for the Institute of Early American History and Culture at Williamsburg, Va., by the University of North Carolina Press, 1948.

Hardin, Achsah. "Volstead English." *American Speech* 7.2 (1931): 81–88.

Harris, Leslie M. *In the Shadow of Slavery: African Americans in New York City, 1626–1863*. Chicago: University of Chicago Press, 2004.

Harrison, Leonard Vance, and Elizabeth Laine. *After Repeal*. New York: Harper & Brothers, 1936.

Hawthorne, Nathaniel, et al. *The American Notebooks*. New Haven: Yale University Press, 1932.

Henderson, Archibald. "An Interesting Colonial Document." *The Virginia Magazine of History and Biography* 28.1 (1920): 54–57.

Henderson, Dwight F. "Treason, Sedition, and Fries' Rebellion." *The American Journal of Legal History* 14.4 (1970): 308–318.

Hildreth, Richard. *The Boston Opposition to the New Law for the Suppression of Rum Shops and Grog Shops*. Boston: Perkins & Marvin, 1838.

Hildreth, Richard, and Martha M. Pingel. *An American Utilitarian*. New York: Columbia University Press, 1948.

Holcomb, Grant. "John Sloan and 'McSorley's Wonderful Saloon." *American Art Journal* 15.2 (1983): 5–20.

Holt, Mack P. *Alcohol: A Social and Cultural History*. English ed. Oxford; New York: Berg, 2006.

Hooker, Richard James. *Food and Drink in America: A History*. Indianapolis: Bobbs-Merrill, 1981.

Horsmanden, Daniel. *The New York Conspiracy*. Boston: Beacon Press, 1971.

Ireland, John. "The Catholic Church and the Saloon." *The North American Review* 159.455 (1894): 498–505.

James, William. *The Varieties of Religious Experience*. Garden City, N.Y.: Image Books, 1978.

Johnson, Harry. *Harry Johnson's New and Improved Bartender's Manual*. New York: Samisch & Goldmann, 1882.

Johnson, W.H. "The Saloon in Indian Territory." *The North American Review* 146.376 (1888): 340–341.

Josselyn, John. *New-Englands Rarities Discovered*. Bedford, Mass., and Chester, Conn.: Applewood Books; distributed by Globe Pequot Press, 1992; 1672.

Kaplan, Michael. "New York City Tavern Violence and the Creation of a Working-Class Male Identity." *Journal of the Early Republic* 15.4 (1995): 591–617.

Kerr, K. Austin. *Organized for Prohibition: A New History of the Anti-Saloon League*. New Haven, Conn.: Yale University Press, 1985.

Kobler, John. *Ardent Spirits: The Rise and Fall of Prohibition*. New York: Putnam, 1973.

Kümin, Beat A., and B. Ann Tlusty. *The World of the Tavern: Public Houses in Early Modern Europe*. Aldershot, U.K., and Burlington, Vt.: Ashgate, 2002.

Laband, David N., and Deborah Hendry Heinbuch. *Blue Laws: The History, Economics, and Politics of Sunday-Closing Laws*. Lexington, Mass.: Lexington Books, 1987.

Launitz-Schurer, Leopold S., Jr. "Slave Resistance in Colonial New York: An Interpretation of Daniel Horsmanden's New York Conspiracy." *Phylon (1960–)* 41.2 (1980): 137–152.

LeMasters, E.E. *Blue-Collar Aristocrats: Life-Styles at a Working-Class Tavern*. Madison: University of Wisconsin Press, 1975.

Lender, Mark E., and James Kirby Martin. *Drinking in America: A History*. New York; London: Free Press; Macmillan, 1982.

Lerner, Michael A. *Dry Manhattan: Prohibition in New York City*. Cambridge, Mass: Harvard University Press, 2007.

"Liquor Saloon a Nuisance Per Se." *Harvard Law Review* 7.8 (1894): 487–488.

Littauer, Amanda H. "The B-Girl Evil: Bureaucracy, Sexuality, and the Menace of Barroom Vice in Postwar California." *Journal of the History of Sexuality* 12.2, Special Issue: Sexuality and Politics since 1945 (2003): 171–204.

Madelon Powers. "The "Poor Man's Friend": Saloonkeepers, Workers, and the Code of Reciprocity in U.S. Barrooms, 1870–1920." *International Labor and Working-Class History*.45, Drinking and the Working Class (1994): 1–15.

Manigault, Peter, and Maurice A. Crouse. "The Letterbook of Peter Manigault, 1763–1773." *The South Carolina Historical Magazine* 70.2 (1969): 79–96.

Marryat, Frederick, and Sydney Jackman. *A Diary in America*. 1 Borzio ed. New York: Knopf, 1962.

Martin, Wendy. *Colonial American Travel Narratives*. New York: Penguin Books, 1994.

McNamara, Martha J. *From Tavern to Courthouse: Architecture & Ritual in American Law, 1658–1860*. Baltimore, Md.: Johns Hopkins University Press, 2004.

Melendy, Royal L. "The Saloon in Chicago." *The American Journal of Sociology* 6.3 (1900): 289–306.

Miller, John Chester. *Sam Adams; Pioneer in Propaganda*. Stanford, Calif.: Stanford University Press, 1960; 1936.

Mitchell, Joseph. *McSorley's Wonderful Saloon*. New York: Duell, Sloan and Pearce, 1943.

Moehringer, J.R. *The Tender Bar: A Memoir*. 1st ed. New York: Hyperion, 2005.

Moore, E.C. "The Social Value of the Saloon." *The American Journal of Sociology* 3.1 (1897): 1–12.

Moore, Frank, and John Anthony Scott. *The Diary of the American Revolution, 1775–1781*. New York: Washington Square Press, 1967.

Murray, Charles Augustus. *Travels in North America during the Years 1834, 1835 & 1836, Including a Summer Residence with the Pawnee Tribe of Indians and a Visit to Cuba and the Azore Islands*. New York: Da Capo Press, 1974; 1839.

Nash, Gary B. *The Urban Crucible: Social Change, Political Consciousness, and the Origins of the American Revolution*. Cambridge, Mass: Harvard University Press, 1979.

Nel, Philip. *Dr. Seuss: American Icon*. New York: Continuum, 2004.

New Plymouth Colony, and Nathaniel Bradstreet Shurtleff. *Records of the Colony of New Plymouth in New England*. Bowie, Md.: Heritage Books, 1998; 1855.

Newman, Paul Douglas. "Fries's Rebellion and American Political Culture, 1798–1800." *The Pennsylvania Magazine of History and Biography* 119.1/2 (1995): 37–73.

Odegard, Peter H. *Pressure Politics: The Story of the Anti-Saloon League*. New York; Ann Arbor: Columbia University Press; University Microfilms, 1966, 1928.

Okrent, Daniel. *Last Call: The Rise and Fall of Prohibition*. New York: Scribner, 2010.

Paton Yoder. "Tavern Regulation in Virginia: Rationale and Reality." *The Virginia Magazine of History and Biography* 87.3 (1979): 259–278.

Pegram, Thomas R. *Battling Demon Rum: The Struggle for a Dry America, 1800–1933*. Chicago: Ivan R. Dee, 1998.

———. "The Dry Machine: The Formation of the Anti-Saloon League of Illinois." *Illinois Historical Journal* 83.3 (1990): 173–186.

———. "Temperance Politics and Regional Political Culture: The Anti-Saloon League in Maryland and the South, 1907–1915." *The Journal of Southern History* 63.1 (1997): 57–90.

Perley, Sidney. *The History of Salem*. Salem, Mass.: S. Perley, 1924; 1928.

Popham, Robert. "The Social History of the Tavern" in *Research Advances in Alcohol & Drug Problems*, vol. 4 ed. Yedy Israel et al. (New York, 1978) 225–302.

Powers, Madelon. *Faces Along the Bar: Lore and Order in the Workingman's Saloon, 1870–1920*. Chicago: University of Chicago Press, 1998.

Pringle, Henry F. *Theodore Roosevelt, a Biography*. Rev ed. New York: Harcourt, Brace, 1956.

Riis, Jacob. *How the Other Half Lives*. 2nd ed. New York: Bedford/St. Martins, 2010.

Ron Rothbart. "The Ethnic Saloon as a Form of Immigrant Enterprise." *International Migration Review* 27.2 (1993): 332–358.

Rorabaugh, W.J. *The Alcoholic Republic, an American Tradition*. New York: Oxford University Press, 1979.

Rose, Kenneth D. "Wettest in the West: San Francisco & Prohibition in 1924." *California History* 65.4 (1986): 284–295.

Rosenfeld, Michael J. "Celebration, Politics, Selective Looting and Riots: A Micro Level Study of the Bulls Riot of 1992 in Chicago." *Social Problems* 44.4 (1997): 483–502.

Salinger, Sharon V. *Taverns and Drinking in Early America*. Baltimore, Md.: Johns Hopkins University Press, 2002.

Sandoval-Strausz, A. K. *Hotel: An American History*. New Haven, Conn.: Yale University Press, 2007.

Ibid., "A Public House for a New Republic: The Architecture of Accommodation and the American State, 1789–1809." *Perspectives in Vernacular Architecture* 9, Constructing Image, Identity, and Place (2003): 54–70.

Sante, Luc. *Low Life: Lures and Snares of Old New York*. New York: Farrar Strauss Giroux, 1991.

Schaack, Michael J., Anarchism Collection, and Paul Avrich Collection. *Anarchy and Anarchists*. Chicago: F.J. Schulte & Company, 1889.

Schoelwer, Susan Prendergast, and Connecticut Historical Society. *Lions & Eagles & Bulls: Early American Tavern & Inn Signs, from the Connecticut Historical Society*. Hartford, Conn.: Connecticut Historical Society, 2000.

Selcer, Richard F. *Legendary Watering Holes: The Saloons that made Texas Famous*. Vol. 10. College Station,: Texas A & M University Press, 2004.

Slaughter, Thomas P. *The Whiskey Rebellion: Frontier Epilogue to the American Revolution*. New York: Oxford University Press, 1986.

Smith, Jessie Carney, and Shirelle Phelps. *Notable Black American Women*. Detroit, Mich.: Gale Research, 1992; 2003.

Smith, Thomas E.V. *The City of New York in the Year of Washington's Inauguration, 1789*. New York: Anson D.F. Randolph & Co., 1889.

St. John de Crèvecoeur, J. Hector, and Dennis D. Moore. *More Letters from the American Farmer: An Edition of the Essays in English Left Unpublished by Crèvecoeur*. Athens: University of Georgia Press, 1995.

Steffens, Joseph Lincoln. *The Shame of the Cities*. New York: P. Smith, 1948; 1904.

Stelzle, Charles. *A Son of the Bowery; the Life Story of an East Side American*. Freeport, N.Y.: Books for Libraries Press, 1971; 1926.

Stivers, Richard. *A Hair of the Dog: Irish Drinking and American Stereotype*. University Park: Pennsylvania State University Press, 1976.

Szatmary, David P. *Shays' Rebellion: The Making of an Agrarian Insurrection*. Amherst: University of Massachusetts Press, 1980.

Thomann, Gallus. *Colonial Liquor Laws*. New York: The United States Brewers' Association, 1887.

Thompson, Peter. *Rum Punch & Revolution: Taverngoing & Public Life in Eighteenth Century Philadelphia*. Philadelphia: University of Pennsylvania Press, 1999.

Thoreau, Henry David, and Ralph Waldo Emerson. *Excursions*. 14th ed. Boston: Houghton, Mifflin and Company, 1800; 1899.

Walton, Stuart. *Out of It: A Cultural History of Intoxication*. New York: Three Rivers Press, 2002.

Warden, G.B. "The Caucus and Democracy in Colonial Boston." *The New England Quarterly* 43.1 (1970): 19–45.

Warner, Harry S., and Intercollegiate Prohibition Association of the United States. *Prohibition, an Adventure in Freedom*. Westerville, Ohio: The World League Against Alcoholism, 1928.

Warner, Jessica. *All or Nothing: A Short History of Abstinence in America*. Toronto: Emblem, 2010; 2008.

West, Elliott. "Thomas Francis Meagher's Bar Bill." *Montana: The Magazine of Western History* 35.1 (1985): 16–23.

Winsor, Justin. *History of the Town of Duxbury, Massachusetts, with Genealogical Registers*. Boston: Crosby & Nichols, 1849.

Wondrich, David. *Imbibe! From Absinthe Cocktail to Whiskey Smash, a Salute in Stories and Drinks to "Professor" Jerry Thomas, Pioneer of the American Bar*. 1st ed. New York: Perigee Book/Penguin Group, 2007.

Woods, Robert A. *The City Wilderness*. Boston: Houghton Mifflin, 1899.

Yenne, Bill. *The American Brewery*. St. Paul, Minn.: MBI, 2003.

INDEX